CAPITAL LONDON

Focus from the Flying Eye

I see London by day and by night, in high summer and
in deepest winter, and in spite of the frustrations and ugliness
that you so often find on the ground, from the air it is
a magical city as it changes with the seasons, grows and renews itself
and undertakes its annual rituals.

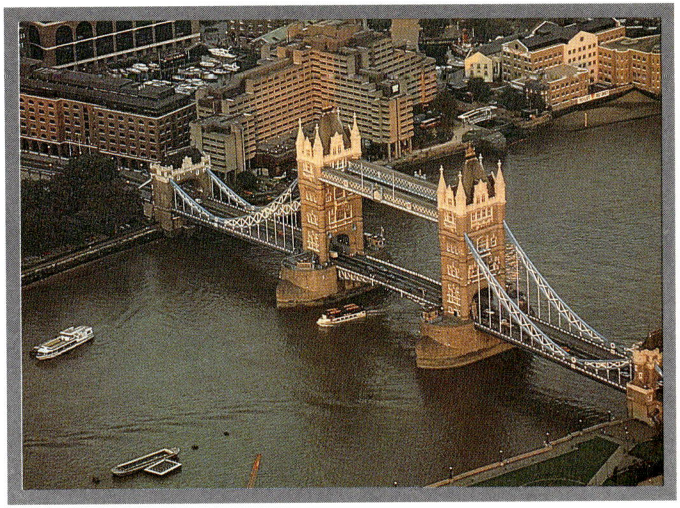

CAPITAL LONDON

Focus from the Flying Eye

Hazel Murray

CASSELL
Published in association with Capital Radio Enterprises

ACKNOWLEDGEMENTS

This book would not have been possible without the help and guidance of Sue and Patrick from Sue Cunningham Photographic, who gave me the confidence to begin, and hours of advice and encouragement along the way. Thanks, also, to Susie Keane and John Pitchforth at Nikon who were brave enough to lend me all the equipment; to Robin, Terry and Martin at Tapestry who, with great care, processed the results; to the Cabair Flying Eye pilots John Ripley, Mike Pearsall, David Hughes and Gareth Trevarthen, who literally turned circles for me; to all the air traffic controllers upon whom we so completely depend; to Chris, Julie and Graham for their unflagging optimism; to everyone at Capital who helped get the idea (and me) off the ground – and to many others, too numerous to mention. Above all, a million thanks to my Mum who always supports me in everything I choose to do.

Cassell Publishers Limited
Villiers House, 41/47 Strand
London WC2N 5JE

First published 1993

British Library Cataloguing-in-Publication Data
A catalogue record for this book is available from the British Library

ISBN 0 304 34338 2

Typeset by Litho Link Ltd, Welshpool, Powys, Wales
Printed and bound in Great Britain by Bath Colourbooks

CONTENTS

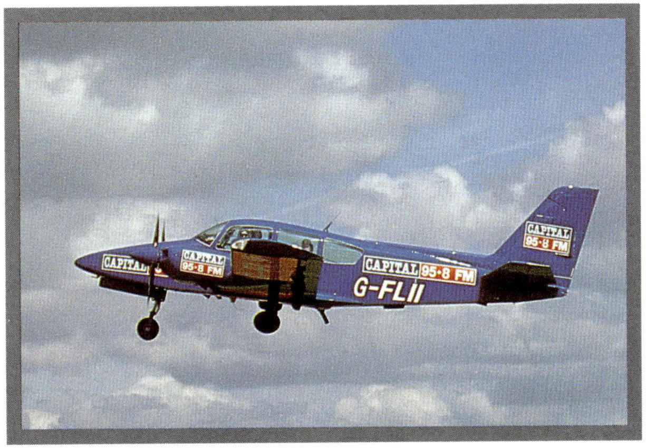

Foreword

by Richard Attenborough, President of Capital Radio

It was crack of dawn, 16 October 1973, when I sat in a small studio in Euston Tower, and announced 'This, for the very first time, is Capital Radio'.

Twenty years later, when I remember my intense anticipation at that moment of birth, I am bowled over at how our child has progressed through its early faltering years, and its difficult puberty, into full and immensely successful adulthood.

As the Capital Broadcasting Organisation has grown, so it has become ever more closely entwined with London, with its wonderful vibrant culture, its excitement, its people and also, in these difficult times, with its problems. However, it has to be said that ever since we first went on air, one of the lesser yet enduring problems that has irritated each and every one of us is London's traffic.

It was with this in mind that, back in 1979, we launched our first airborne traffic spotting plane, to soar the skies over the city to identify and report those jams faster and more accurately than any land service would have found possible. We named it the 'Flying Eye', and it has been keeping watch over our capital ever since.

When it started, the Flying Eye flew for a couple of hours each day. Now it is in the air for nearly thirty hours a week, reporting mornings, evenings and weekends on London's snarl ups.

In total, the Eye covers roughly 161,000 miles every year (that's almost five times round the earth!) criss crossing 1,000 feet over London, giving it a spectacular bird's eye view of the capital.

The wonderful aerial photographs that follow, chosen from literally thousands, give an insight into what the greatest city in the world looks like from that height, both by day and by night. We've also asked some of our presenters from Capital 95.8 FM and Capital Gold 1548 AM to pick their favourite pictures and explain which parts of London have a special significance for them.

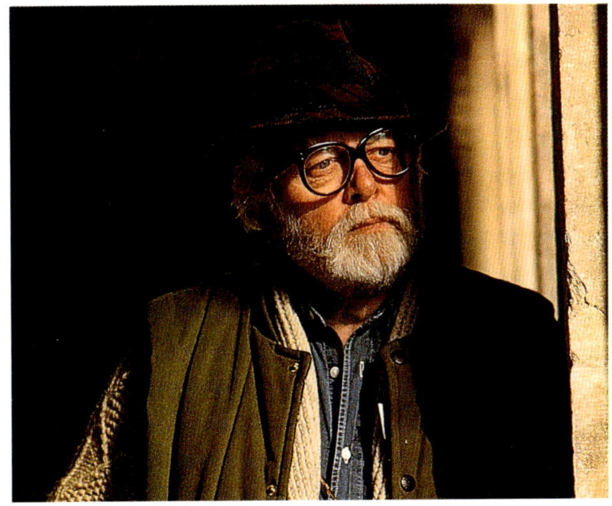

PHOTOGRAPHED BY KEITH HAMSHERE

So settle back, and let us take you on a magical flight through the pages of this book. And, as you look down, tune your radio to Capital so you have the real sights and sounds of the city!

London's great new monument

Introduction

When I joined Capital it never really occurred to me to wonder if I would enjoy flying around in a small plane for a couple of hours every day. Luckily I do, but it wasn't that easy in the beginning.

My broadcasting career began with Piccadilly Radio in Manchester – a natural progression, you might think, for a girl with a First in mathematics from Warwick University. Be that as it may, I had seen an ad for a researcher at Piccadilly demanding that applicants be 'very talented'. I wrote to say that I was incredibly talented, which got me an interview, and then a fair amount of bluff got me the job.

My first broadcast was at 5.30 one Sunday morning, an epic debut, heard by as many of my friends as remembered to set their alarm clocks and probably by no one else. Even so, I got to do more and more broadcasting, and I had a great time. All in the call of duty, I took my advanced motorists' certificate, learned to play the bagpipes and flew in a hot-air balloon. I interviewed Sir John Mills, Billy Connolly and a man from Bury who kept a 12-foot python in his back bedroom. I was even the film reviewer for a year or so, which was a wonderful experience. It really is amazing how many bad films are released.

After Piccadilly came a life of adventure (mostly misadventure, to be honest) in Africa, where I taught A-level maths in Kenya for a year and became an enthusiastic photographer. Then it was back home to England and my earlier career. I joined AA Roadwatch as a traffic broadcaster, and from there it was a short and lucky step to being asked if I would like to join Capital Radio to be the Flying Eye. Well, of course I would!

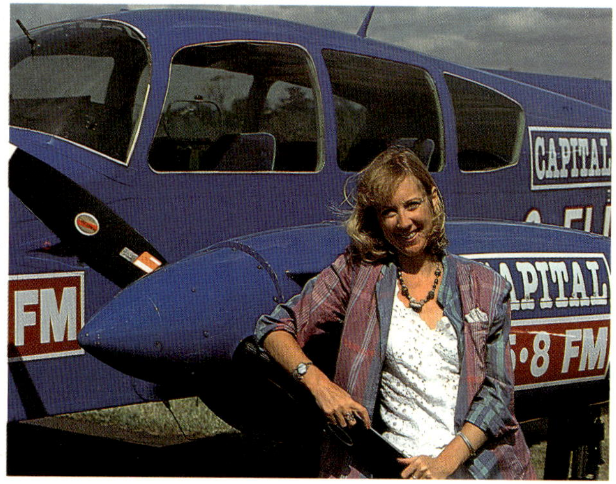

Hazel Murray and G-FLII.
Photographed by Fred Mullane

I had to go up in the plane to see if I could survive without being sick – and I have to admit that it was touch and go. Despite not having lunch and dosing myself with various travel pills, I started to feel decidedly queasy. Russ Kane was with me, showing me how everything worked, and he asked how I was feeling. 'Fine,' I replied, 'just a bit hot.' I know now, from some of our more unfortunate passengers, that this is a dead giveaway and that breaking out in a sweat usually comes just before turning green and reaching for a paper bag. Luckily I survived with dignity intact, and a new career in the capital's skies.

The Flying Eye covers London's traffic in both the morning and evening rush hours. My friend Russ Kane conducts proceedings in the mornings, as everyone travels in to work, while I would take over for the

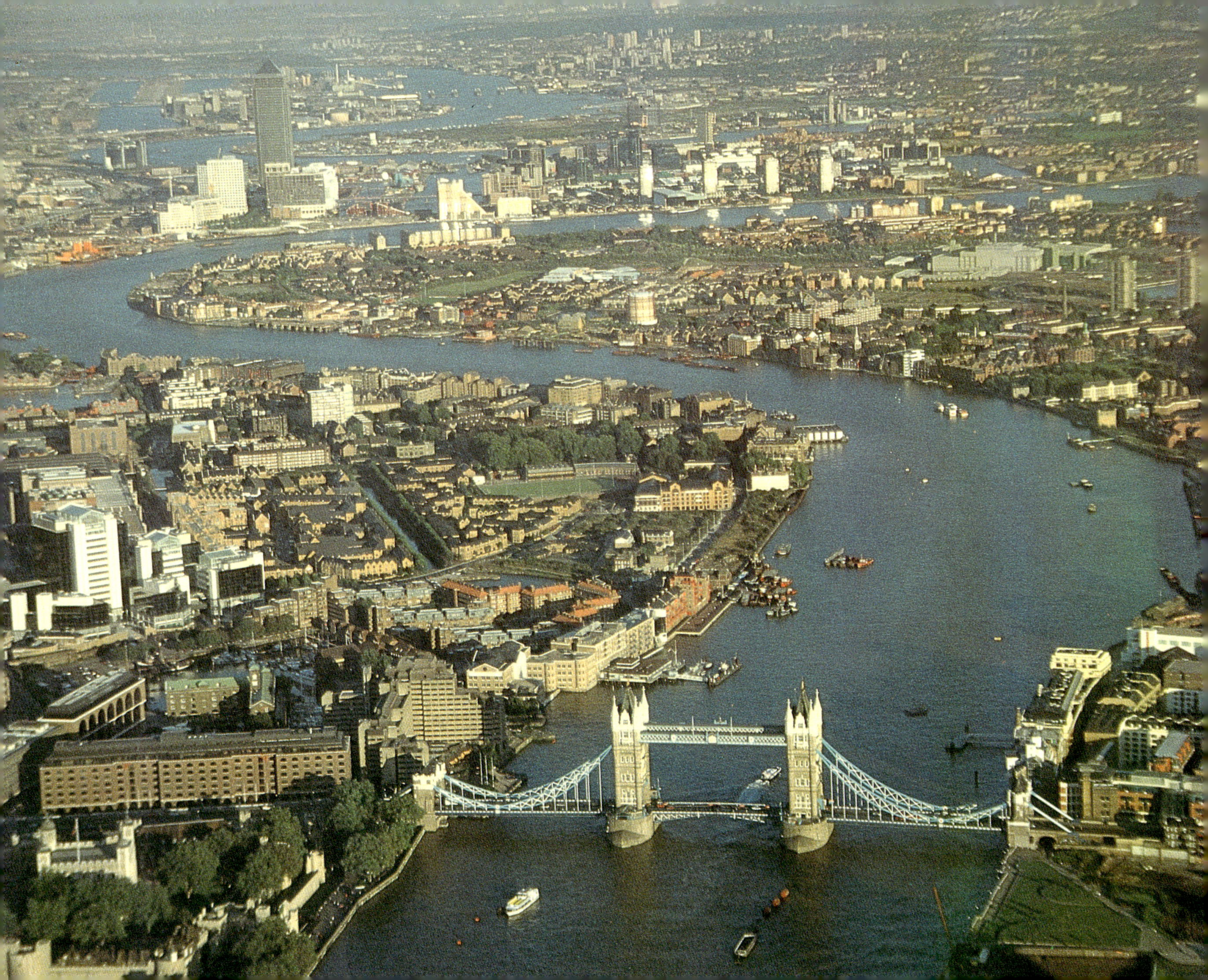

homebound shift. We take off from Elstree, about 14 miles northwest of the Capital Tower on Euston Road, at 4.30 and land at 7.00. In that two and half hours we make ten broadcasts, five on Capital FM (95.8) and five on Capital Gold (1548 AM).

Sometimes there are extra reports to do for the news programme *The Way It Is* if they are covering a traffic story or if there is a major jam somewhere. It can be really busy, dashing from one place to another, trying to keep on top of several incidents at once, although other evenings can be much quieter, especially during school holidays when traffic is comparatively light and there is time to enjoy the view.

Of course, between broadcasts the presenter always listens to Capital. I'm a great one for singing along. My mother was an opera singer, so it's not fair that I should be tone deaf, but I am, and people are forever telling me to shut up. Up in the plane the pilot has his headphones on, so I could yodel away to my heart's content with no one to complain. Unknown to me, this habit caused great amusement down at Capital, where they sneakily listened in from the master control room. The first I knew of this was when David Jensen told me one day on air that he was going to play a special record for me, a remix of the Michael Bolton cover of 'Sitting on the Dock of the Bay', which he knew I loved. I settled down to enjoy it, only to hear the truly ghastly sound of myself screeching away like a demented cat. This awful wailing seemed to go on for an eternity. They had recorded it a few days previously, and you can imagine how they teased me about it. At about the same time Russ Kane was caught giving his version of Free's 'All Right Now', which I must admit had me in fits of laughter. You would think that this might have cured my compulsion to sing, but no, and since then Chris Tarrant has broadcast my version of 'Bachelor Boy', and Capital Gold listeners have been forced to endure my rendition of 'Son of a Preacher Man'. I know the tunes, I can hear them in my head, but somehow they just won't come out of my mouth.

Very occasionally, chance remarks got broadcast from the Flying Eye when, for some reason or other, I forgot I was on air. Once, when we were flying low over the BT Tower, I said to JR, my pilot, 'my bottom always feels funny when we do this'. I have no idea what Capital's listeners made of that. On another occasion one winter our last report was delayed, and we were actually circling over Elstree waiting to land by the time I made it.

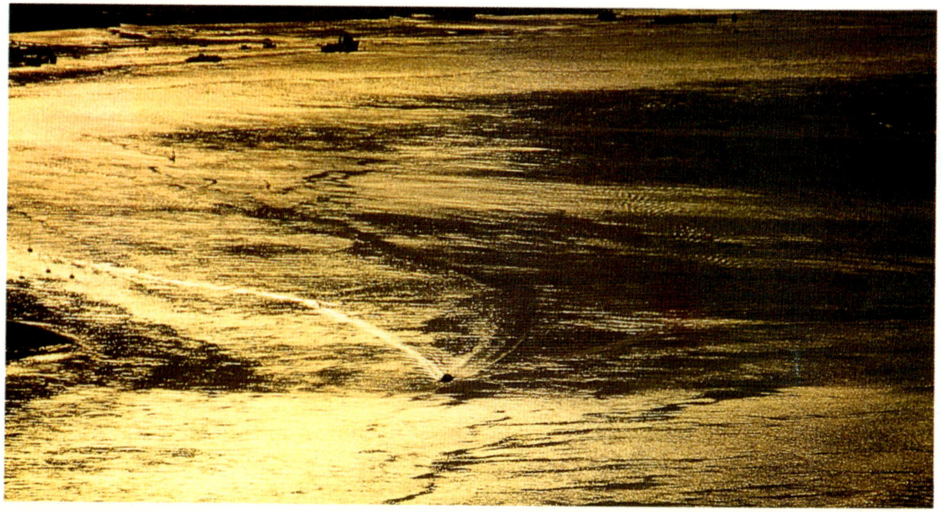

Dirty old Thames, beautiful in the sunset light.

Red skies and bright lights

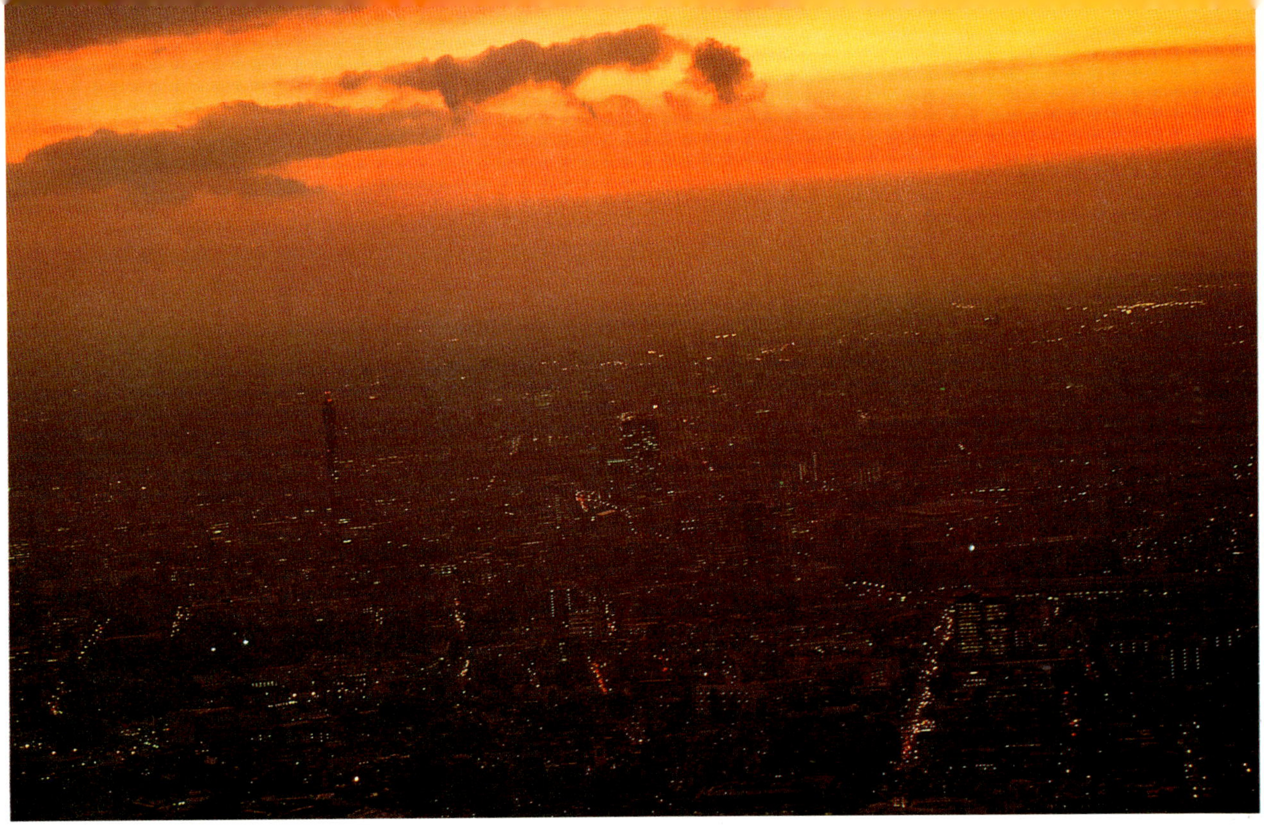

Obviously, I need a light when I broadcast so that I can see my notes, but the pilots generally prefer to have the interior lights down when they land. I finished the report and, thinking I was no longer on air, said to the pilot 'you can turn the light off now if you want'. Needless to say, Mike Read had a field day with that one.

Some people think that being the Flying Eye must be a very glamorous job; others think it must be hell on earth (or a thousand feet above the earth, to be exact). In fact, it's probably a mixture of the two. On a summer afternoon, when everyone else is stuck in offices or in queues below us, we fly around in blue skies, seeing London green and serene.

On the other hand, it can be pretty unpleasant, especially in winter. If it's raining we are wet before we get into the plane, and often the seats are wet as well. On windy nights we really get thrown around, and despite the seat belts we sometimes have to hang on with both hands to stop our heads bumping on the roof – then the clipboard on the lap is likely to bounce up and hit you in the face. Writing is difficult, and deciphering the hieroglyphics afterwards is well nigh impossible. But that's all part of the job. Unless the weather is so bad that we can't take off, Capital's Flying Eye is up there looking down on the traffic and reporting back to the millions listening to the two Capital Radio frequencies. Next time you see the plane, buzzing past, not all that high in the sky above your part of London, you'll have a good idea of what it's like to be part of the Flying Eye team and what we can see of Capital London.

LONDON TRANSPORT

The Flying Eye sets off from Elstree each afternoon at 4.30, and for two and a half hours it circles above London, on the look out for queues, congestion, accidents, roadworks and jams – for anything, in fact, that may delay London's homebound commuters.

People are always surprised by the amount of detail we can see from the Flying Eye. We can pick out an individual vehicle blocking a junction or the fire brigade clearing up an oil spill, but I think we are at our most useful when there is a big accident on one of the motorways. Then, when there are horrendously long queues, we are really the only people who can get a complete overview of the situation.

I remember in particular an accident on the Surrey section of the M25. A tanker was on fire midway between two junctions, both carriageways were completely blocked, and there were tailbacks of at least 10 miles in both directions. The police had closed several junctions so that no more traffic could get on to the motorway, and vehicles were being diverted off at the first junction they came to. At the scene of the accident itself there were still queues of about 3 miles each way, and we watched as the police, starting at the back of each queue, patiently helped each car to do a U-turn and drive the wrong way back along the motorway until it could escape at the next junction. I felt sorry for the people at the front of the queues, because it was clearly going to be several hours before they would be able to move. From our position we could tell drivers exactly how far the queues stretched, how the roads approaching the motorway were doing and what were the best routes to

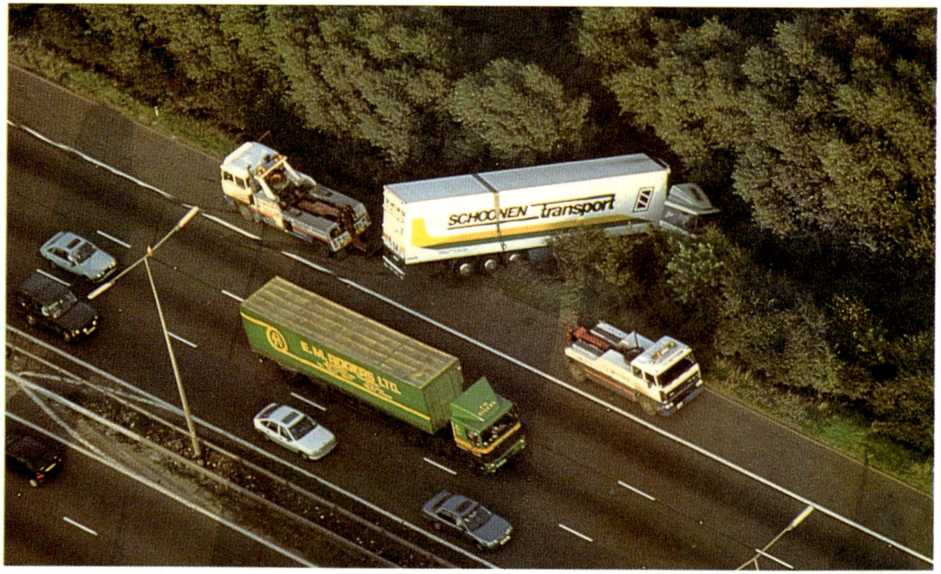

take to avoid the worst of it. It took us more than 10 minutes to fly from the back end of the clockwise queue to the end of the one on the anticlockwise carriageway – and we fly at over 120mph . Of course, we were also in a position to see the details of a very nasty accident, something I try not to concentrate on too much. Certainly, as far as the Flying Eye broadcasts are concerned, the job is reporting information relevant to motorists rather than accounts of the accident itself.

Naturally, any major accident will involve the ambulance service, but the ensuing congestion sometimes makes it difficult for an ordinary ambulance to reach the scene of a crash, and one of the most

MAYBE DANGEROUS?

An AA report suggests that motorists on the M25 are more likely to break down or have an accident in May: 47 incidents caused serious delays in May 1992 compared with a monthly average of 34.

M25

London's orbital motorway carries more than 200,000 vehicles a day on its busiest sections; no wonder queues like this build up so often.

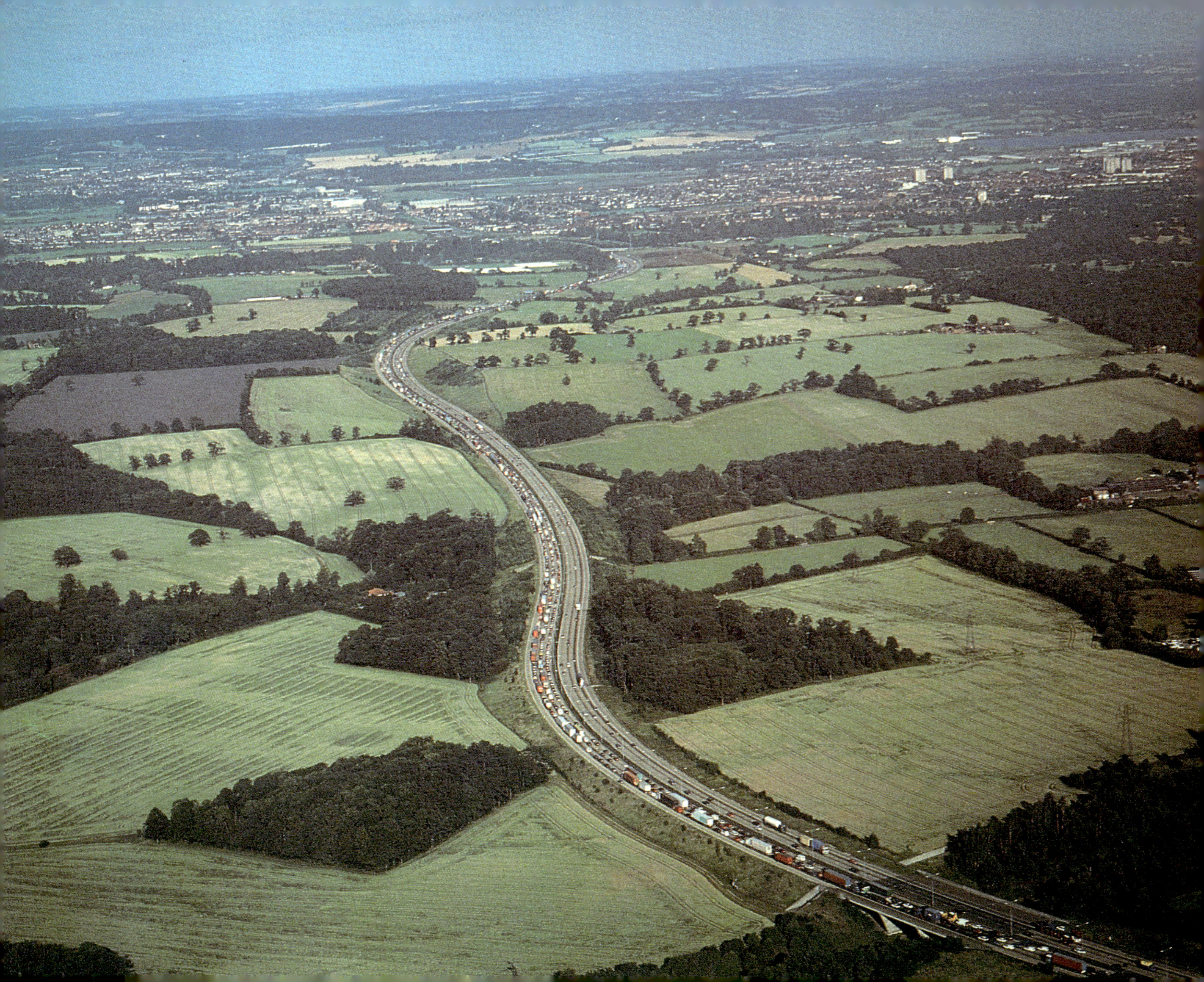

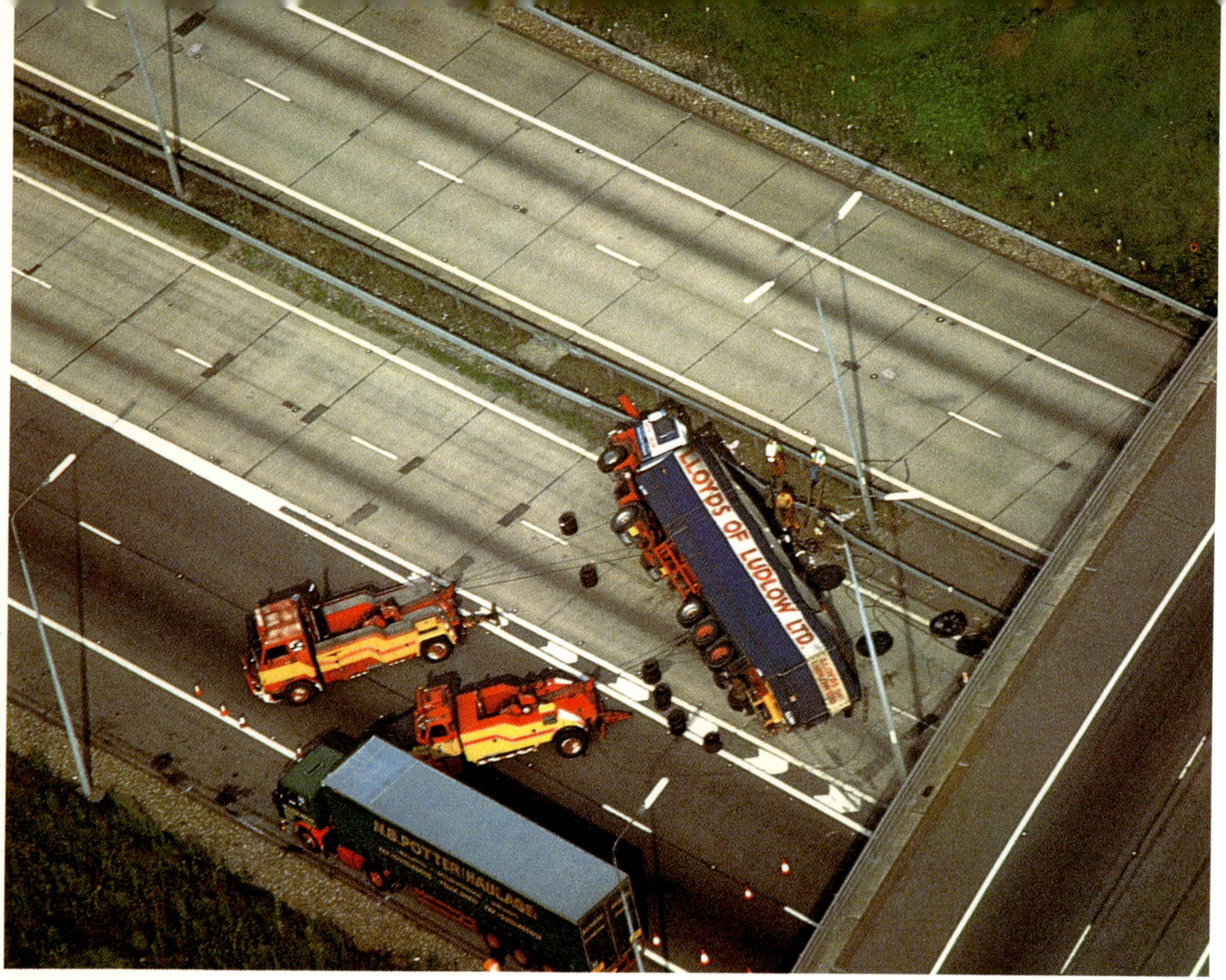

JUNCTION 27

An articulated truck falls victim to the most accident-prone stretch of the M25. There were 39 crashes between junctions 27 and 28, the M11 and A12 intersections, in 1992 alone.

extraordinary sights we see – though thankfully not too often – is the Medevac helicopter landing on a motorway to airlift casualties to hospital with the minimum delay.

What often frustrates drivers sitting in a jam is when they finally get to what seems to be the front of the queue there doesn't appear to be any reason for the delay. Of course, we are all familiar with lanes that are coned off for no apparent reason – that's another story – but there is also the phenomenon of the shifting queue. What happens is that an accident or breakdown causes a tailback, and in due course the vehicles are cleared on to the hard shoulder. The traffic then starts moving, but because there are now so many vehicles all clogged together, they move quite slowly. Meanwhile, the back of the queue is increasing rapidly as more and more vehicles reach it and come to a halt. Gradually, the front of the queue eases, but the back is still growing, so that, in effect, the position of the queue moves backwards

RESCUE FROM THE AIR

The Medevac ambulance helicopter can reach any part of the M25 within 10 minutes of call out. The team, which consists of two pilots, a doctor and a paramedic, flew 974 missions in 1992. Air traffic control gives them priority.

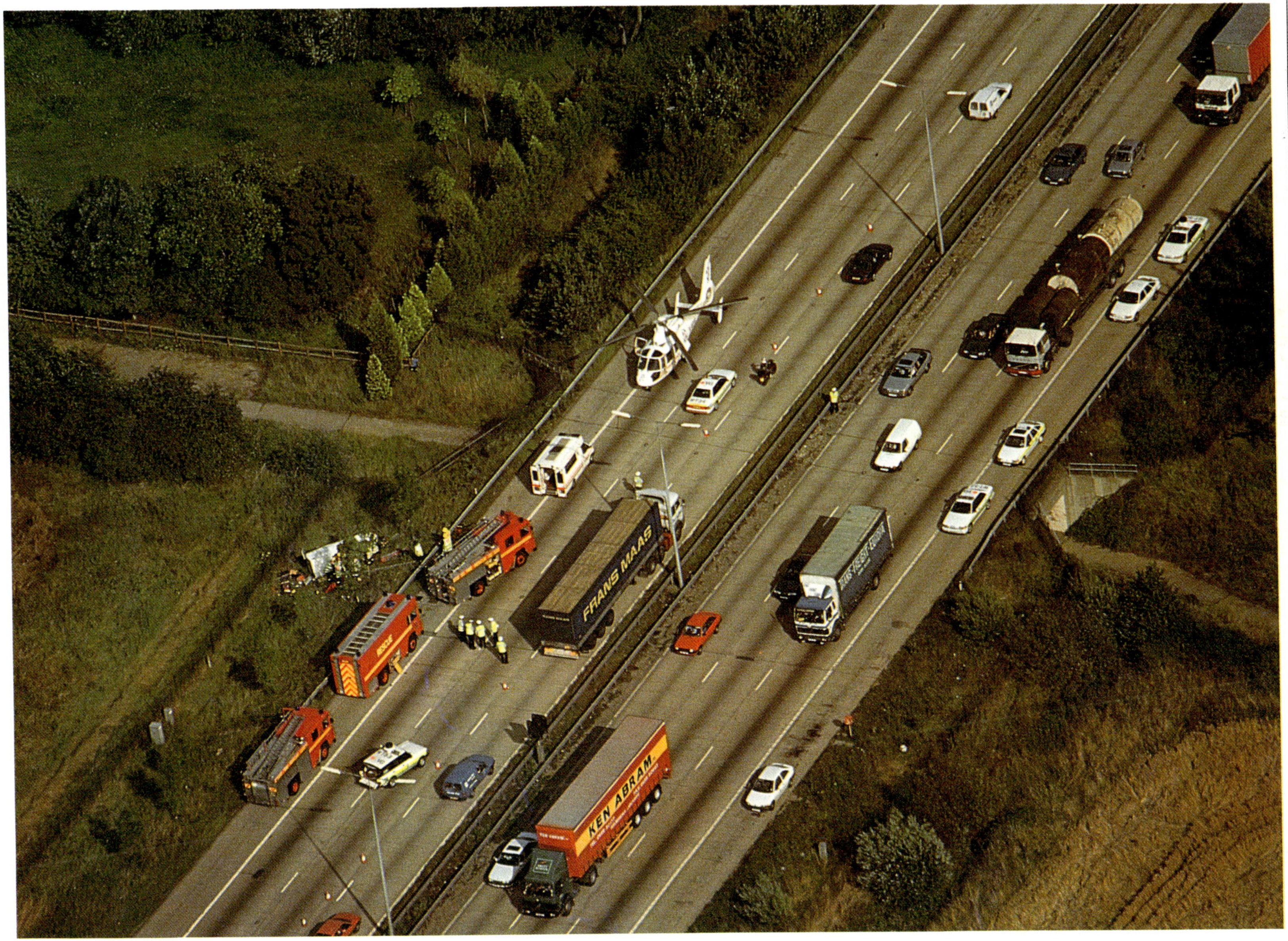
FRANS MAAS
KEN ABRAM

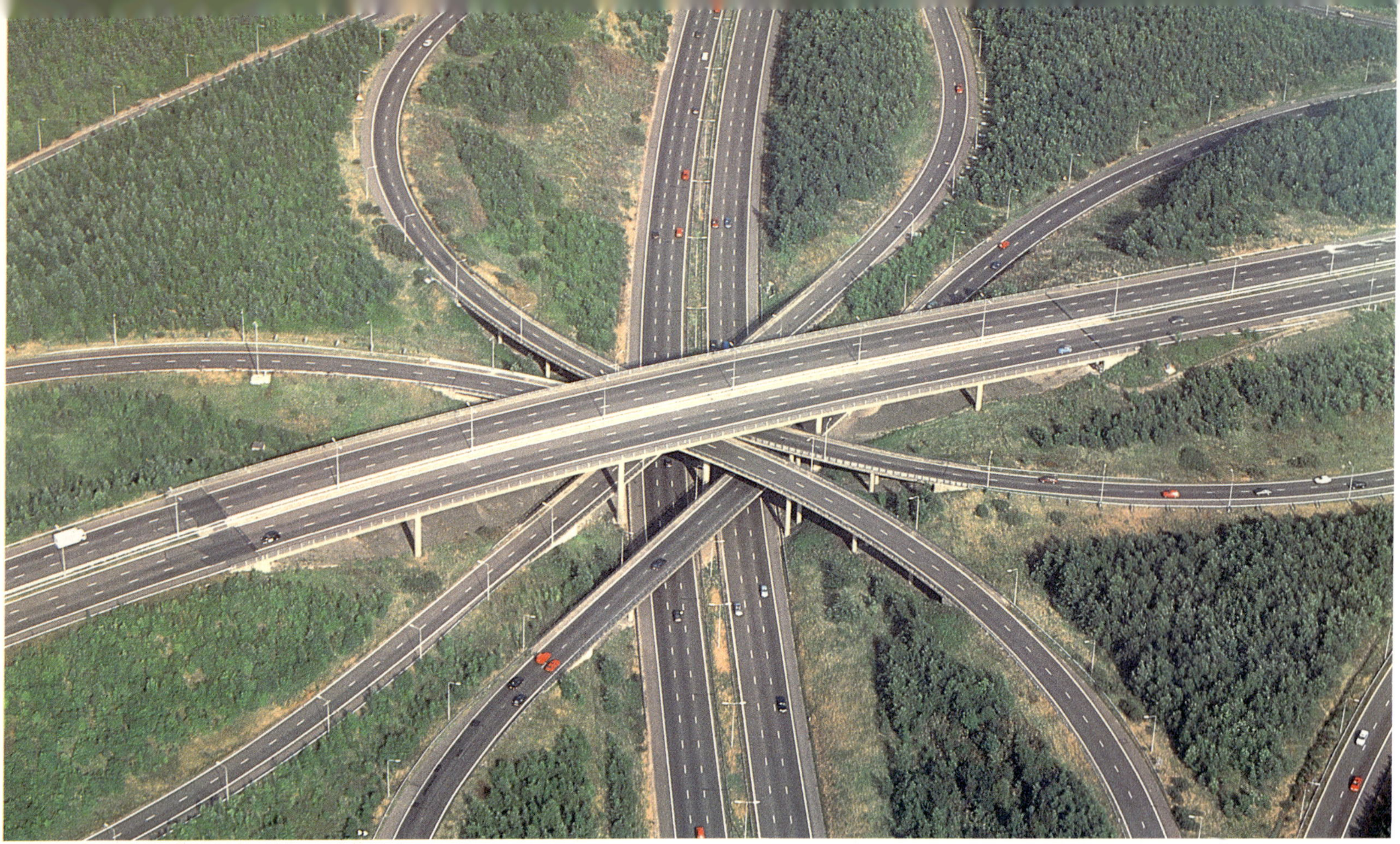

along the motorway. Often, when you reach what feels like the front of the jam, you are in reality several miles further back from the incident that started it all.

Something that we are seeing more and more often is the gridlock, where nothing at all moves. A prime example of this is the Hanger Lane gyratory system, a mega-junction that comes in for a lot of stick, which I don't think it really deserves. There's nothing intrinsically wrong with the roundabout; it's the North Circular on either side that causes the trouble. If there is an incident on the North Circular or if traffic gets clogged up as it tries to change lanes because of the seemingly perpetual roadworks, queues can tail back on to the roundabout. This stops other traffic moving freely around the junction, and eventually the whole thing becomes one massive circular queue . . . nothing moves, so nothing can move, so nothing moves. Then horrendous queues build up on all the approach roads, not just on the North Circular, but on the A40 and Ealing Road as well. Typically this kind of gridlock happens

LONDON SPAGHETTI

At 117 miles, the M25 is the world's largest city by-pass to get you back where you started. It has 32 junctions, six badger tunnels, and one underpass and one flyover especially for deer!

‘AAAH, THE M25! Once I’m inside its circumference I know I’m in London. Once I’m on it I know I’m late. Even at six o’clock in the morning the traffic flashes on my early morning breakfast show always feature a problem on London’s orbital motorway.

It’s not wide enough, and believe me I know – I met the guy who built the M25. On a Greek island I once spent a whole week one evening listening to how this surveyor levelled the carriageway and calculated the curves that weave around the M4 junction at Heathrow.

And it never stops! The M25 by-passes everything, so I can drive all day and not get anywhere. Getting caught in a jam leaves me feeling utterly hopeless, without any control over my destiny.

I remember driving a prize-winner’s car over a specified route as part of a Capital FM ‘Win a Car Contest’. The Flying Eye warned me a of 5-mile jam on the M25, and Hazel Murray advised us to take Exit 16 to avoid the jam. I checked in the mirror to see Exit 16 disappearing in the distance. I looked ahead to see three lanes of red brake lights. Five miles later I was still saying to myself ‘If only I’d tuned in earlier’.’

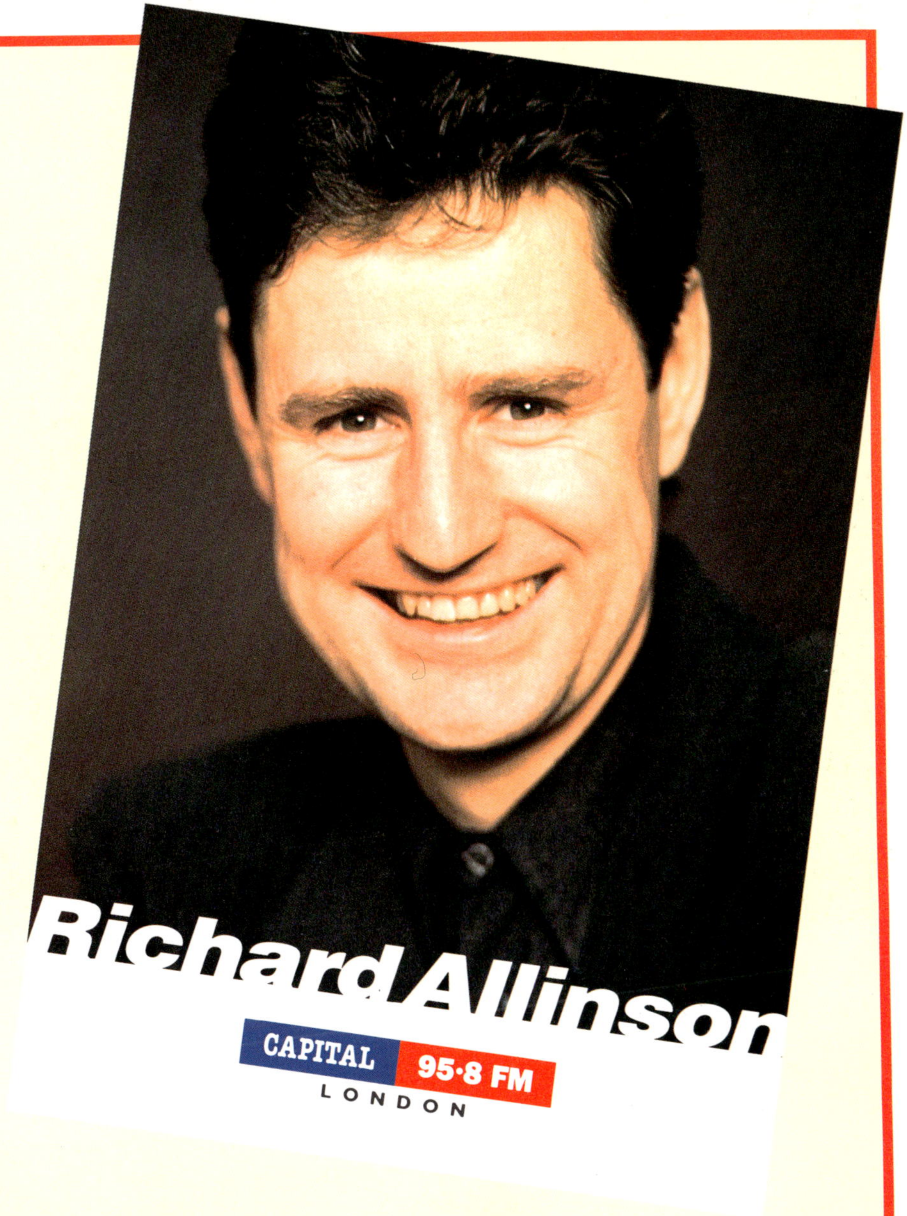

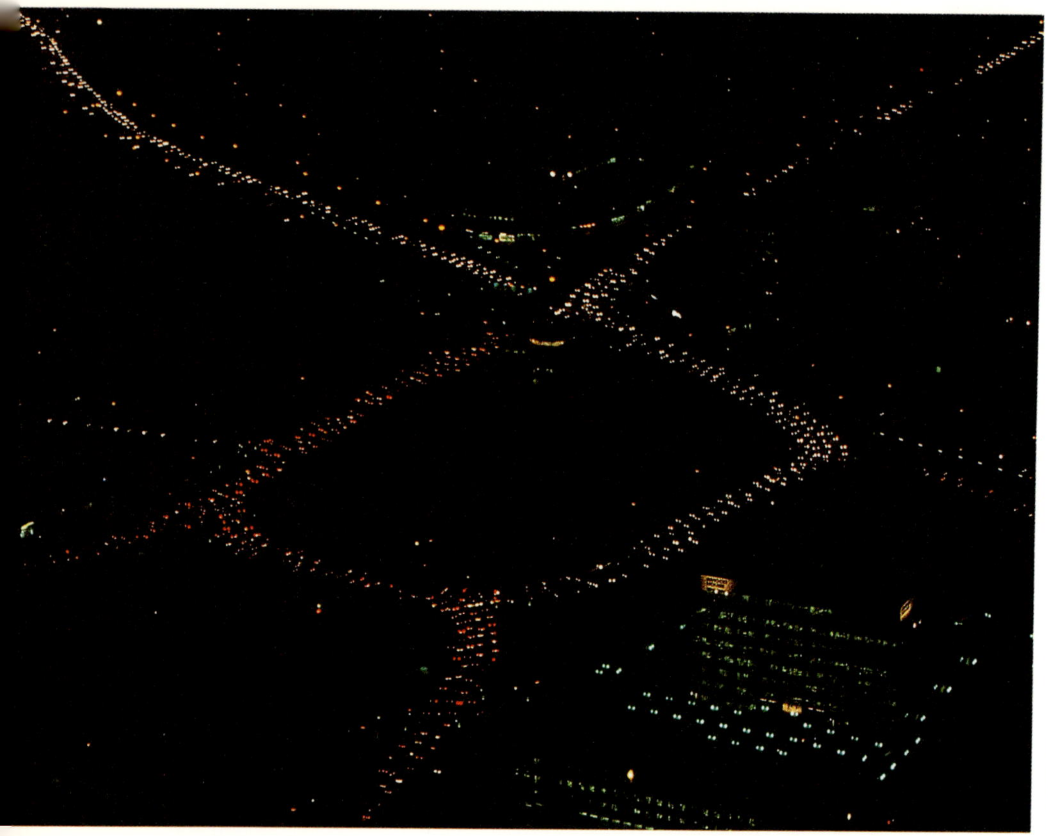

GIANT GRIDLOCK
This is the gyratory system at Hanger Lane, where our old friend the North Circular meets our other old friend the A40. The traffic is more jammed than gyrating, and very pretty it looks too, at night – as long as you're not in it!

when a major event is taking place at the Wembley Complex, but it frequently occurs at Hammersmith, too, and even sometimes to quite large areas of London.

Traffic experts often prophesy that the whole of London will one day turn into one vast traffic gridlock. We haven't seen it yet, even though it might feel like it, but we have come close to it. For instance, the combination of the closure of the Westway because of an accident and a broken-down lorry on Hammersmith Broadway successfully gridlocked west London for a couple of hours one night. Situations like this are normally caused by something unexpected, but the day-to-day grind of London's roads is generally due to a combination of roadworks and just too many vehicles.

A report by the Select Committee on Metropolitan Communication said: 'The requirements of the existing traffic of the metropolis far exceed the present facilities provided for it; the rapid increase of that traffic is constantly adding to the amount of inconvenience and loss thus caused.' And that was in 1855!

Six out of ten London households own at least one car, and that figure is increasing fast. The Department of Transport estimates that well over two million journeys are made on Central London's roads each day, and this amount of traffic makes hold-ups inevitable. The commonest causes of jams, however, are roadworks. More than 30,000 holes are dug each year in the Borough of Westminster alone, and an estimated 500,000 across London as a whole. Up to 60 per cent of these are caused by British Gas; Thames Water and British Telecom account for another 30 per cent; and the electricity companies, Mercury and Cable TV are responsible for the rest. Of course, all this work has to be done, but the problem is the time it takes to restore the roads after the work has been completed and the lack of coordination between the various organizations digging the holes. Local councils are trying to tighten things up, even to the extent of prosecuting companies with 'improper' holes, but there is still a long way to go.

London's 23 river crossings carry more than 900,000 vehicles a day, and the last couple of years have seen drivers facing major delays as a result of a series of

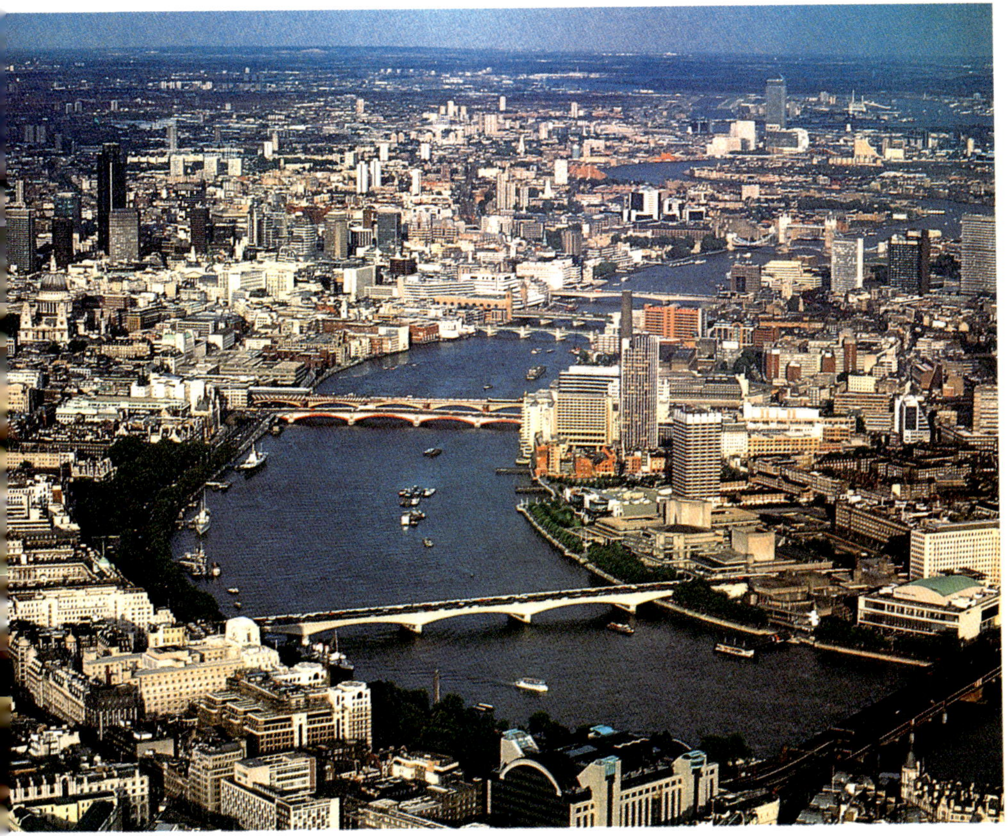

LONDON'S BRIDGES
The 23 river crossings carry more than 900,000 vehicles a day. Bridge traffic is often seriously disrupted by repairs and accidents.

repairs to the city's bridges. Much of this work has been the strengthening made necessary by the juggernauts now using our roads. The good news is that new solutions to the problems of congestion are being found – we now have two companies operating river buses and taxis, BR assures us that it's getting there, trams may soon be returning to the capital's roads after an absence of 40 years (they are already planned for Croydon), and even a helicopter service has been proposed.

The Department of Transport is working on a £40 million, 300-mile red route network across London, which should be in place by 1997. The Department estimates that on routes where the system has already been introduced, journey times have been reduced by up to one-third and the number of accidents cut dramatically. However, red routes are often unpopular with local businesses, and it is doubtful if there is sufficient manpower to enforce the regulations effectively anyway.

Perhaps ironically, at the same time that attempts are being made to accelerate London's traffic, speed cameras have been introduced over the last couple of years in an effort to slow it down. Police hope that the cameras will cut road deaths by up to 50 per cent, which has to be good news.

The Confederation of British Industry estimates that the ever-mounting congestion in London and the Southeast costs industry and business about £10 billion a year in wasted fuel, lost time, late deliveries and so on. Although the Department of Transport claims that in 1991 traffic speeds in inner London averaged about 13mph in rush hours, London Transport says that its buses are frequently reduced to an average speed of less than 4mph.

The first traffic signal, which was hand operated, was set up in Bridge Street in Westminster in 1865 – but the light exploded! On the whole, things have gone downhill from there. Clearly the problems of London's traffic are not about to go away, and it even seems likely that we may soon have to pay for the privilege of driving on the capital's roads. Only one thing is certain – the Flying Eye will remain an essential part of London's *air* traffic for some time to come.

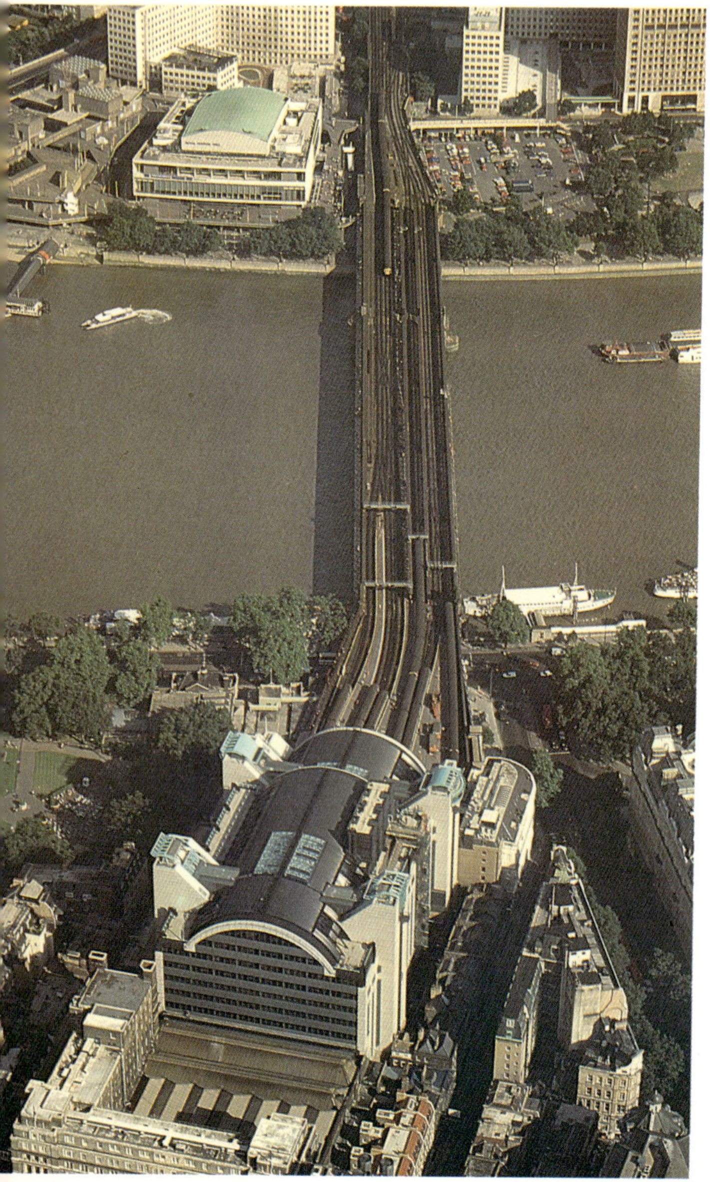

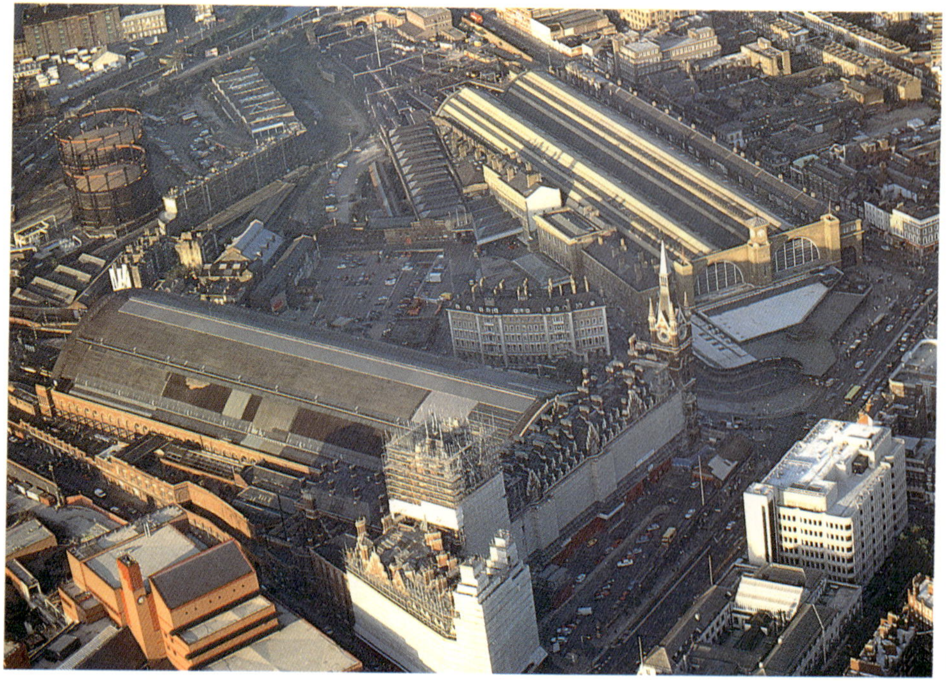

TO TOWN BY TRAIN

Those who don't drive in come by train. Charing Cross, newly adorned, accounts for 138,000 passenger (sorry, BR, *customer*) journeys every day. St Pancras hides behind the builders' screen for a complete restoration, with the clean brick lines of the new British Library alongside. From our view in the Flying Eye, King's Cross might have been built only yesterday.

GOT A NEW MOTOR, JOHN?

The British love for red, white and blue is perfectly displayed by these new cars waiting their turn in the showrooms.

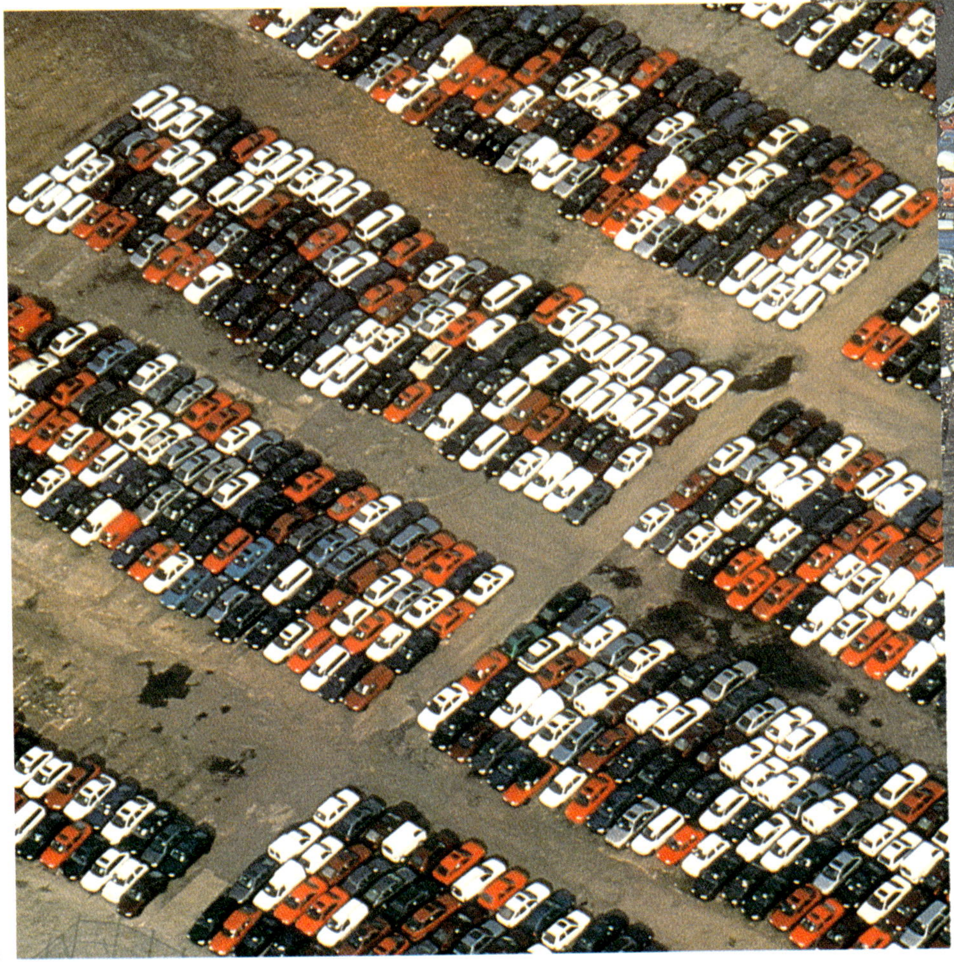

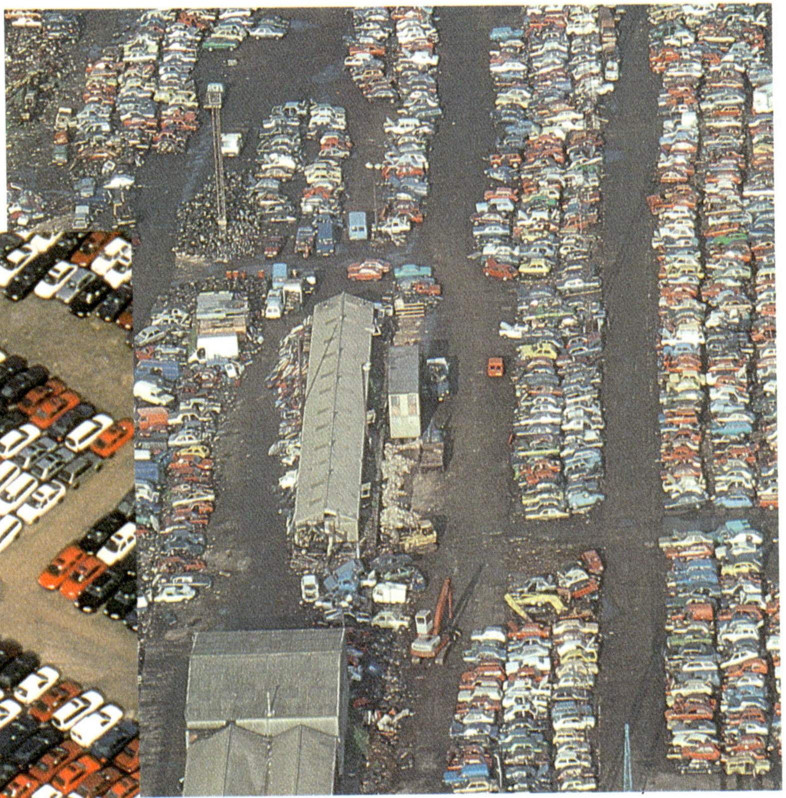

THE END OF THE ROAD!

Alas, a sad end is inevitable.

Capital City

When we have guests in the Flying Eye we always do our best to show them what they want to see. The most important thing for most people is to spot their own house, but this is much more difficult than it sounds, and it is amazing how many people have trouble pinpointing their home. One passenger who lived in a particularly built-up area had thoughtfully attached a banner to his chimney to make sure we spotted it – very sensible – and we were even able to make out his wife, jumping up and down like a lunatic in the back garden. After we have spotted their house and waved at the neighbours, our passengers generally like to see the traditional tourist sights of London, although from a viewpoint that few tourists ever get the chance to experience. We have worked out a route through London that includes a look at most of the landmarks and that at the same time gives a view of most of the traffic trouble spots.

I suppose that Buckingham Palace is one of the very special sights, probably because until recently so few people had had the chance to see much of it from the ground. Although we never overfly the Palace, we still manage to get a peep at the Queen's back garden – now that's what you call a lawn! In the same area there is also Trafalgar Square – it's surprising how small Nelson and his lions look down there. On the same circuit are Westminster Abbey, Big Ben and the Houses of Parliament. In summer you can see the two awnings, one green and one red, that are erected on the terrace of the Palace of Westminster, and as the sun sinks the shadow of Big Ben on the river almost touches the shimmering reflection of County Hall on the opposite bank.

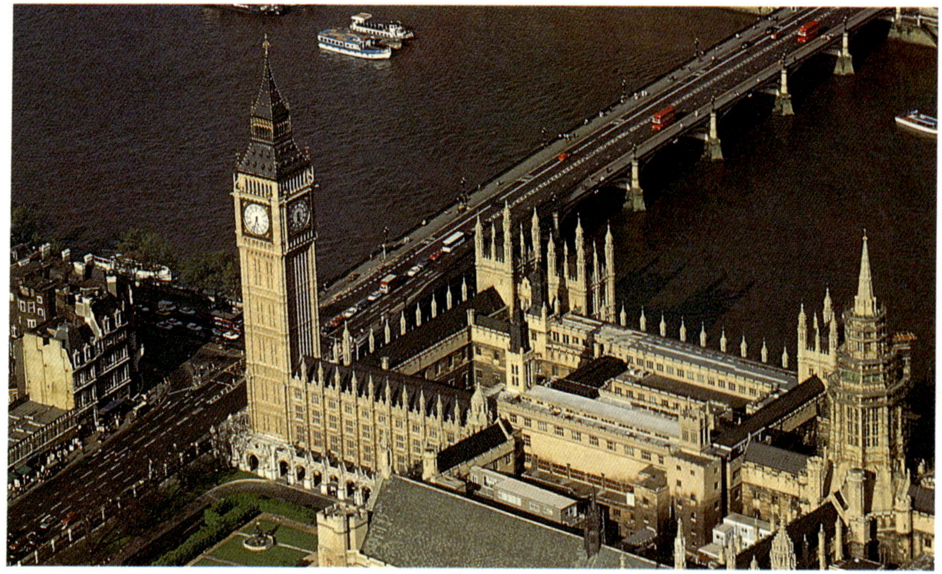

BIG BEN ABOVE THE HOUSES OF PARLIAMENT

The most famous clock face in the world, but not the biggest in London – that's down river on the Shell building. It is the largest striking clock in the world, though. The minute hands are 14 feet long and travel 120 miles each year at their tips. Fine tuning is carried out by placing old coins on the pendulum. Positively no quartz in this mechanical movement.

At the heart of the West End are Piccadilly Circus and Leicester Square, surprisingly not that spectacular from the air. I suppose that's because they are open spaces rather than impressive buildings. Oxford Street, though, is quite unmissable, with its wall-to-wall buses and taxis.

Hyde Park Corner and Marble Arch are frequently the scene of some fairly hefty traffic jams, and then it's on to Marylebone Road and Euston Road, which are always good for spotting a queue, but it's only worth a mention if the tailback is through the underpass. As we pass Euston Tower, the home of Capital, we give it a wave and check out the BT Tower. Apparently it changes its height on a regular basis – like most tall buildings, it contracts in cold

BUCKINGHAM PALACE

The official residence of the sovereign since Queen Victoria made it so in 1837, the Palace is now open to the public each August and September to help raise funds for the restoration of Windsor Castle.

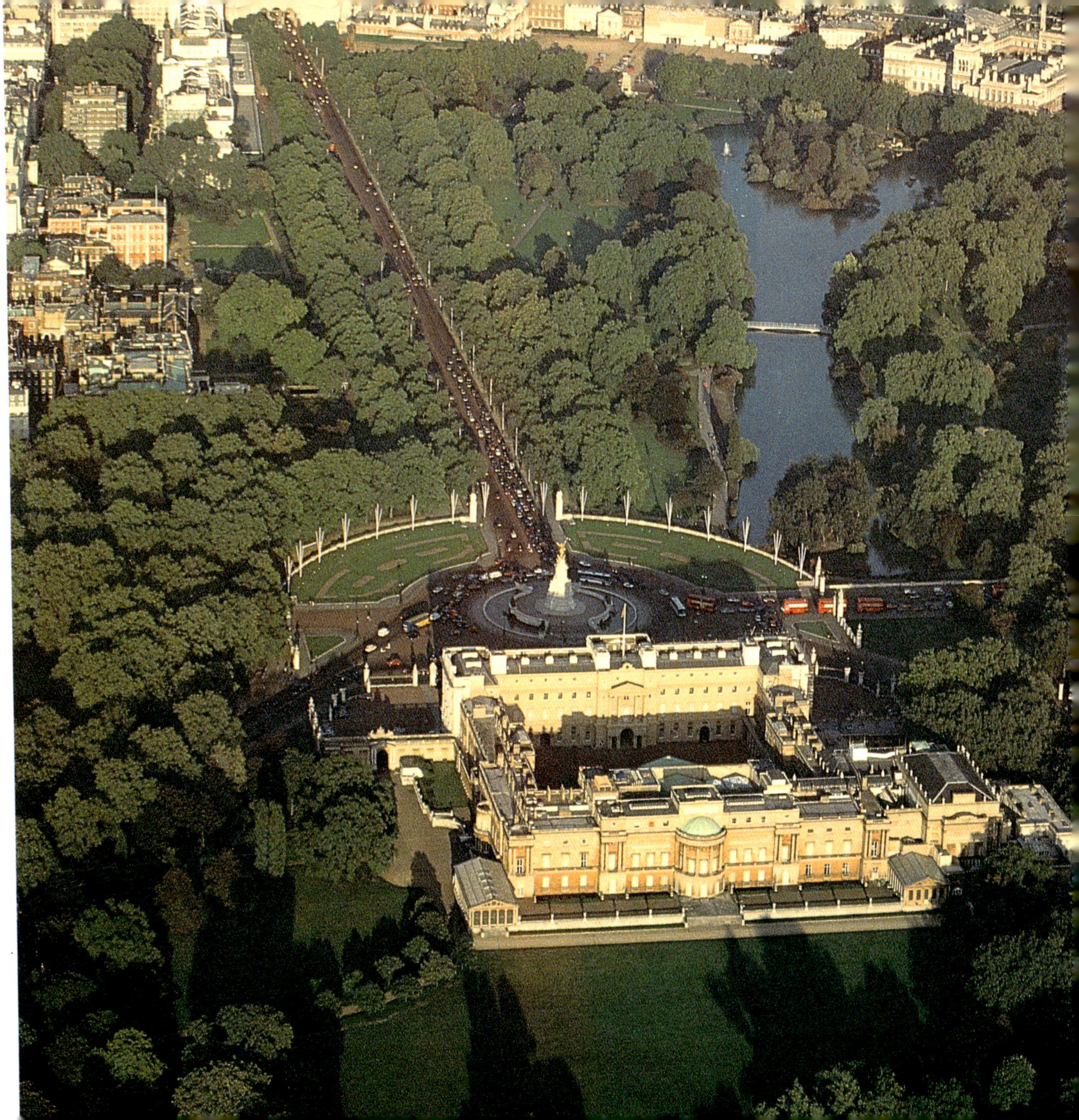

TOWER BRIDGE

The magnificent Victorian bridge was opened in 1894, when it carried 8,000 horse-drawn vehicles and 60,000 foot passengers across the river every day. The bridge used to be raised up to 150 times a week – now it's only 10 times a week – to let vessels in and out of the Pool of London. For a good part of 1992 a 30-strong team was at work 140 feet above the Thames repainting Tower Bridge. One painter by the name of White stumbled and spattered paint of the same colour over fifteen tourists below.

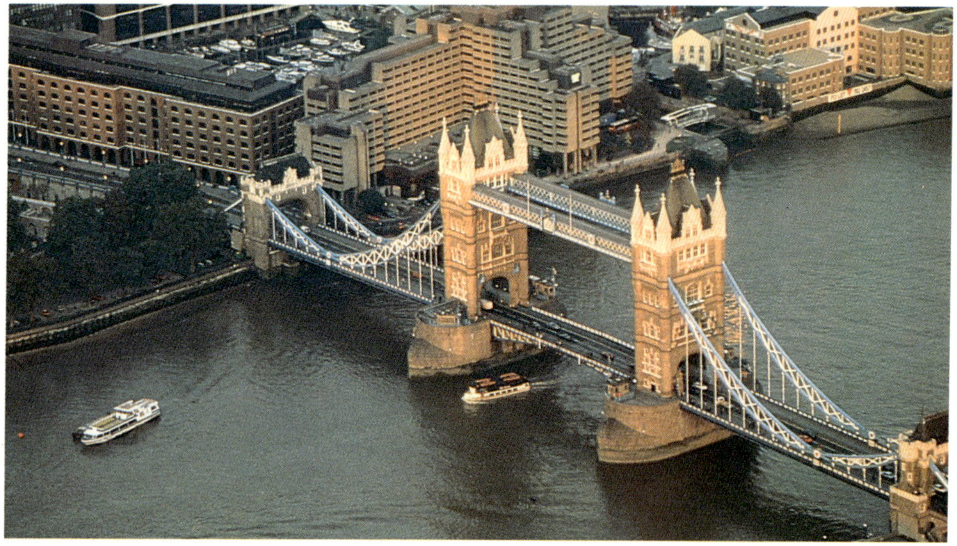

weather, and in winter it can be up to 9 inches shorter than it is in summer.

Heading back towards the river we find St Paul's, 365 feet high – one foot for every day of the year. Tower Bridge is worth looking at; although the bridge is raised about ten times a week, it doesn't stay up for long, so it's always exciting when we catch it open. Nestling alongside there's the Tower and St Katharine's Dock. We might take a turn around the NatWest Tower, built in the shape of their logo, and, almost huddling in its shadow, the unmistakable Lloyds building, all pipes and bits and pieces, and quite spectacular at night.

And then there is Canary Wharf. If ever a building could be said to have a split personality this is it; on a grey day it broods over London's skyline, a great hulking monolith, but on a summer's evening, when it catches the setting sun, it turns into a fairy-tale palace of gold. Sadly, the road the leading to it, the A13, is not only not paved with gold but can claim to be one of the most dug-up roads in London and, therefore, one of the most congested. Thank heavens (and the Department of Transport) for the new Limehouse Link – at £225 million for just over a mile, it's the most expensive road in Europe, if not the world.

To the south of the river there is not quite so much to see, but the Elephant and Castle forces itself on your attention, if only for its subtle colour scheme – is it a twist on the idea of pink elephants or was the designer the victim of 'pink elephantitis' the day he picked the paint? And just up the river is Battersea Power Station, still waiting for a future. Travelling northwest we pass over the top people's store, take a twirl around the Albert Hall and check to see if traffic in Hammersmith and Shepherd's Bush has tied itself into its usual tangle.

From there we might head south down the A3 to the M25 or maybe cruise up around the North Circular to Alexandra Palace. Wherever we go, it's almost certain we'll find a jam that needs reporting.

THE TOWER OF LONDON

The Tower has been a tourist attraction since at least the sixteenth century – in 1599 a German tourist bitterly complained about continually being asked for tips! It is visited by two and a half million people each year, more than the entire population of England in 1066 when William the Conqueror began the building. The last execution at the Tower, the shooting of a spy, took place in the moat on 15 August 1941.

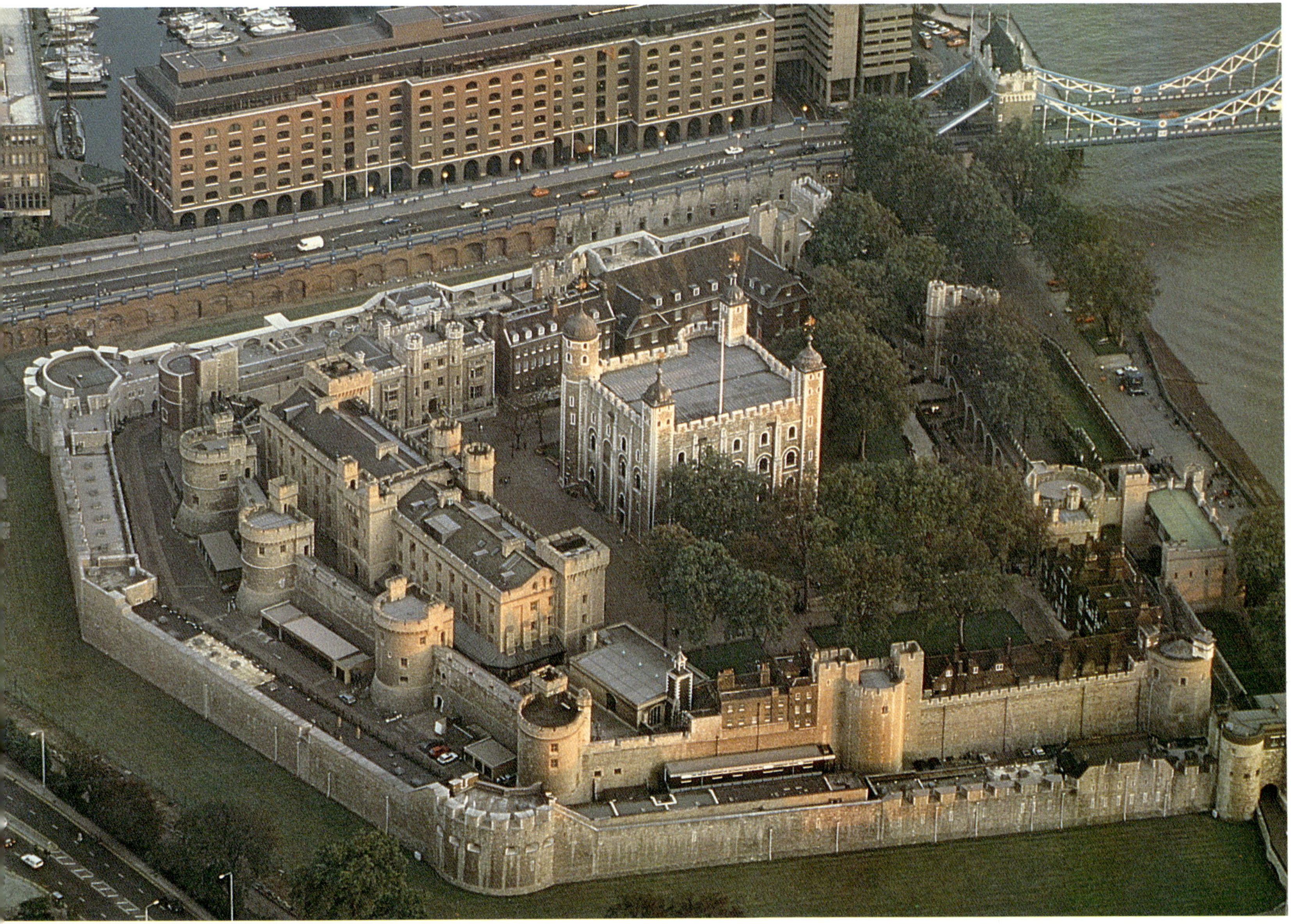

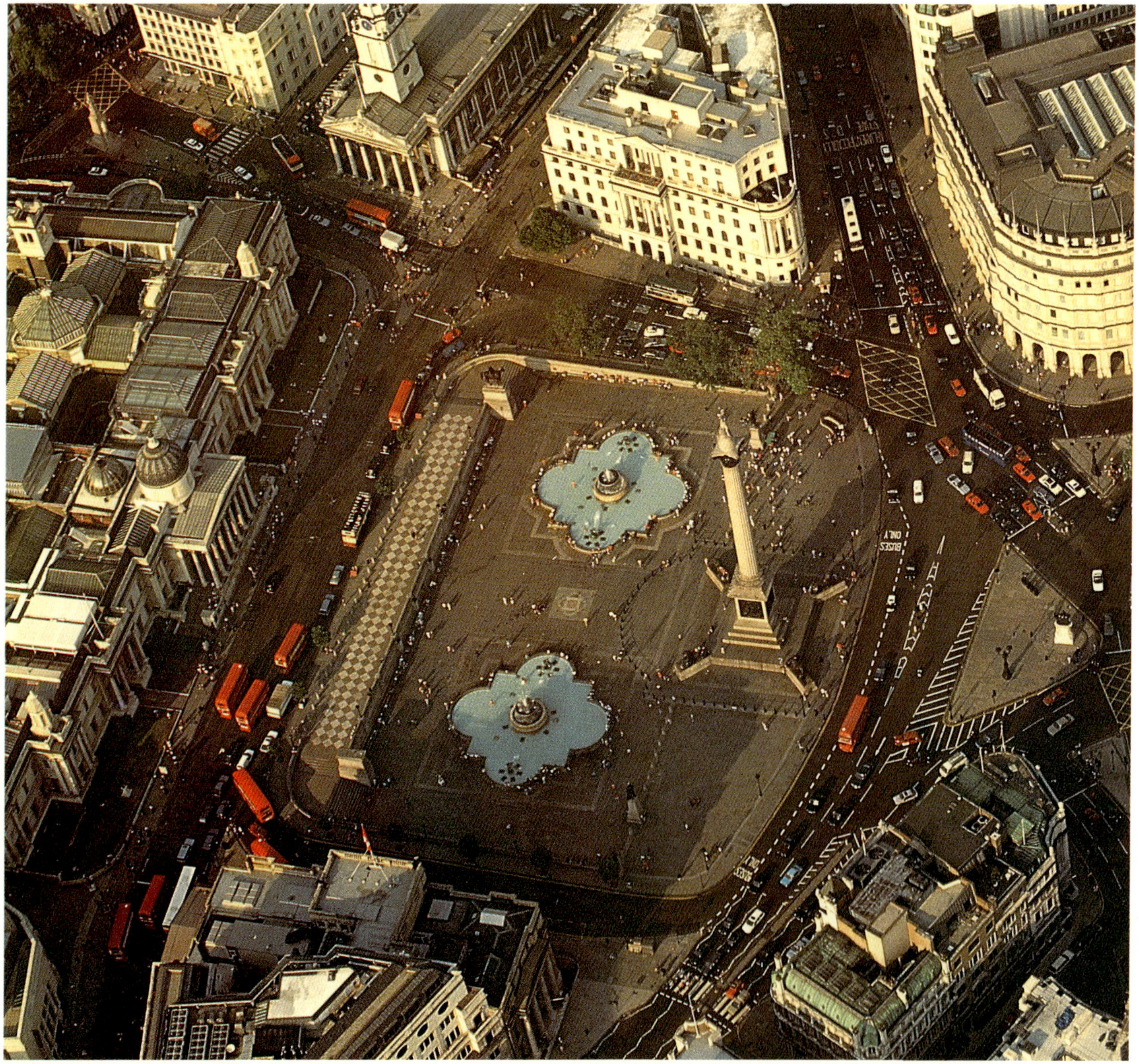

TRAFALGAR SQUARE

An imposing open space in the heart of London. The column was completed in 1843, a memorial to Lord Nelson, who died victorious at the battle of Trafalgar. Landseer's lions arrived in 1868, and St Martin's, in the northeast corner of the Square, is scarcely In-the-Fields.

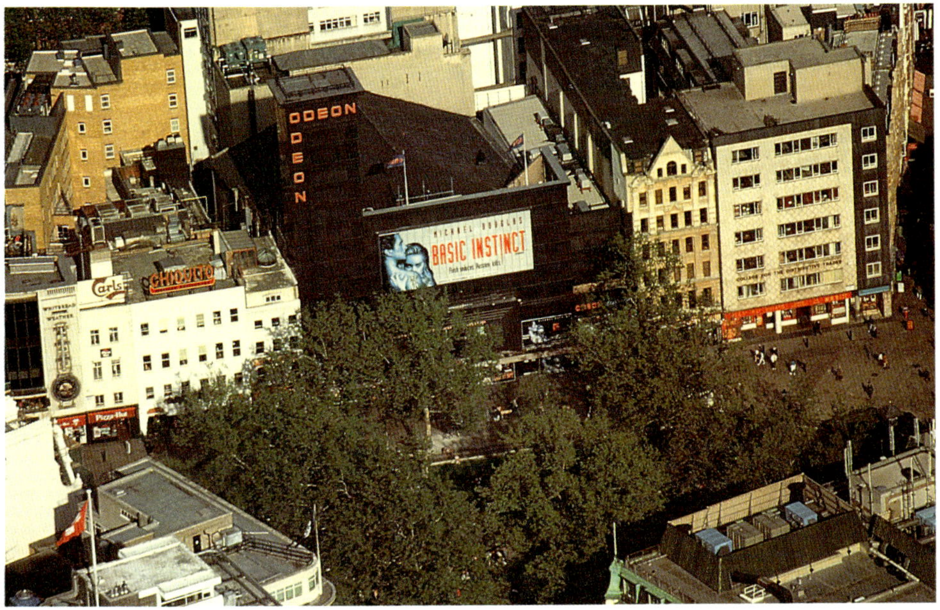

LEICESTER SQUARE

Once a residential square, but for generations synonymous with the bright lights of the West End – cinema, dancing and the good life. Now showing at the Odeon, Leicester Square: *Basic Instinct*.

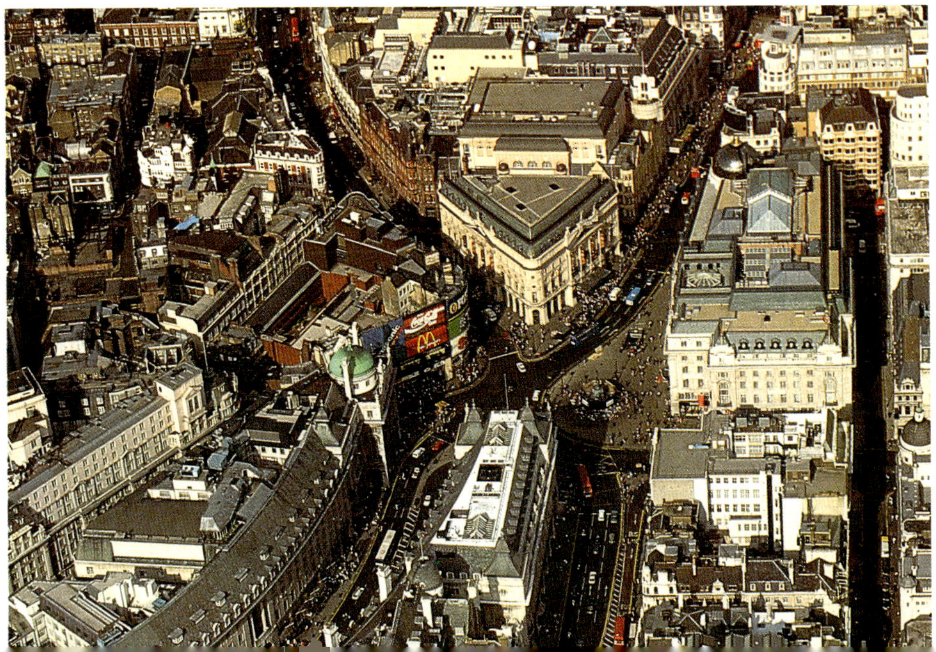

PICCADILLY CIRCUS

Not so special from the air, all the world passes by this fabulous place. Nor can we solve from the Flying Eye the controversy about which way Eros, with his newly mended broken leg, is facing: towards Piccadilly or up Shaftesbury Avenue in tribute to the philanthropist Lord Shaftesbury. Eros is more properly called the Shaftesbury Memorial.

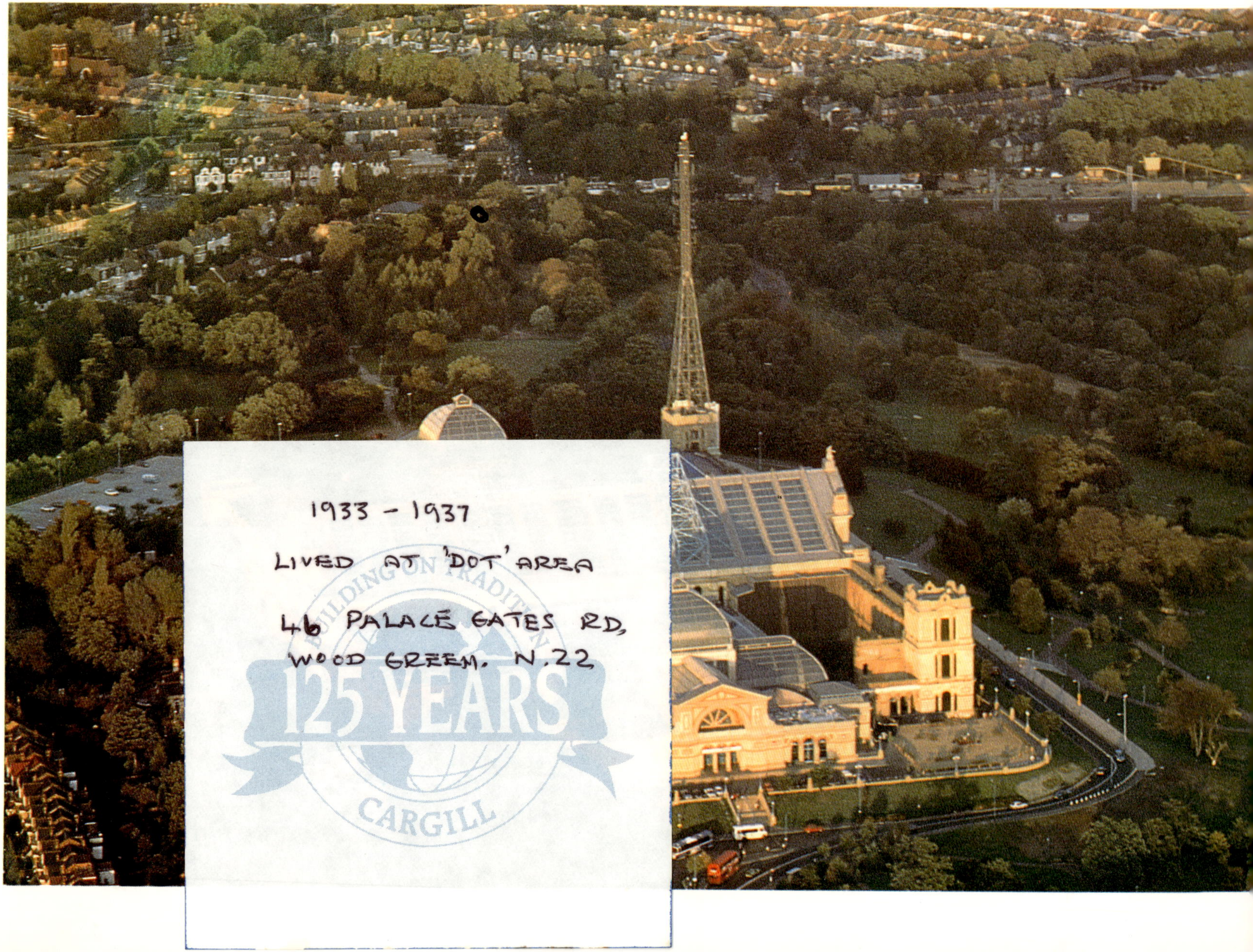
1933 - 1937
LIVED AT 'DOT' AREA
46 PALACE GATES RD,
WOOD GREEM. N.22

ALEXANDRA PALACE

The first television broadcast came from Ally Pally on 2 November 1936. There were approximately 350 viewers. It took time, but the idea caught on . . .

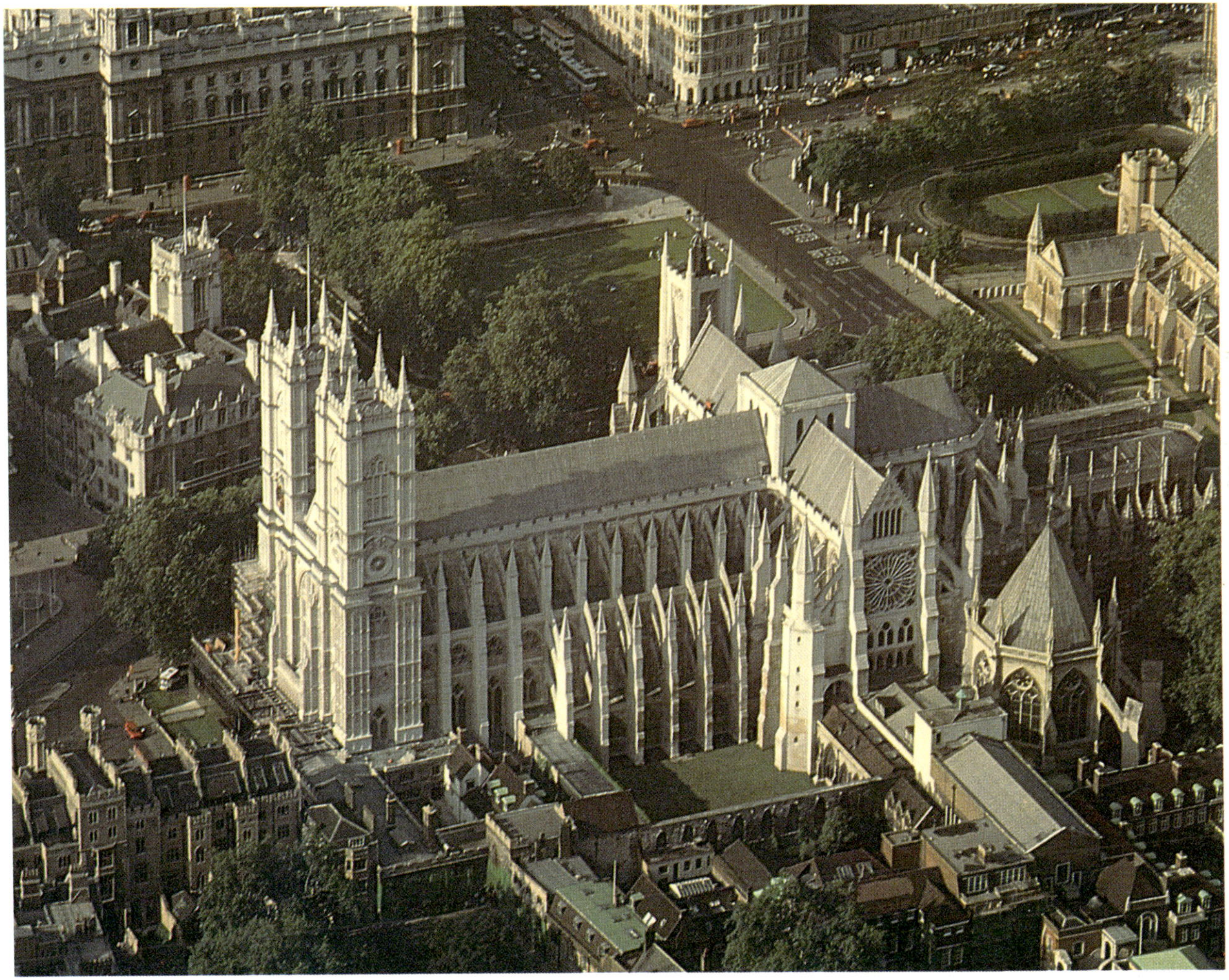

WESTMINSTER ABBEY

Cleaned and restored, the Abbey shines in the afternoon sun as though it had just been built. Westminster gets its name from the Abbey; founded by Edward the Confessor well to the west of the existing city, it came to be known as the 'church in the west' or Westminster.

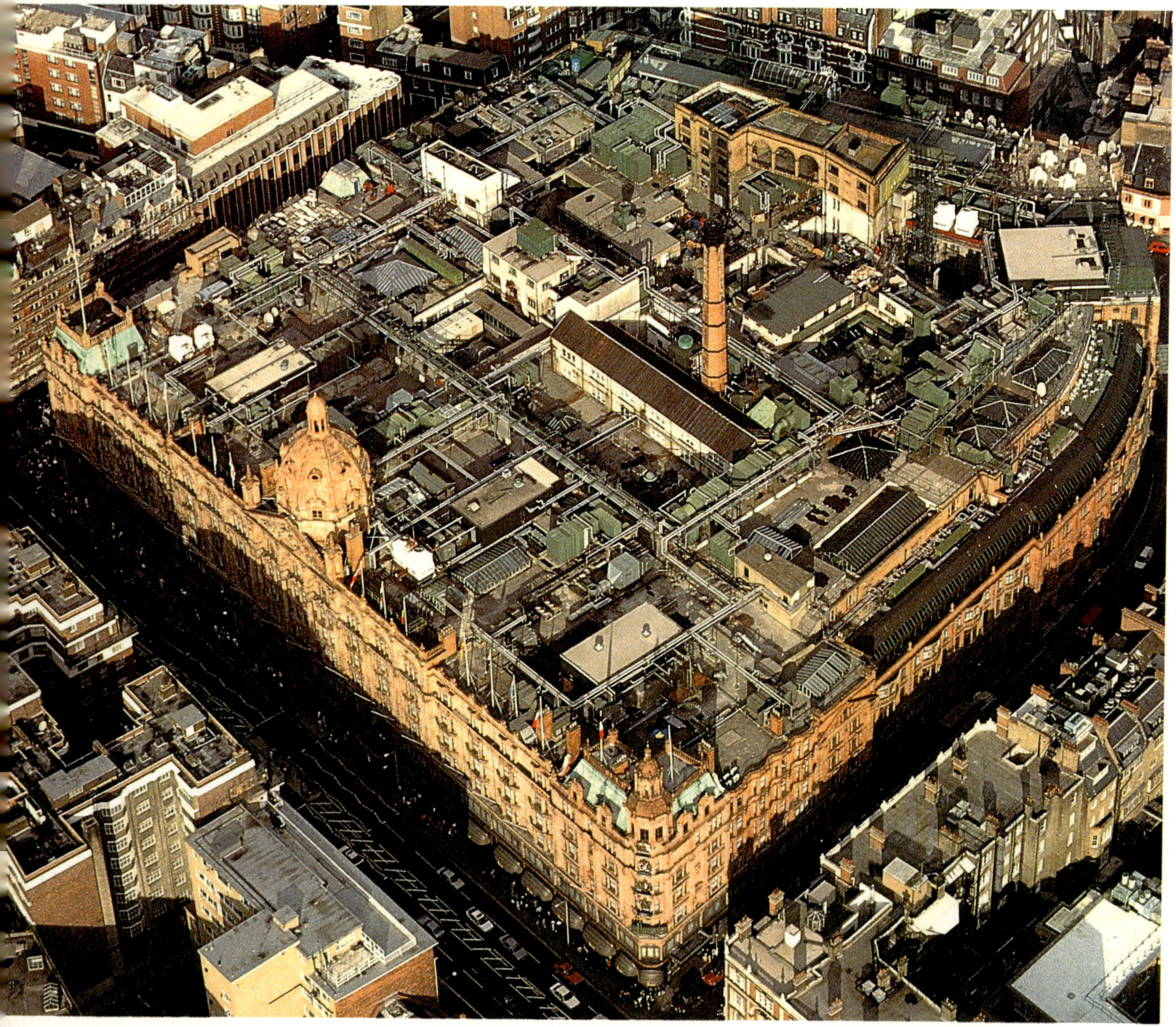

HARRODS

Charles Henry Harrod opened up shop in Stepney in 1800, moving the business to a small 'country' shop in Knightsbridge after the cholera epidemic of 1849. The country shop grew to an empire, with 50 lifts covering nearly 50,000 miles a year. Customers walk out with six million carrier bags a year.

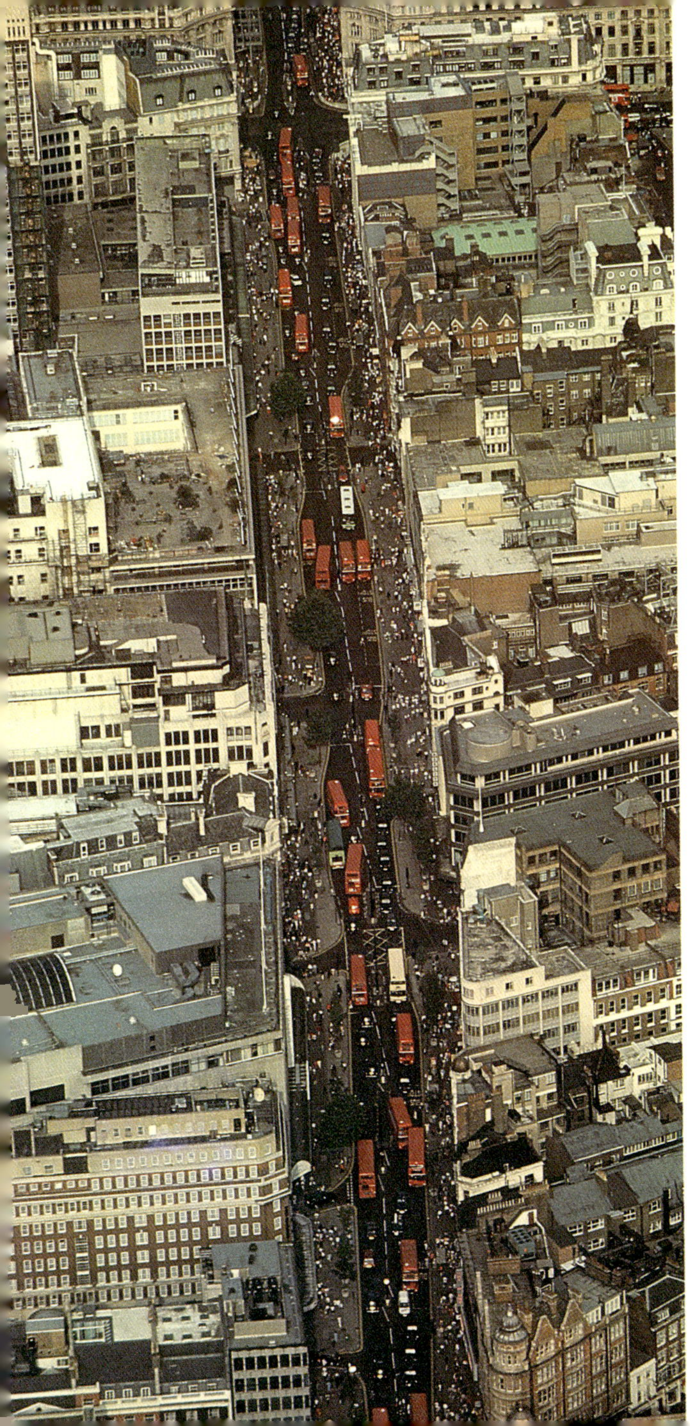

OXFORD STREET

London's most famous shopping street, with over 60,000 pedestrians entering per hour at busy times. All is bus and bustle; but will the fleets of red double-deckers disappear with the deregulation of London's buses?

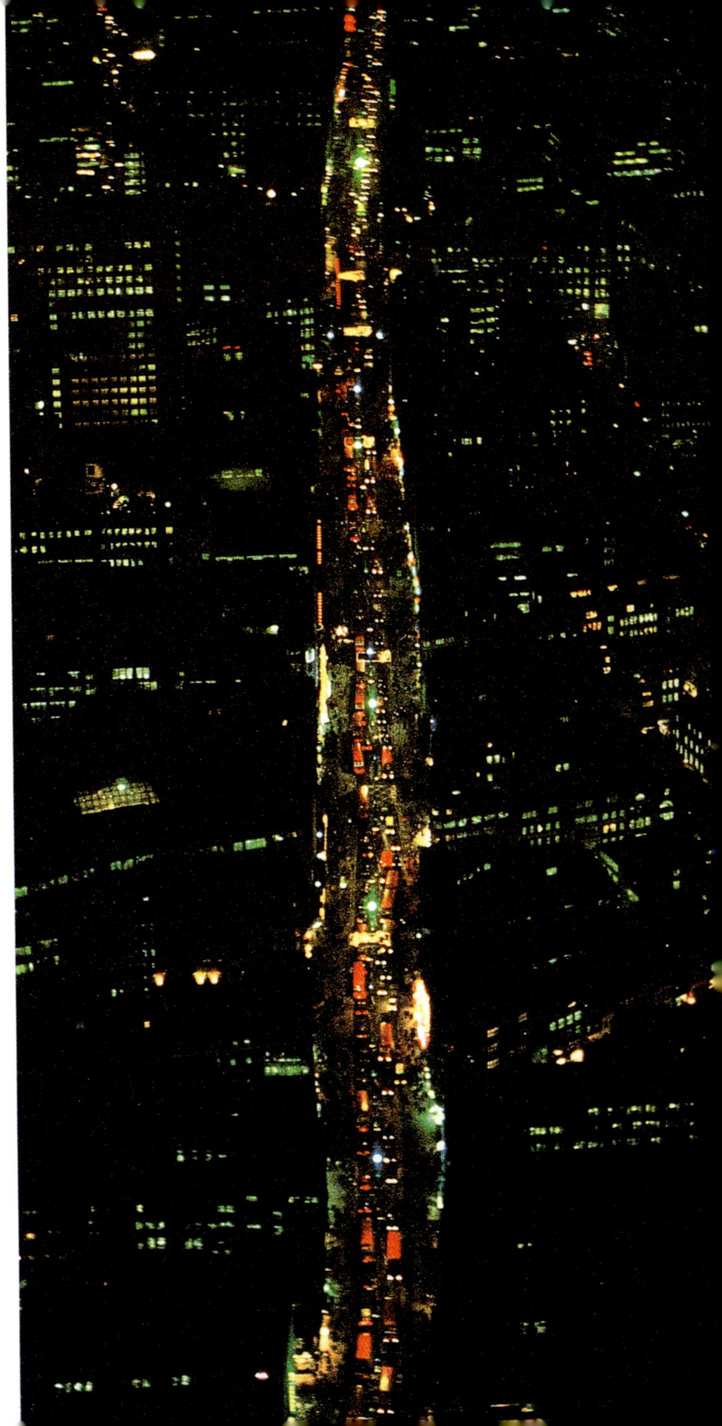

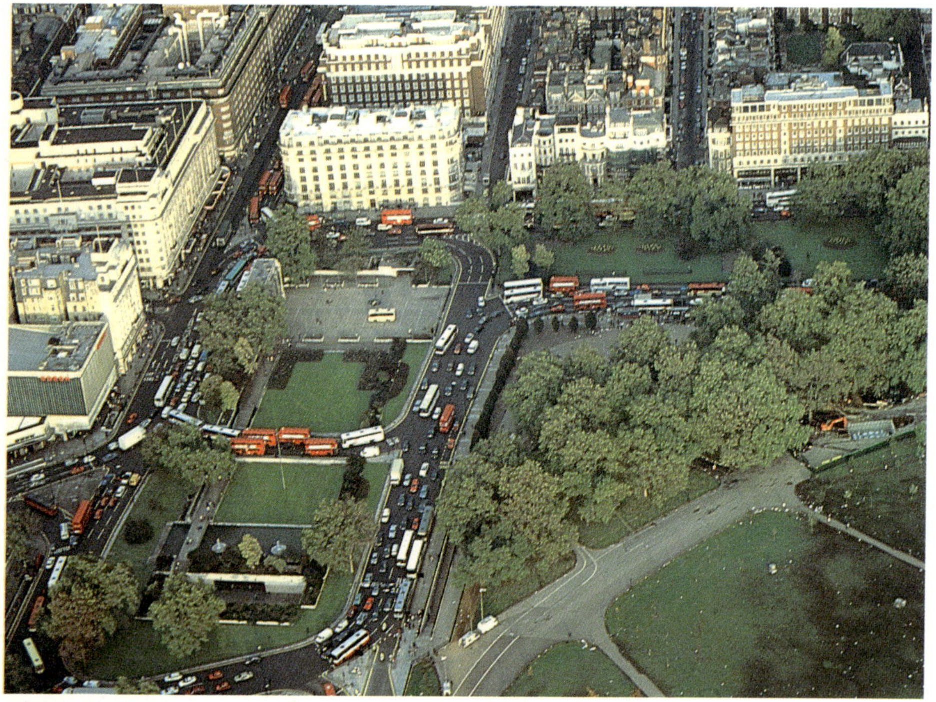

MARBLE ARCH

This was the location of Tyburn Tree, London's traditional place of public execution. The congestion here is the aftermath of the miners' rally in Hyde Park in October 1992.

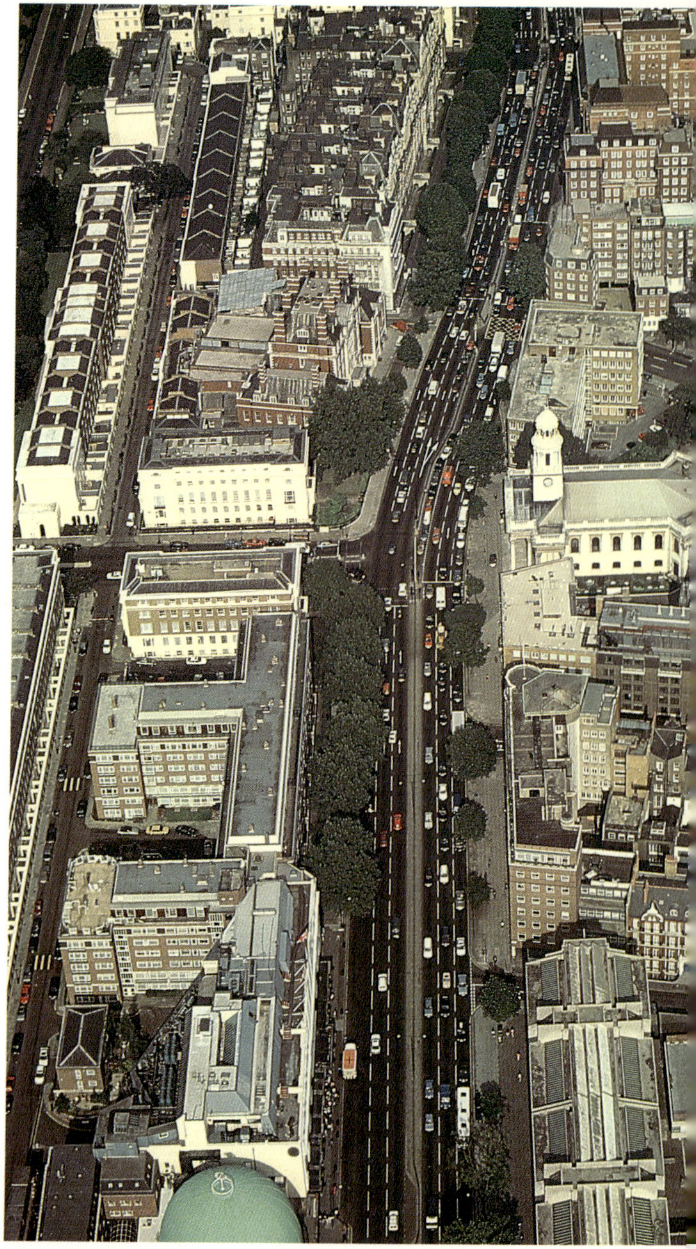

MARYLEBONE ROAD

Another of London's traffic hot-spots and always ready to keep us busy in the Flying Eye. This is the view east from the green dome of the Planetarium towards Euston Road and the underpass.

'I've chosen Marylebone Road because I know it as well as I know my own flat – I know every brick and every pothole! I've seen Marylebone Road 3,460 times: my producer and I worked out the other day that over my years with Capital I've done 1,730 shows, in fact probably more by the time this book comes out – it's only June now, folks!

I go right along the length of it from the Westway to Euston Tower, and it's like a recurring nightmare: every time I look up I seem to be on the Marylebone Road. And even worse, of course, a lot of the time I'm stationary because all the traffic has got clogged up in the Euston underpass outside Capital Gold. As you come over the Westway you can see the whole thing stretching out ahead of you, and one day, as I was coming in to do my show, all I could see, right the way up to Euston Tower, was solid traffic – absolutely nothing moving. Time went on, and I'd moved exactly 2 feet 3½ inches. I could hear old Fluff (Alan Freeman), who in those days did the show before mine, starting to sound a bit panicked because I hadn't arrived, so I thought 'Oh dear, I'd better do something about this or the boss will be livid'. I got out my mobile phone and phoned up the control room, and they put me on air. I went round with my phone to all the cars in the jam, asking if anyone wanted a request on the radio, so I did a sort of live broadcast from the traffic jam until the traffic started moving again. In the end, I was about 20 minutes late, but as traffic jams go it was quite a lot of fun – perhaps we should make it a regular feature of the show.'

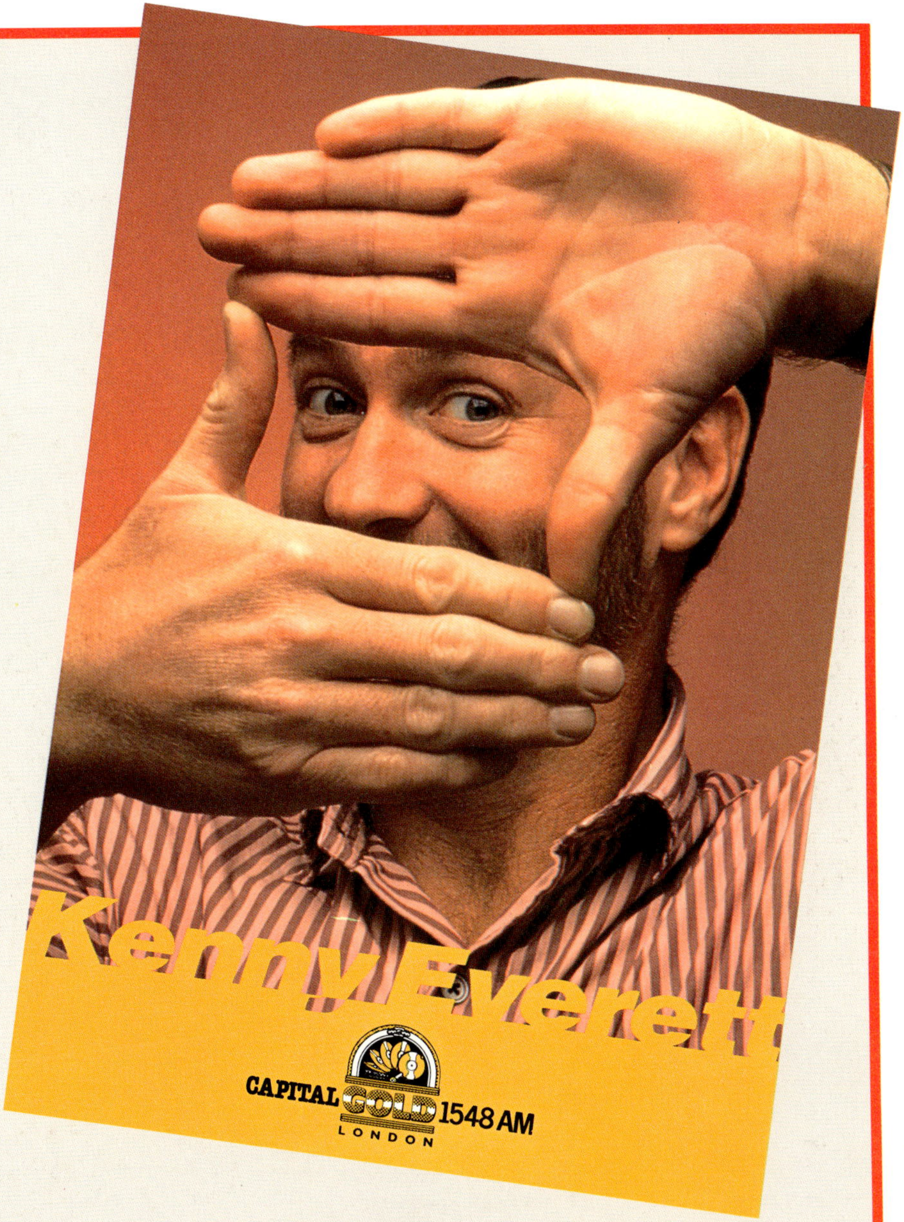

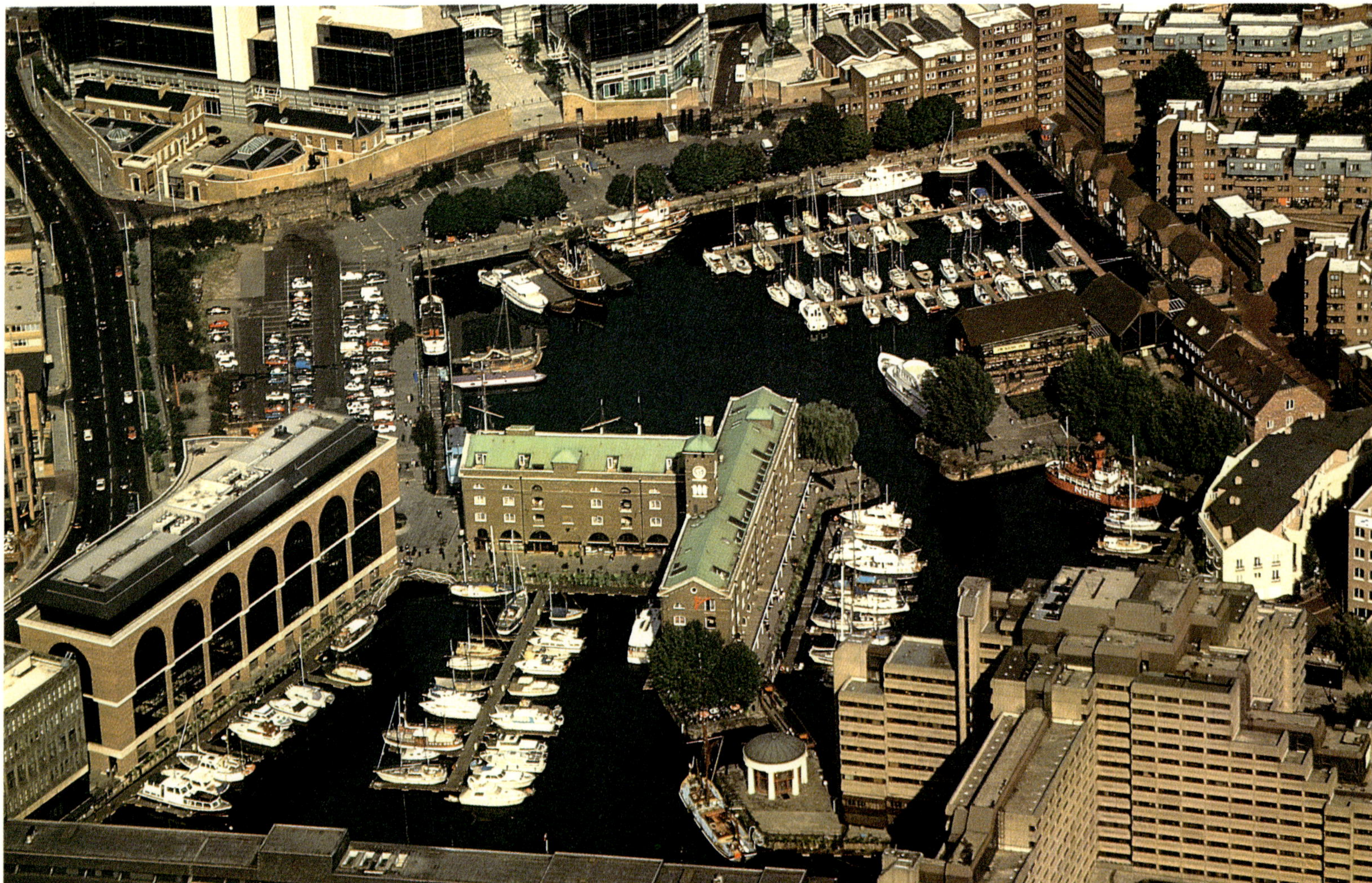

ST KATHARINE'S DOCK

The dock, properly known as the Haven, was, with the World Trade Centre, the first urban renewal project to be undertaken in Docklands in the early 1970s. A short walk 'on the other side' of Tower Bridge, the whole area is now a popular and agreeable tourist attraction.

THE CITY OF LONDON

Over a quarter of a million people commute daily to work in the narrow streets and tall buildings of the world's leading financial centre.

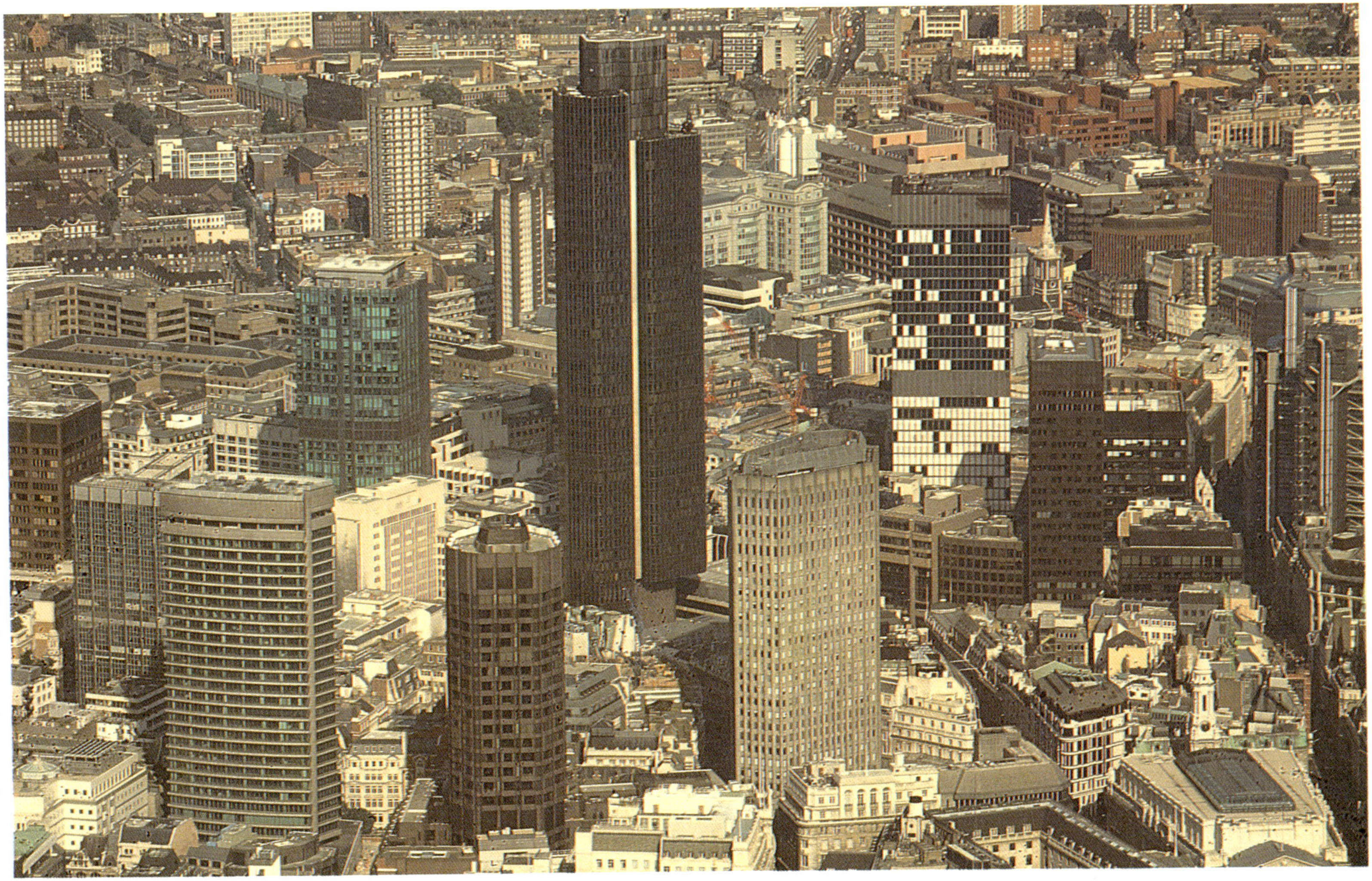

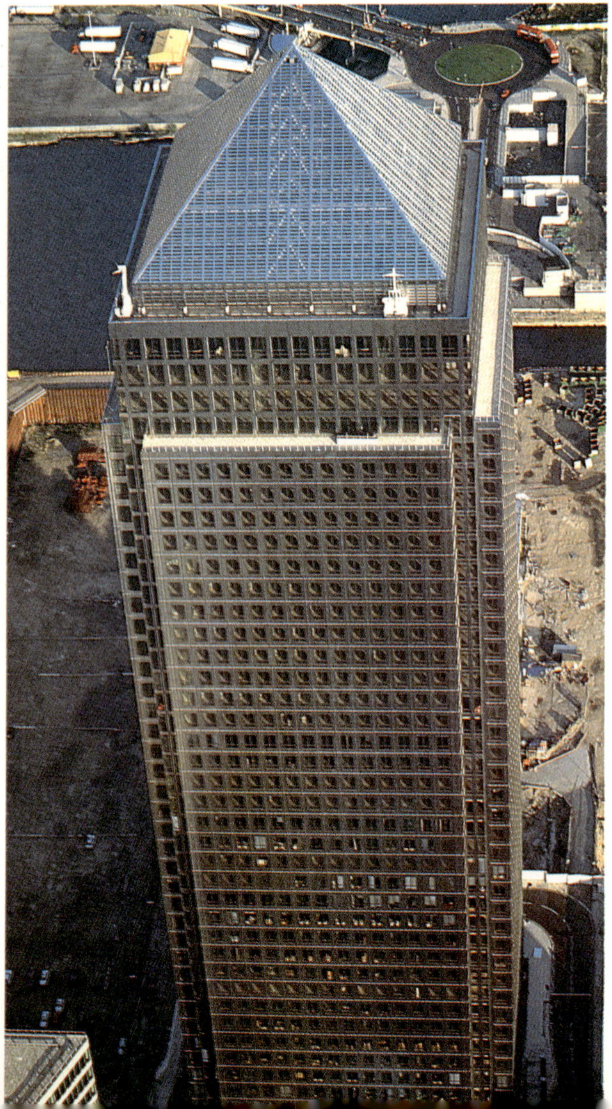

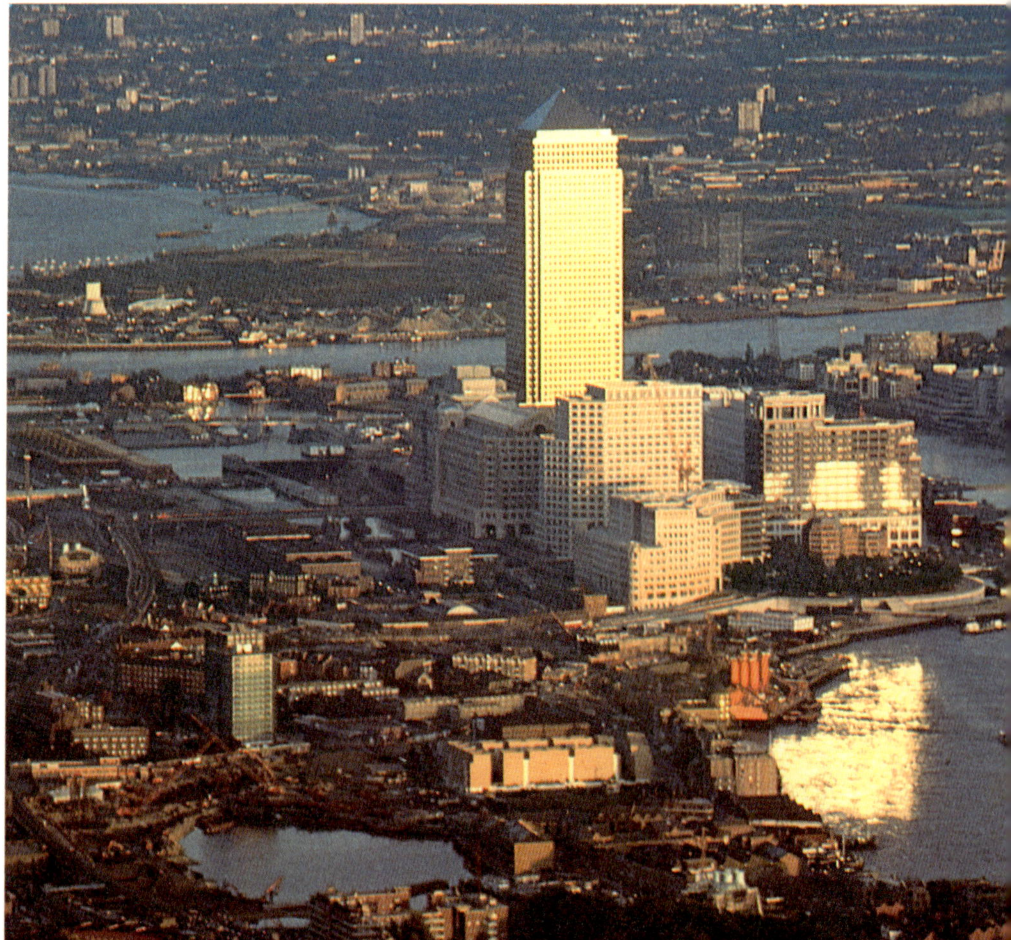

ONE, CANADA SQUARE

Flying over London's tallest building, better known as Canary Wharf: as near to Mammon as we ever get. As befits such a huge construction, it dominates the whole London landscape.

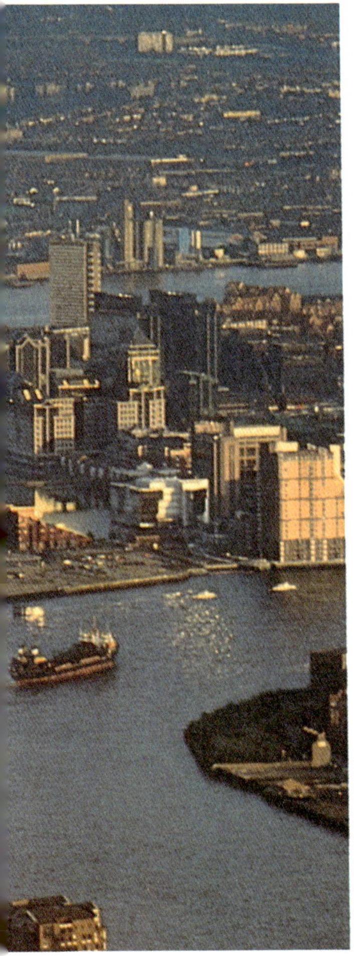

THE ELEPHANT AND CASTLE

Not, perhaps, quite so splendid is this pink pachyderm of a south London 1960s shopping centre.

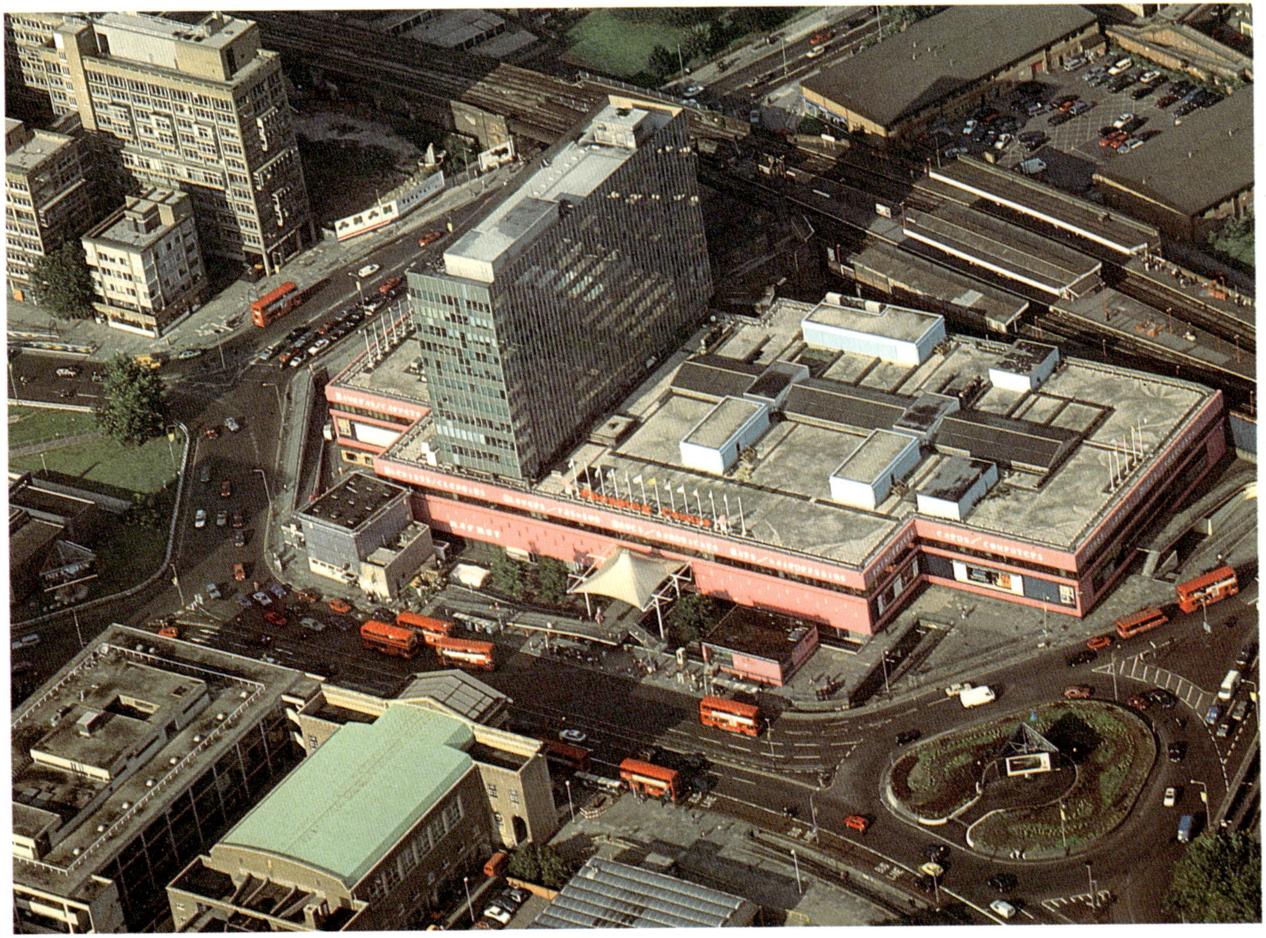

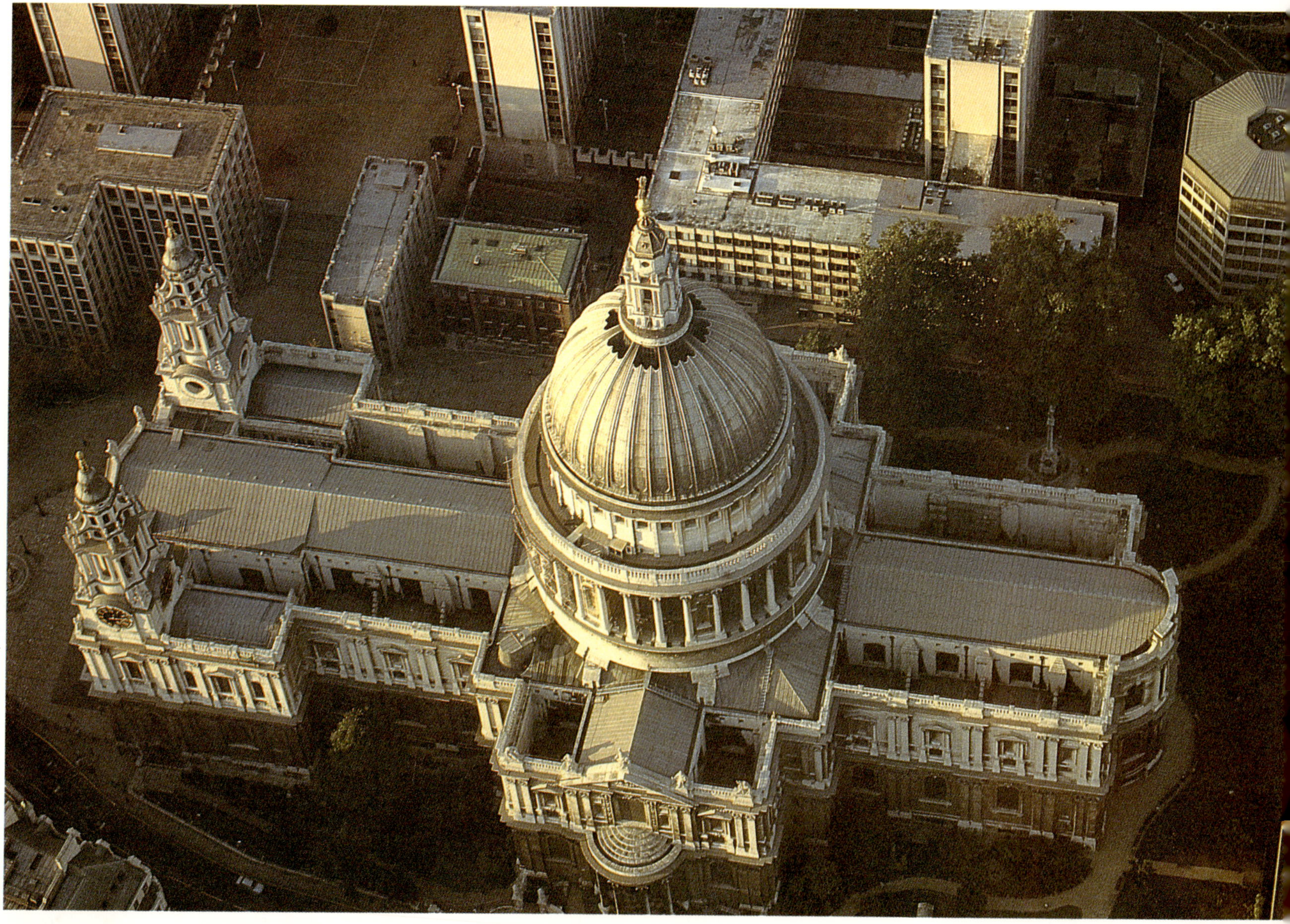

EUSTON ROAD

The two towers of London: on the left, Capital's home in the Euston Tower, on the right, the BT Tower. Tall buildings are susceptible to wind and temperature. In a high wind the BT Tower sways up to 8 inches off vertical, and in winter it contracts to be up to 9 inches shorter than in summer.

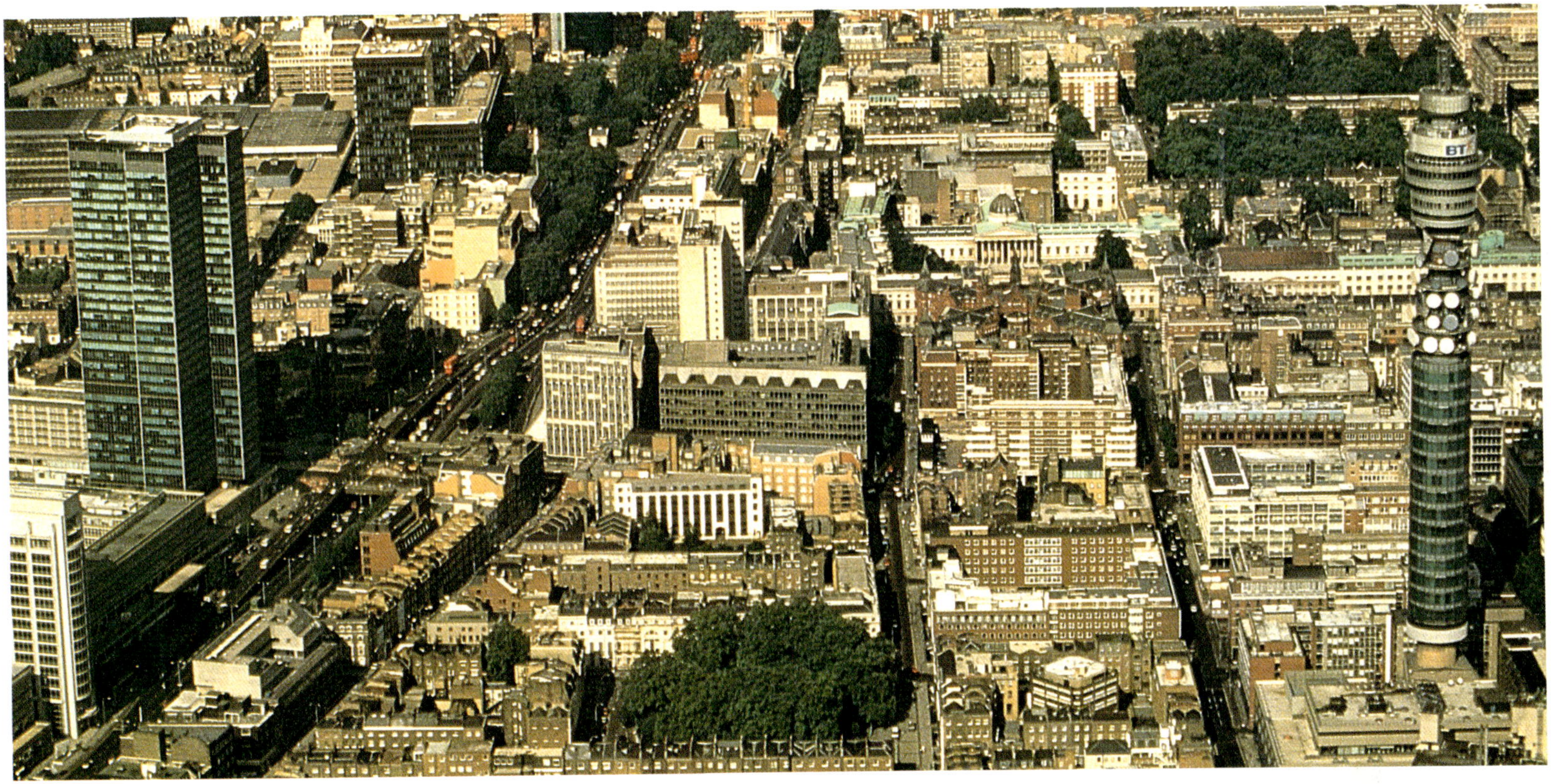

ST PAUL'S CATHEDRAL

The outside wall that hides the buttresses can be clearly seen in this aerial shot. Buried under the dome is Nelson, who was brought back from Trafalgar in a container filled with rum. The 40,000 visitors on a summer day give off 1,500,000 kilocalories of heat inside the cathedral, enough to boil around 10,000 kettles!

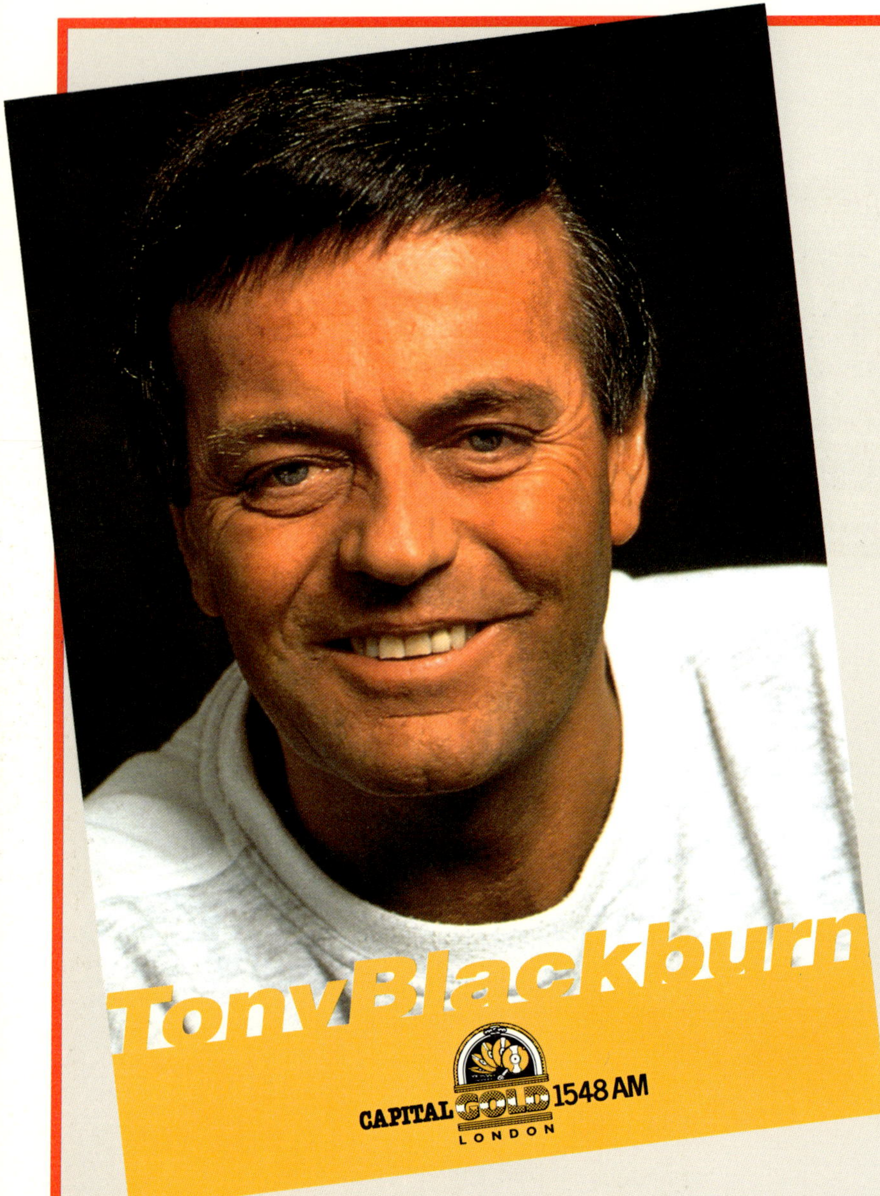

'I LOVE the BT Tower because for me it's really the true centre of London. When I drive in to do the Breakfast Show at about 5.30 in the morning, particularly on one of those wonderful summer mornings, it really does look very impressive, silhouetted against the sky. In a way, it's the landmark we look at all the time at Capital Gold – it's more or less the next-door tower to our very own Golden Tower.

And, of course, it brings back many happy memories for me because, years ago, when it was open to the public, the top was a revolving restaurant and many a happy evening was spent in it. We used to call it the revolving teeth because so many people were noshing and gnashing away up there. And it was right back then that I thought what a wonderful place it would be to broadcast from – an ambition I realized in September 1992, when Capital Gold asked me to do just that. I remember it all so well: it was a beautifully crisp, clear morning, and as I was driving towards it I could see that they had put my name in lights all round the tower – quite a unique experience, seeing that.

The views from there are fantastic, only to be beaten, I suppose, by the ones from the Flying Eye. I went up with Hazel a couple of years ago, and I'm proud to say that I didn't feel at all ill, even when we circled over my flat a few times so that I could take some photos. Of course, in the morning it's Russ Kane up in the plane, and on that particular day, while I had breakfast out on the deck of the Tower with a couple of prize-winners, he circled around us in the Flying Eye. It was all a bit like King Kong: I suppose I was the gorilla – or was it Fay Wray?'

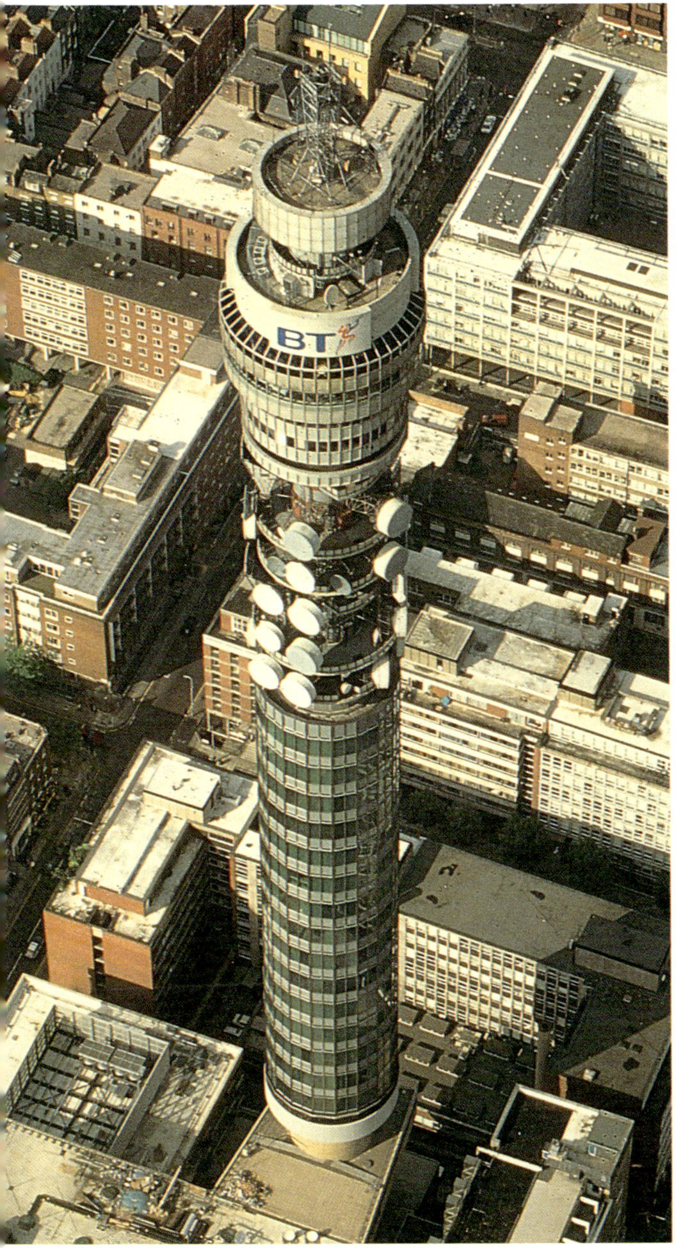

BT AND THE GOLDEN TOWER

This would have been Russ Kane's view of two towers when Tony Blackburn was playing his King Kong role. Even the tallest building (and the BT Tower was, for a long time, London's tallest) seems to shrink down into its surroundings when seen from the air.

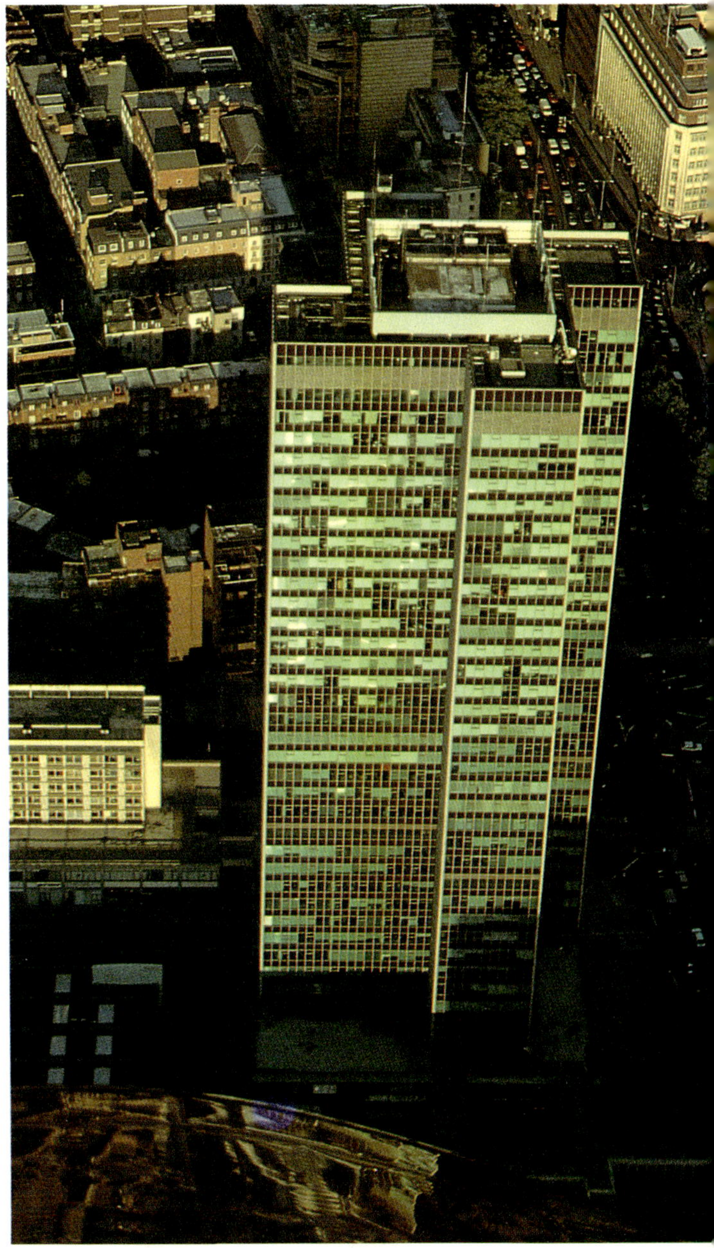

Capital Contrasts

When we take guests up in the Flying Eye in summer the frequent comment is 'how green it all looks'. When you are plodding along the grimy pavements, with the grey tower blocks rearing up on all sides, it's easy to forget that London is crammed full of squares and parks and that it is one of the greenest capitals in the world.

One of the joys of flying in high summer is to see the acres of fields spread out below us like a patchwork: suddenly the green is studded with a whole palette of colours – the rape fields burst into bloom with slashes of sunshiny yellow; the poppies give a flash of red; and cool blue is added by the linseed.

London is a city of colour and contrasts – looming skyscrapers, serried rows of houses, five million trees, rivers and reservoirs – and everywhere you look are the stylized patterns of daily life.

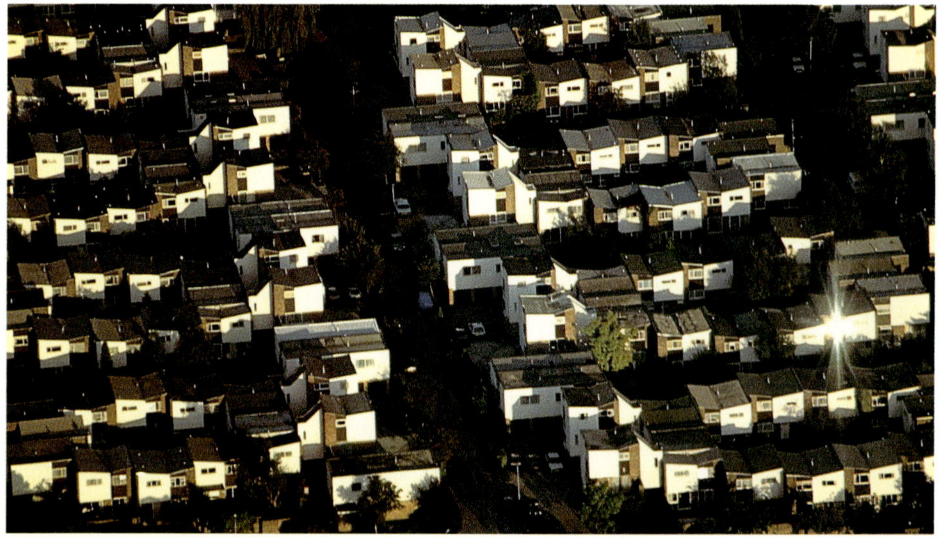

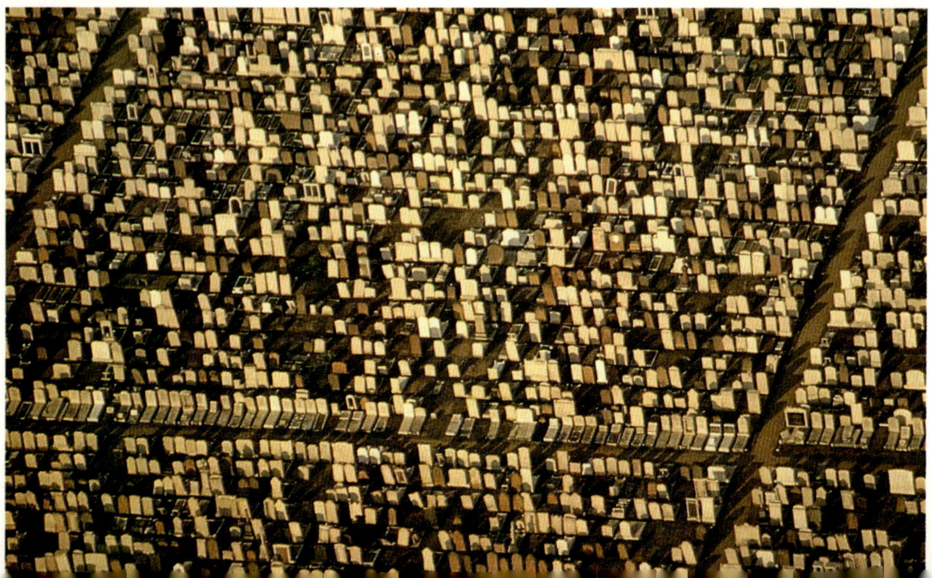

THE RHYTHM OF LIFE
London is more than just tower blocks and housing estates. From the air it is a city of pictures and patterns. The living (and here the dead, too) are arranged in neat rows, in vast crescents, in bright, shining little boxes, and they all look just the same. Elsewhere, fields and crops, reservoirs and floods, even the sewage plant, make their mark and from 1,000 feet up become a wonderful patchwork of colour and shapes.

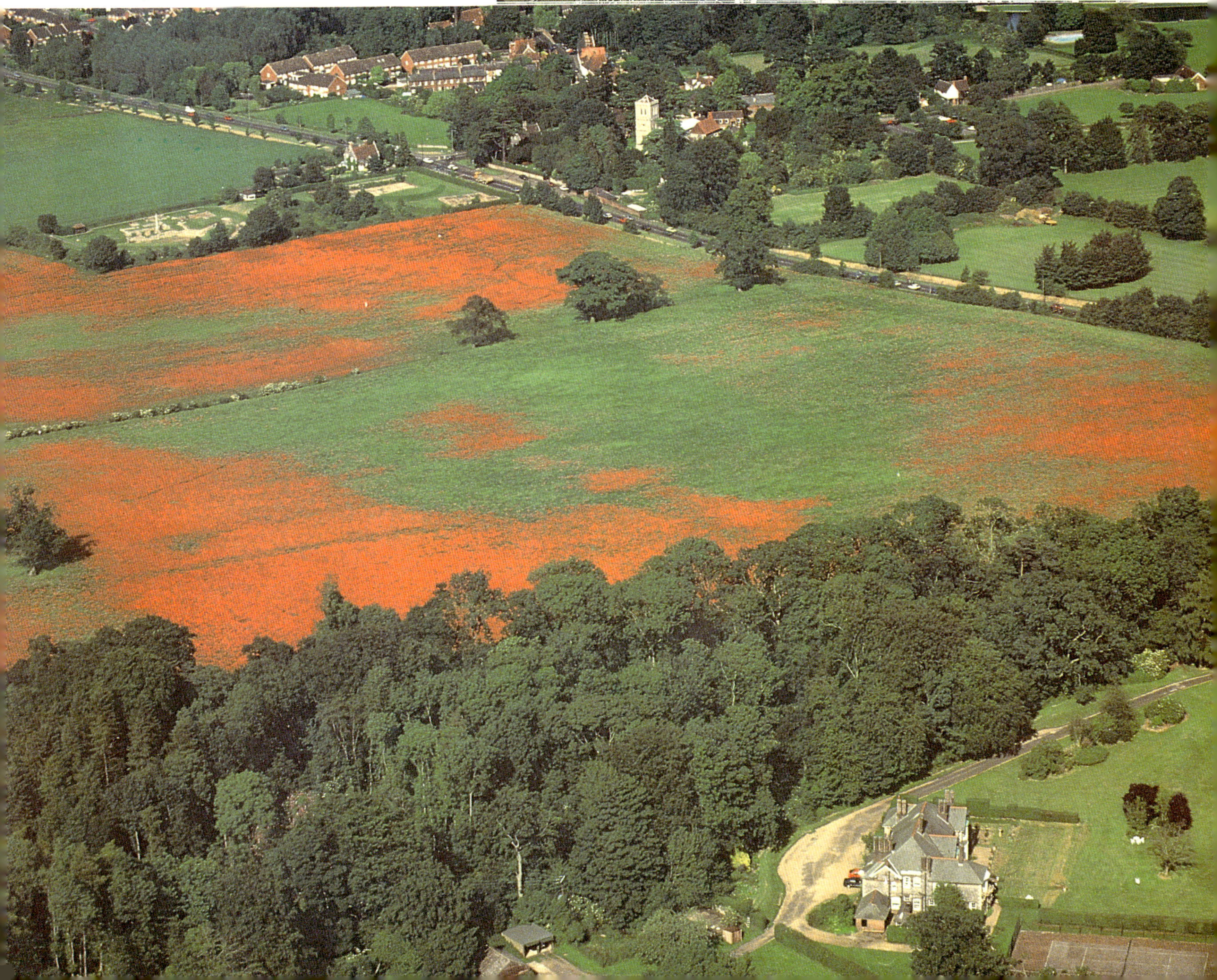

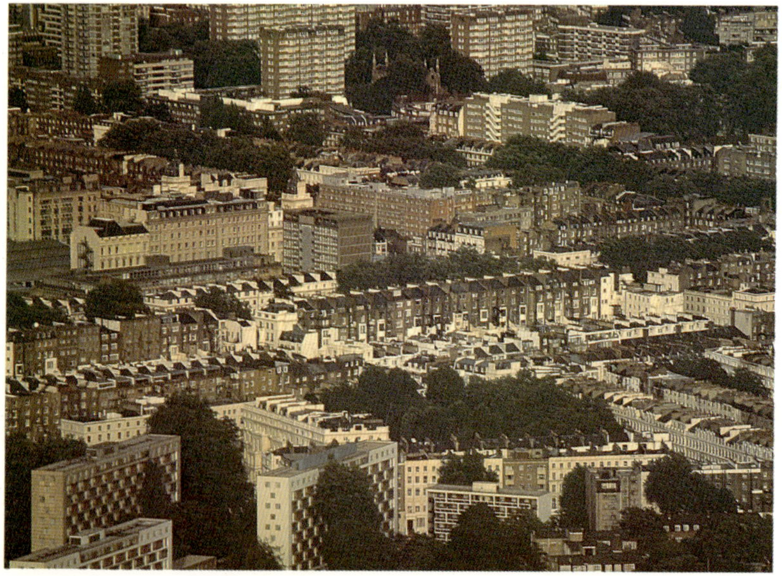

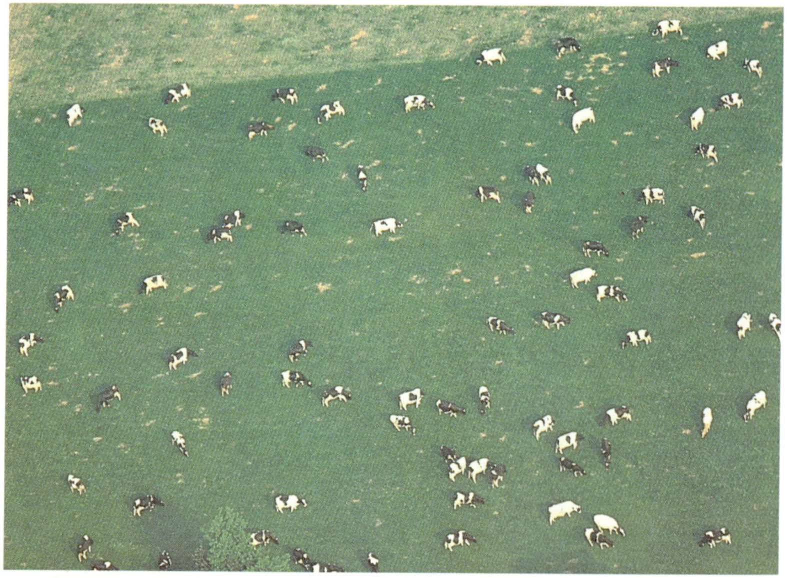

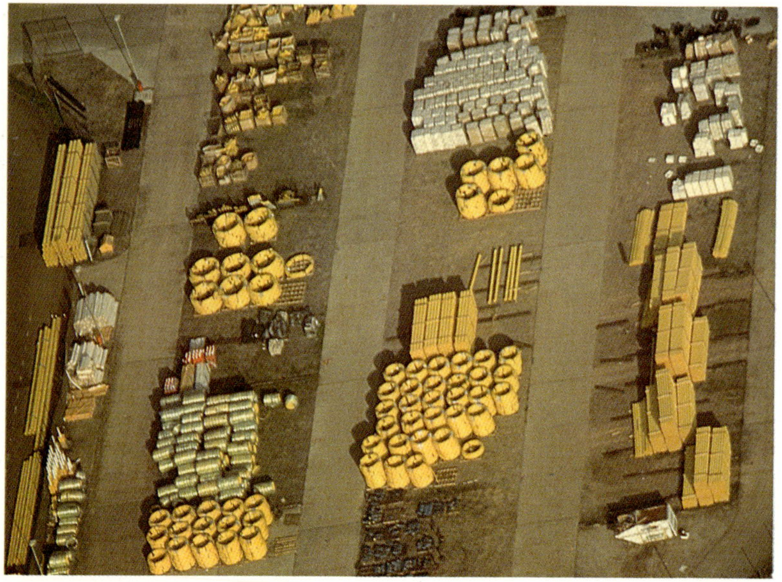

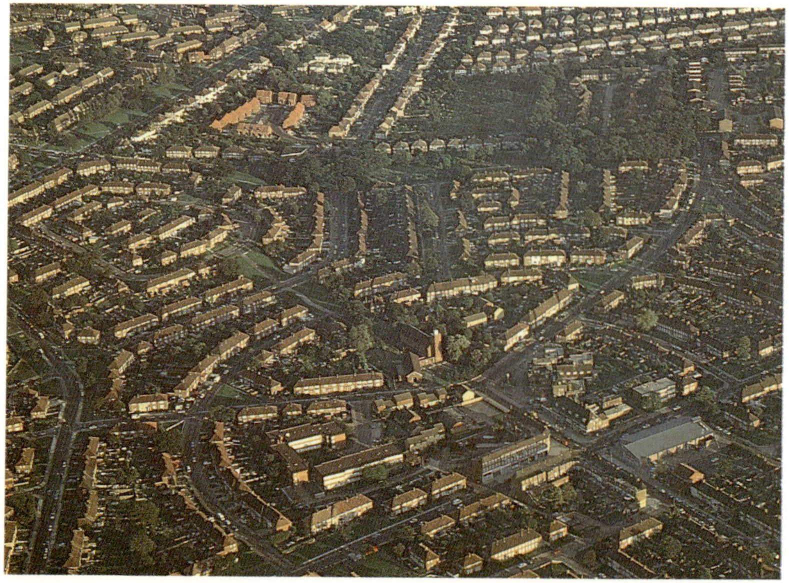

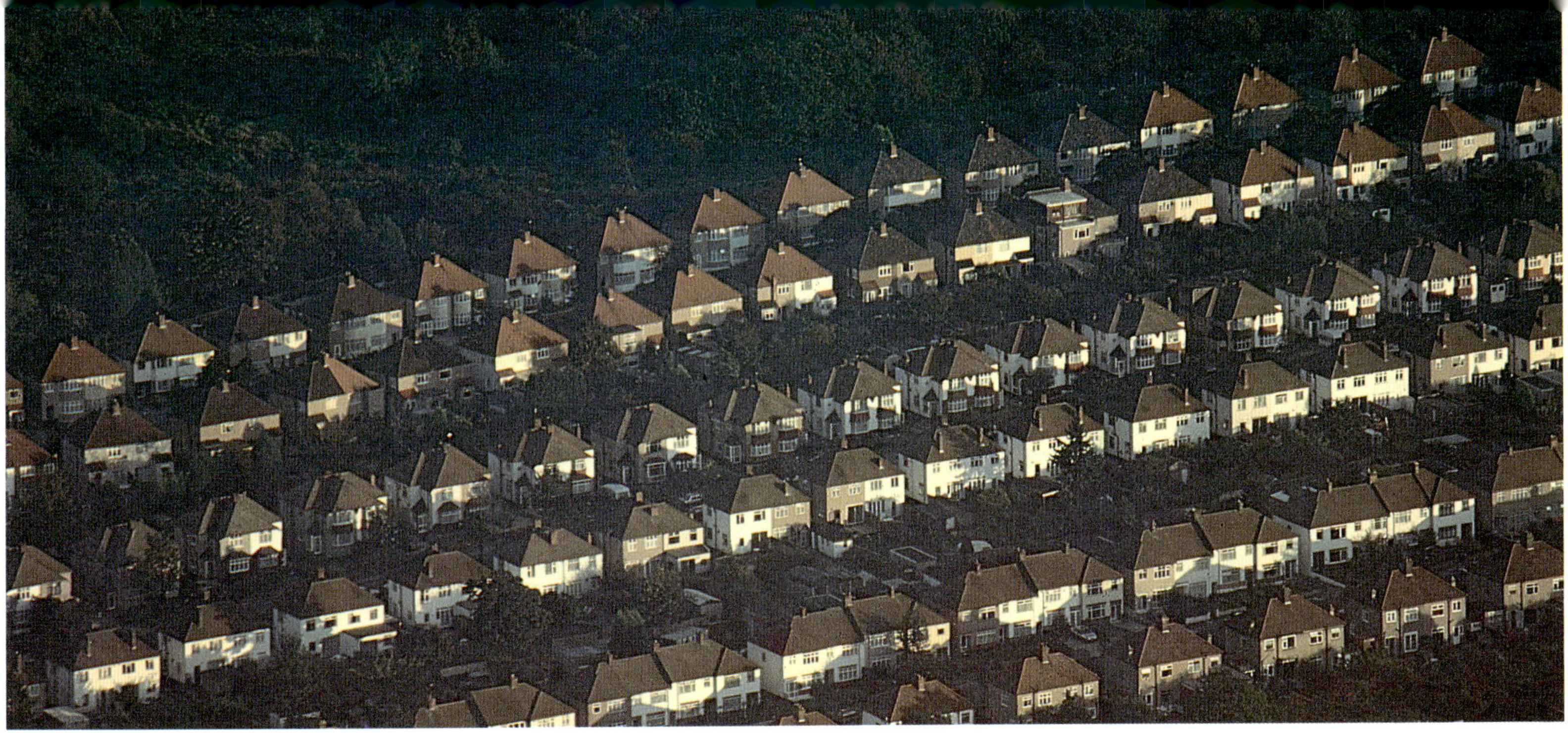

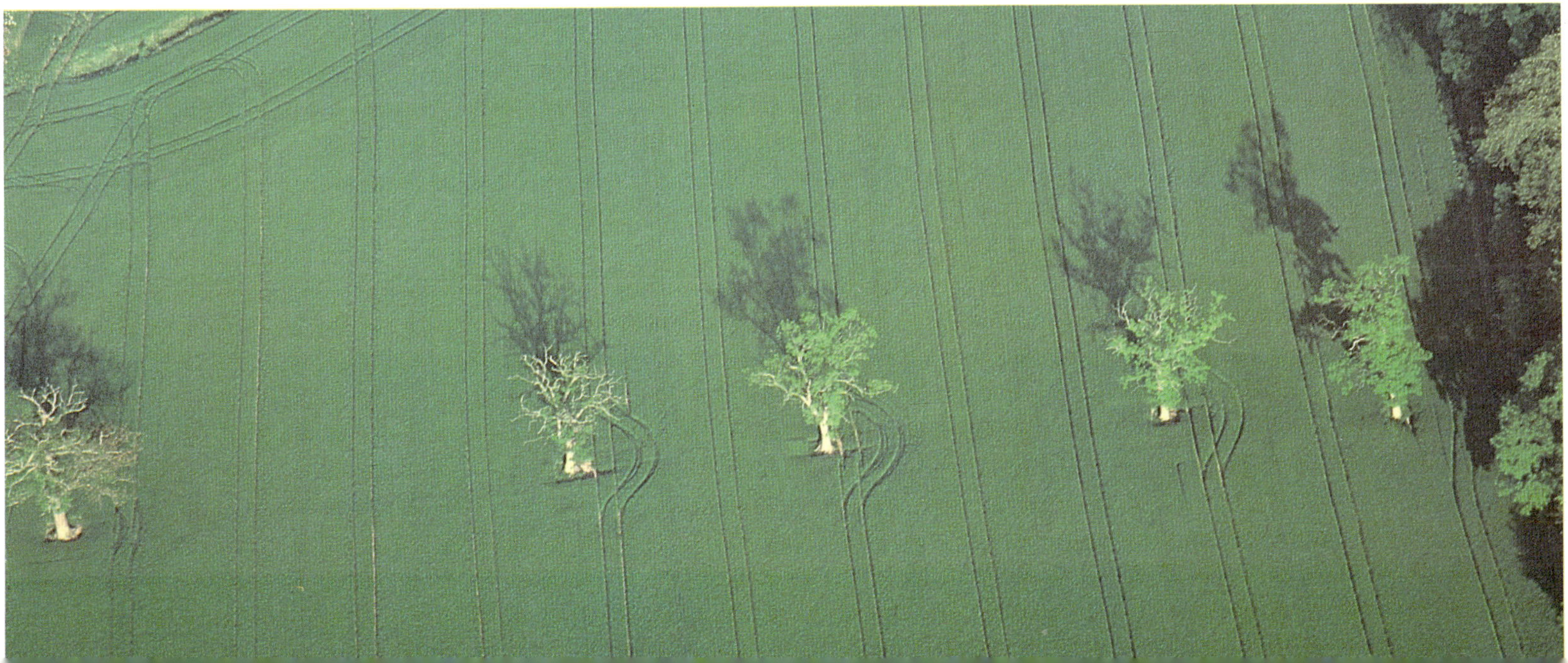

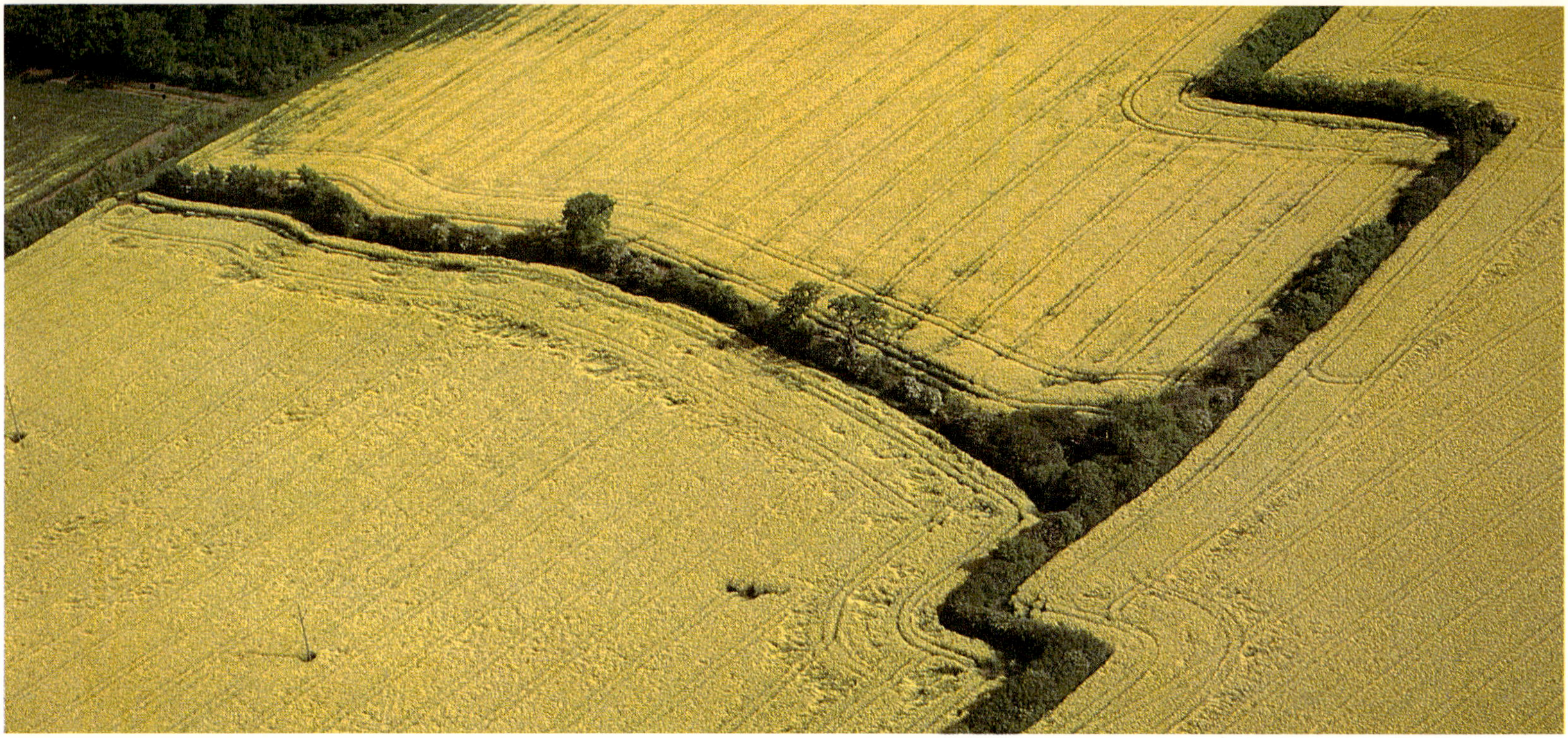

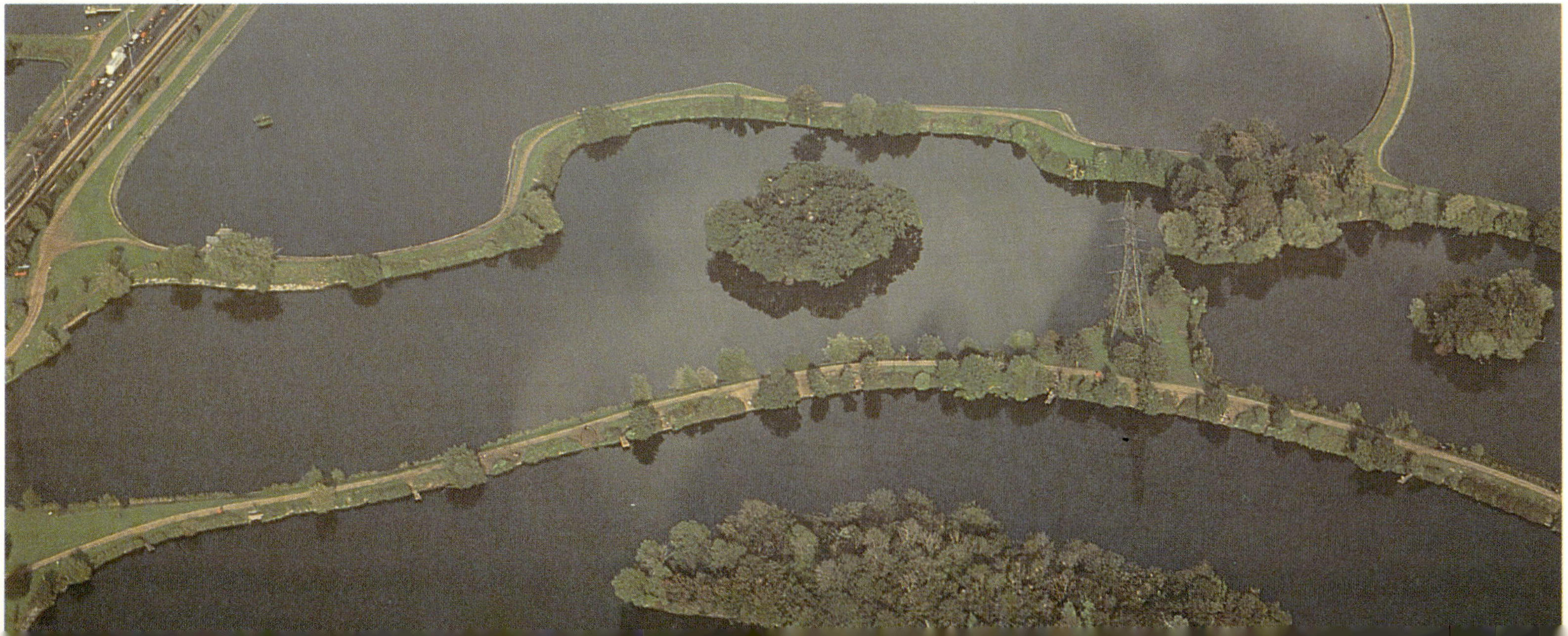

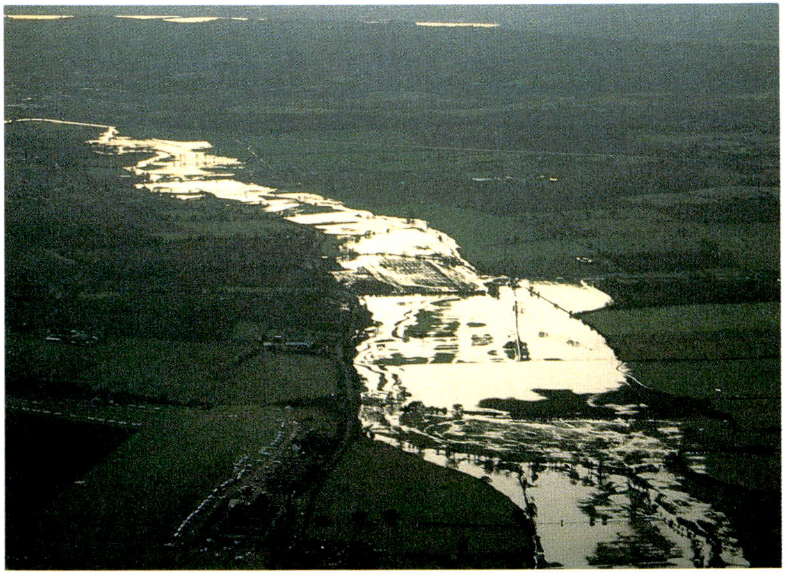

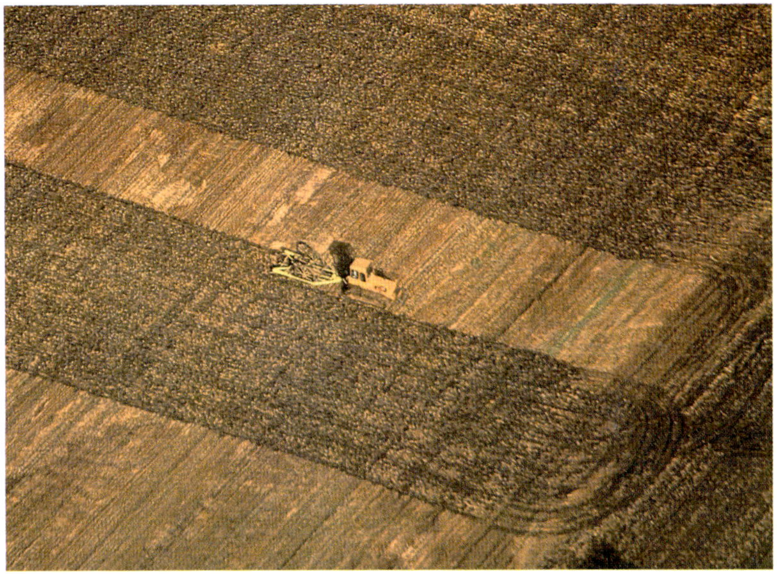

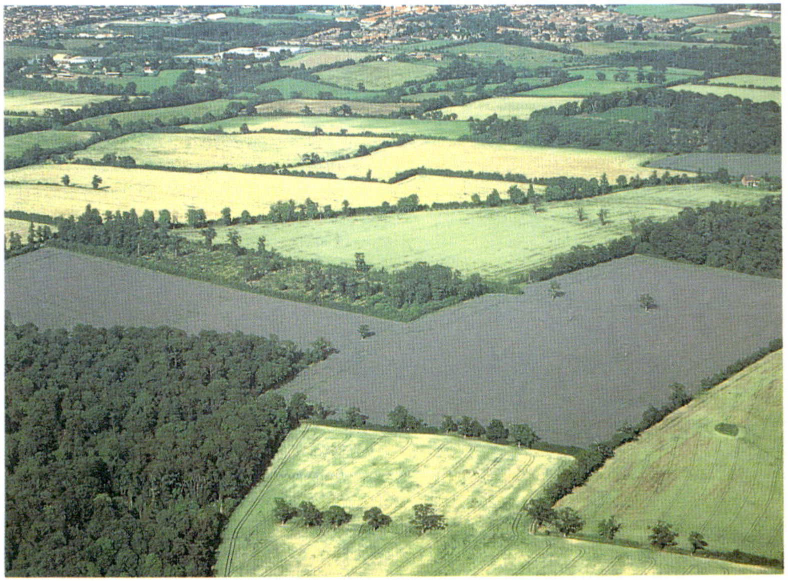

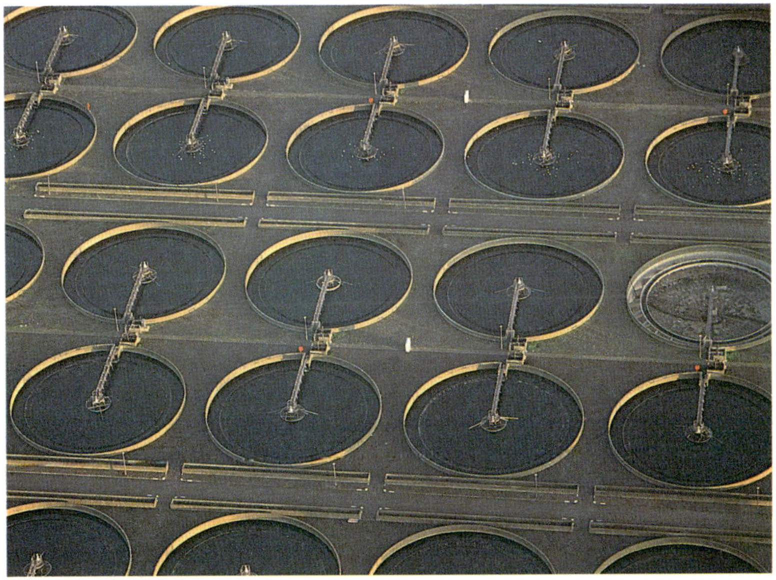

CHANGING LONDON

Over the past few years the face of the capital has altered dramatically, and from our eagle's eye view we have witnessed the transformation in the city's skyline. We watched the Dartford Bridge grow, inching its way across from each bank, its vast pillars rising from the river and its network of cables and girders gradually interlinking to form the massive structure now spanning 765 yards of the Thames. My pilot and I often toyed with the idea of flying under it, but needless to say we never tried to put the plan into practice.

Canary Wharf has risen from a squat stump on the Isle of Dogs to the majestic monolith that now dominates the city skyline. Together with City Airport will it revitalize Docklands or become a sad white elephant, a reminder of a boom that finished too soon?

In Hammersmith the Ark has arisen on one side of the A4, while on the other side the Broadway has been variously a hole in the ground and a giant building site (not to mention a giant traffic jam) until the new Centre West emerged from the confusion.

At Wimbledon the roof of Centre Court was stripped

CITY AIRPORT

A water-skier's paradise complete with a single runway and only a few miles from the city centre. City Airport opened in October 1987 and serves cities within a thousand-mile radius.

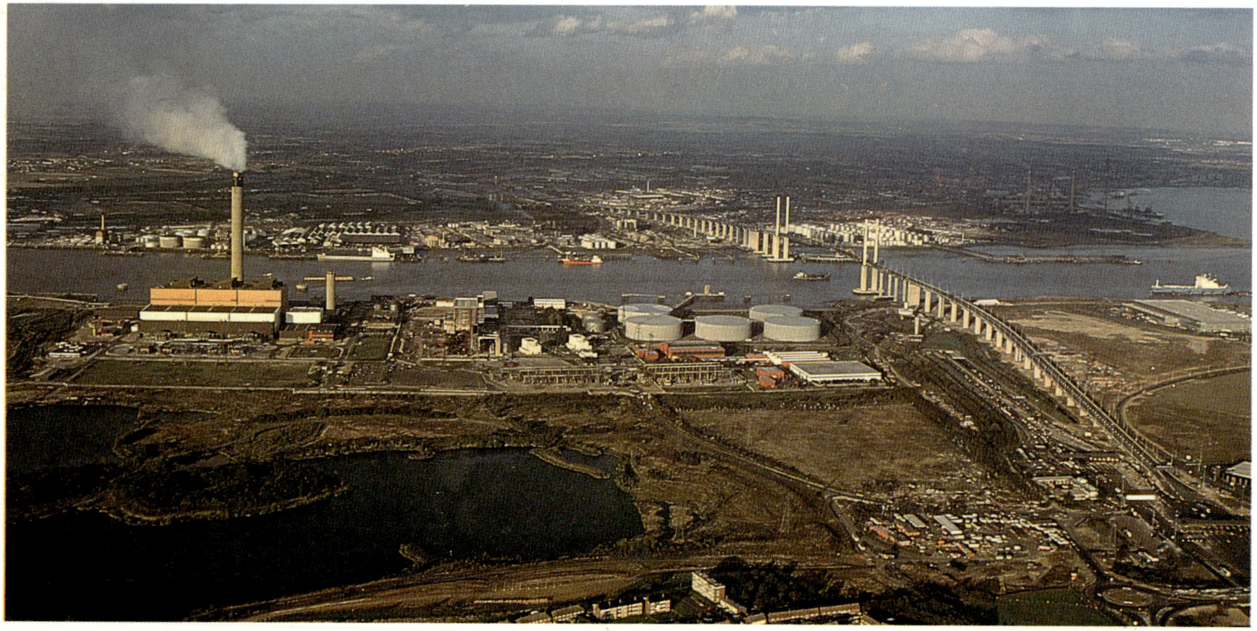

OVER THE THAMES AT DARTFORD

The Queen Elizabeth II Bridge spans about 2,300 feet of water and carries up to 50,000 vehicles a day, all from north to south, 210 feet above the river. This photo shows it before it opened in October 1991.

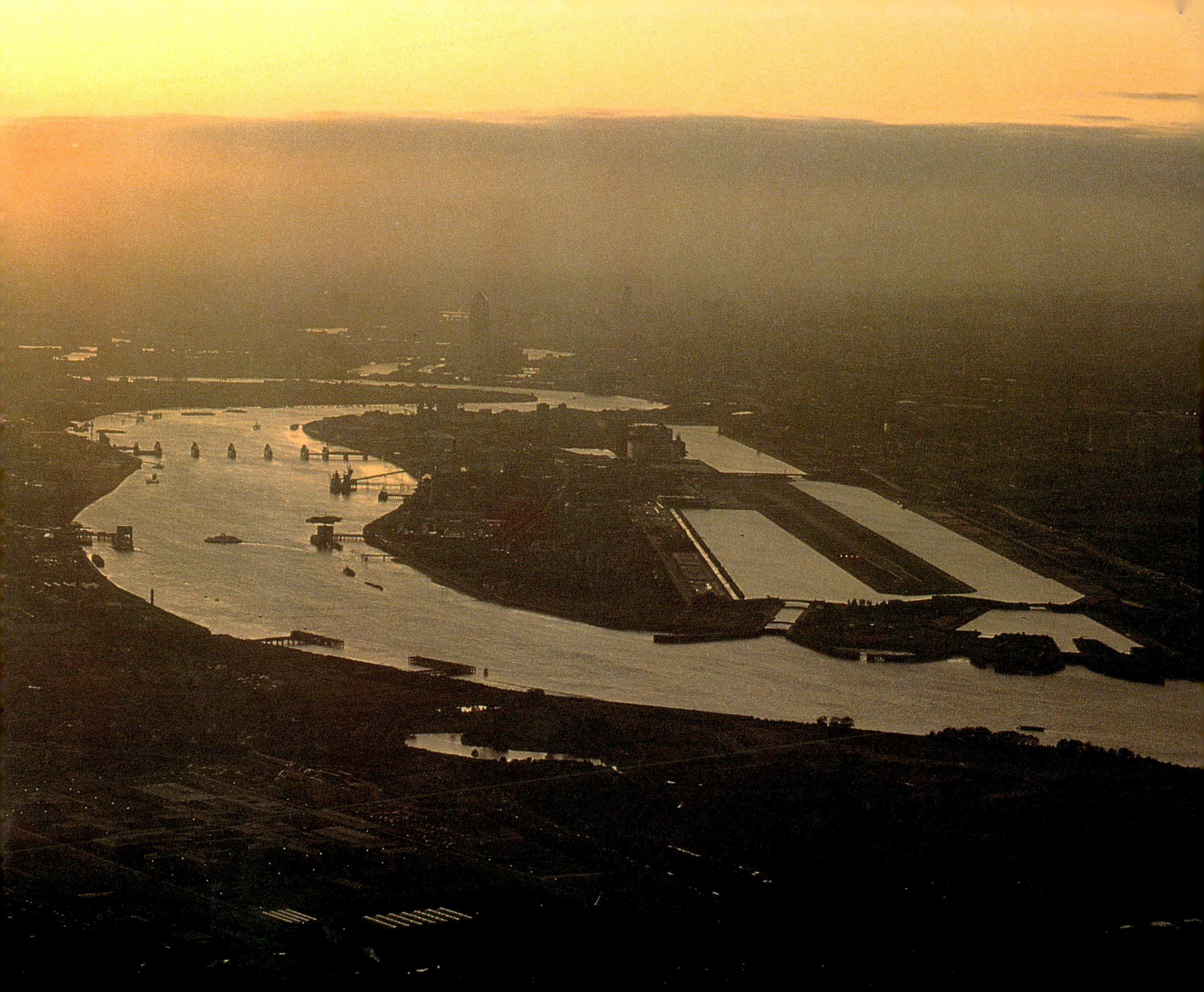

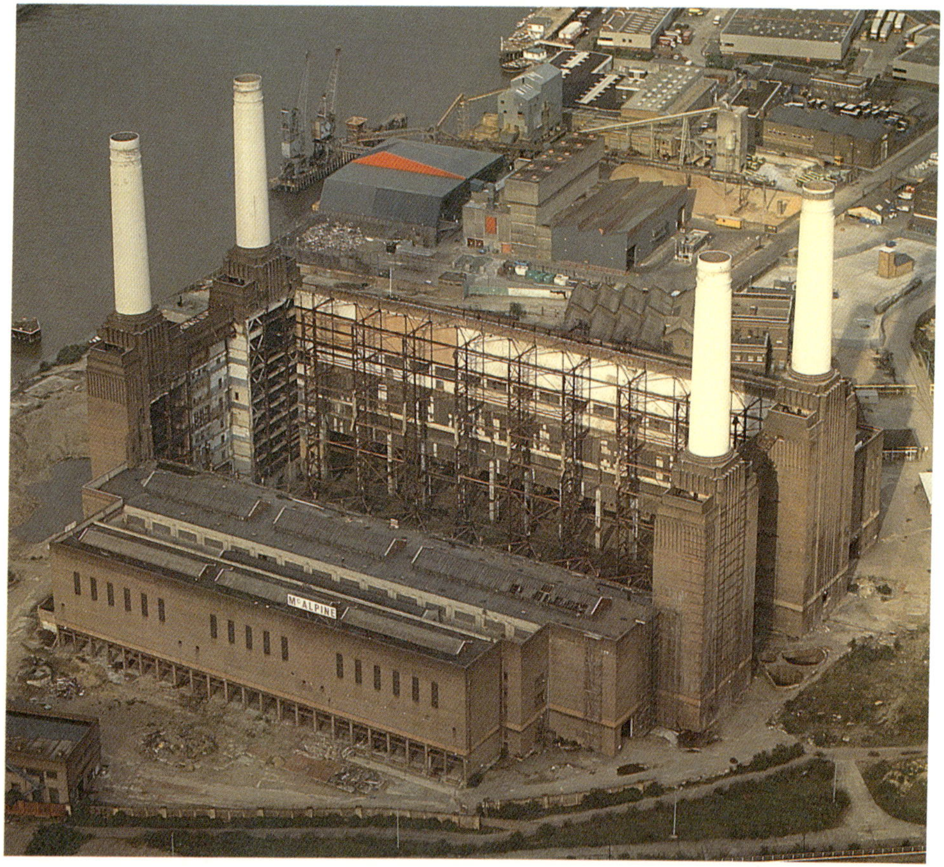

BATTERSEA POWER STATION

Open to the skies, down but not out, and now awaiting a new beginning.

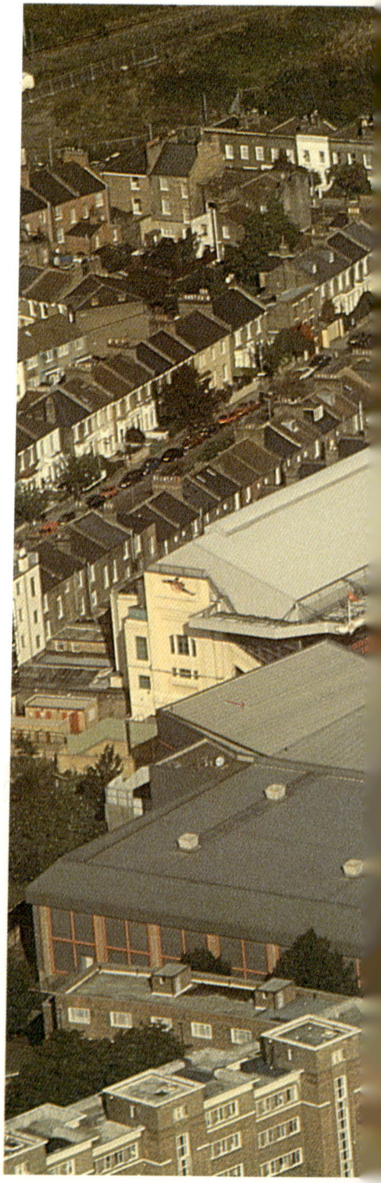

away like the peel of an orange and then replaced; the Palace of Westminster has been giving a good impression of a bandaged thumb; and the Albert Memorial has disappeared from view.

Albert Bridge got lit up, while Tower Bridge had a new paint job. Arsenal gained an audience, and Hyde Park Corner got its gates – or is that just a façade?

Waterloo International is born, County Hall is turning Japanese, the old Hoover building on the A40 finds a new lease of life, but will the Wang brothers of Singapore save Battersea Power Station? And the shattered reflections of terrorism tell their own sad tale. On the M25 a new service station is built and extra lanes are tacked on, and all across London roadworks bloom like blisters.

Some changes are good, other may be not so good; some are temporary, others we'll just have to live with. But London continues, ever in a state of flux, ever changing, ever basically the same.

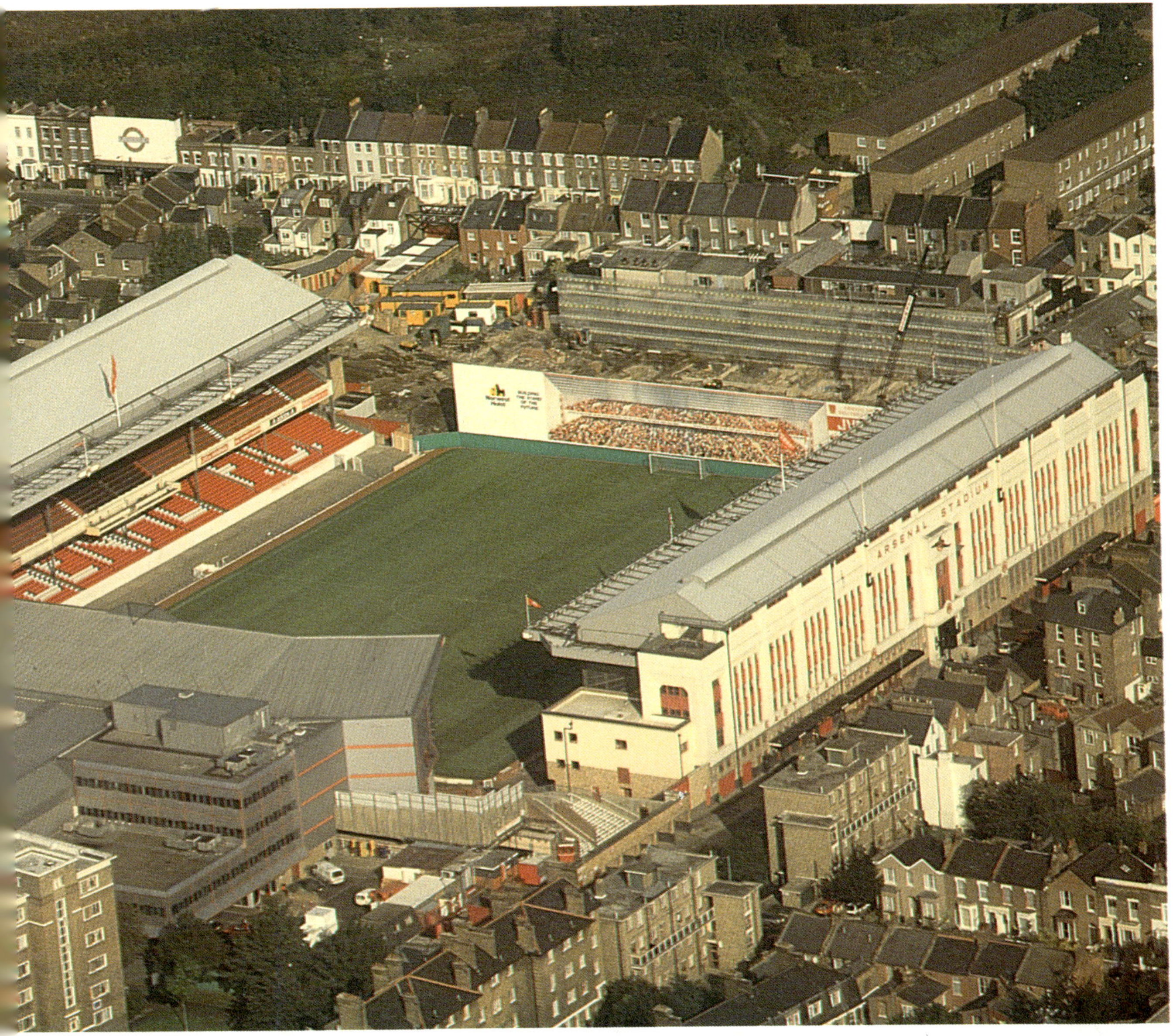

FOOTBALL FOR ALL

An unacceptable crowd at Arsenal. After many complaints, the hoarding had to be repainted to include black and female faces.

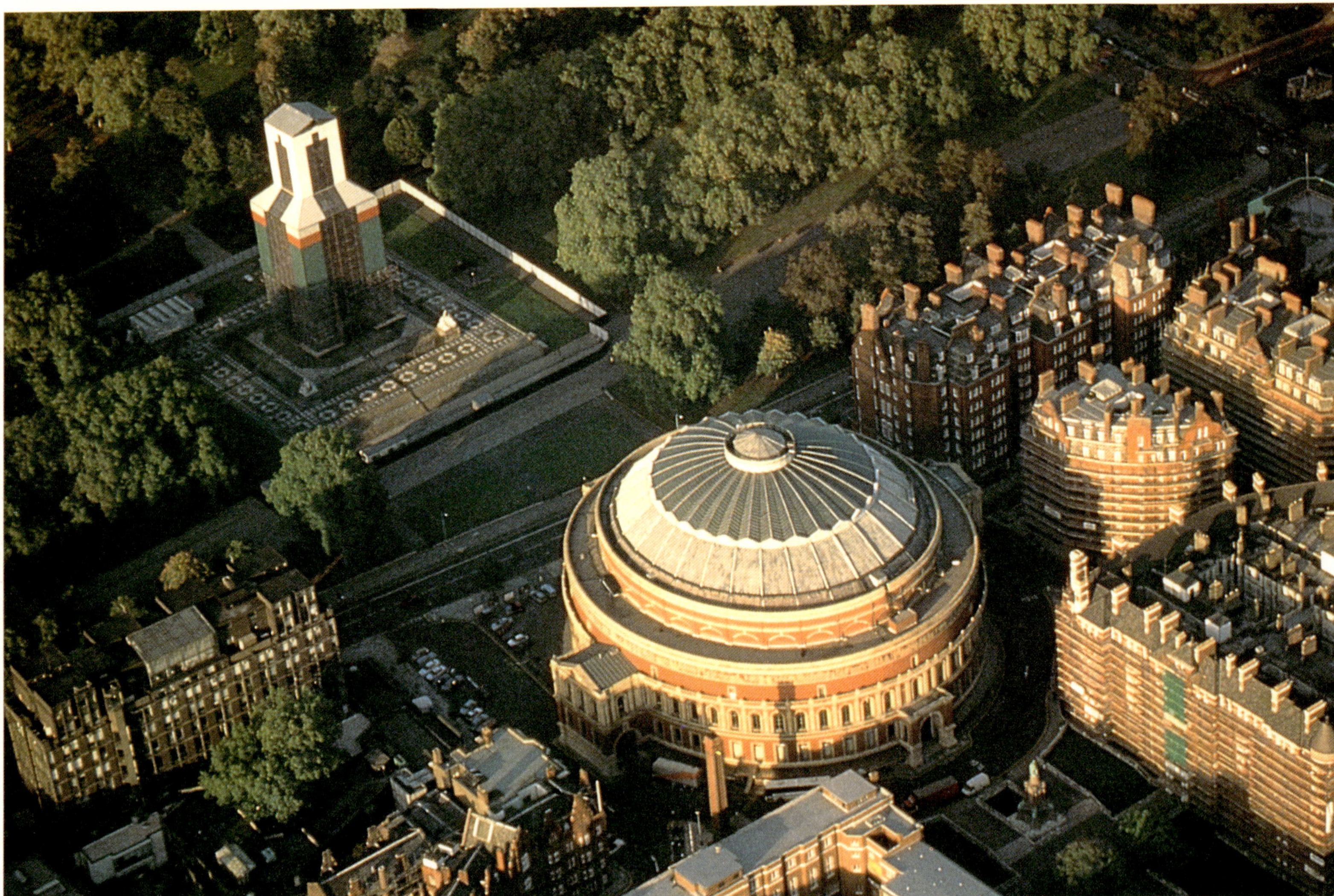

ALBERT HALL

Queen Victoria commented: 'it looks like the British Constitution.' Quite what she would have said about the Albert Memorial disappearing behind a screen of scaffolding and plywood, apparently forever, is another matter. About £10 million is needed for its restoration. Will we see it again this century?

'I'VE APPEARED at the Albert Hall several times, most recently for Capital Gold gigs, but my strongest memory is of November 1978, when I presented the Miss World Contest there. It was a really big event in those days. I hadn't done much television, and this was live, with the whole world watching – or at least, that's what it felt like. I was very nervous, and for the three days of rehearsal I hardly slept at all. The big night came, and I was backstage, feeling not too bad, when I suddenly got this dreadful nervous tic in one eye. Well, at that point there was nothing I could do about it – Sacha Distel was already warbling away with a sexy French accent, and I was about to run down this big flight of stairs on to the stage. Sacha finished his song and said 'and now I would like to introduce my vairy good friend Paul Burnett' (actually we had never met), and I ran down these stairs, convinced I was going to trip, with this convulsive twitch, which by then seemed to have taken over the whole of one side of my face. It felt like I was having some kind of huge facial seizure! Somehow or other I managed not to fall. I made it to the camera and said my lines, wondering all the time what on earth everyone was thinking about this grinning, twitching idiot, and then staggered off into the wings. There I apologized profusely to the floor manager, who looked completely blank and obviously didn't know what I was talking about – apparently nothing at all had showed up on camera, it was all in my head! So after that I could relax a bit, and it turned out to be one of the best nights of my life. And no, the girls weren't at all bitchy. They were really incredibly supportive of each other – no one ever believes that, but it's true.'

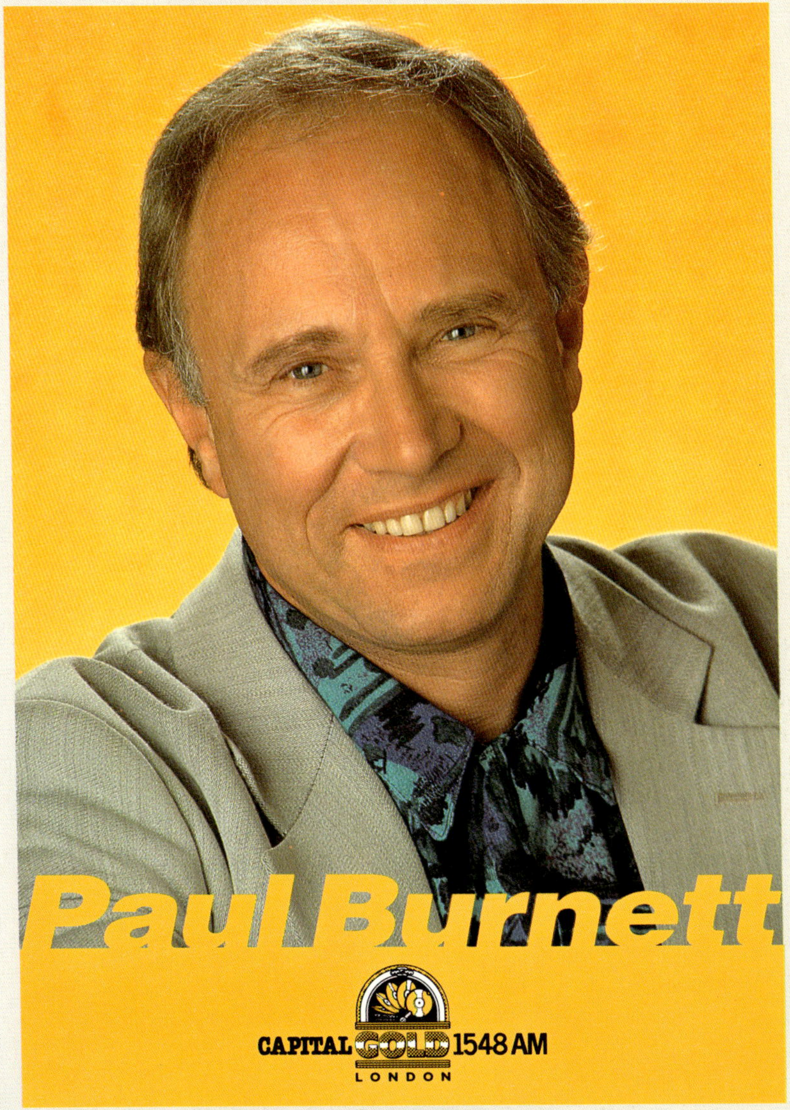

WATERLOO INTERNATIONAL

A much admired new station snakes its way alongside the old Waterloo, allegedly to receive those £24 million, quarter-mile long trains from the Continent via the Channel Tunnel. Or will they go to St Pancras?

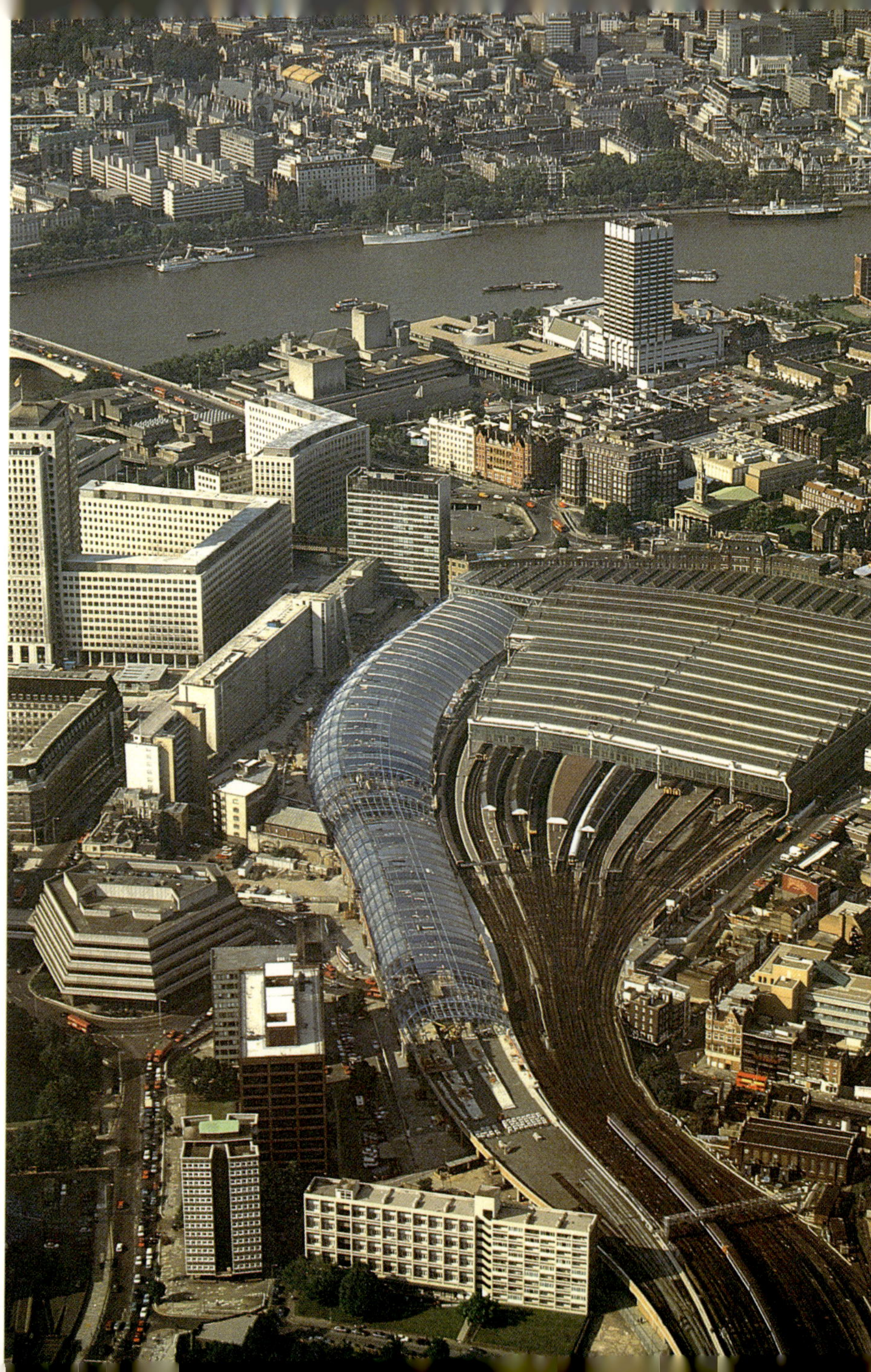

HYDE PARK CORNER

Work proceeds behind the hoardings on the Queen Mother's Gates, built in late celebration of Her Majesty's 90th birthday in 1990.

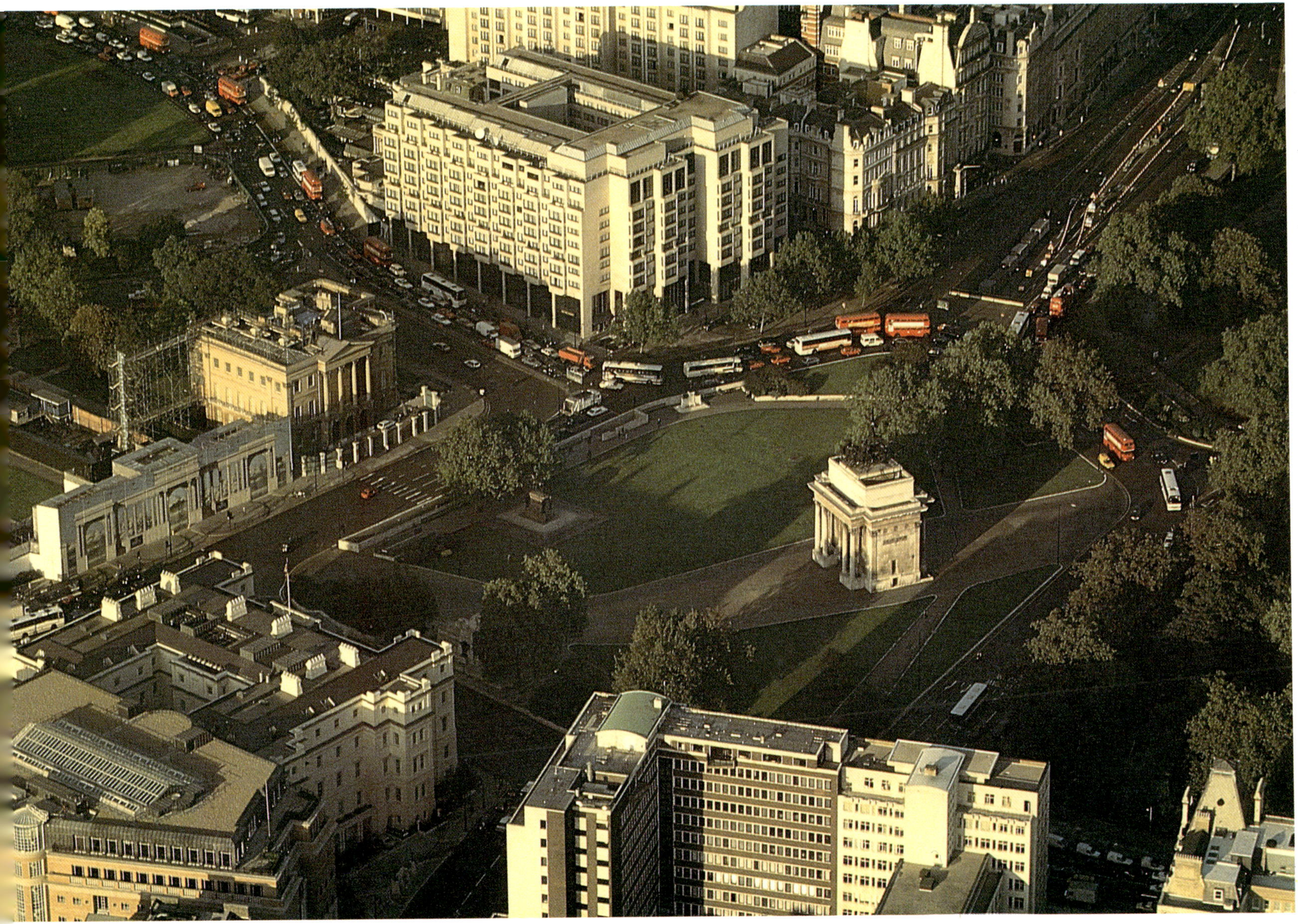

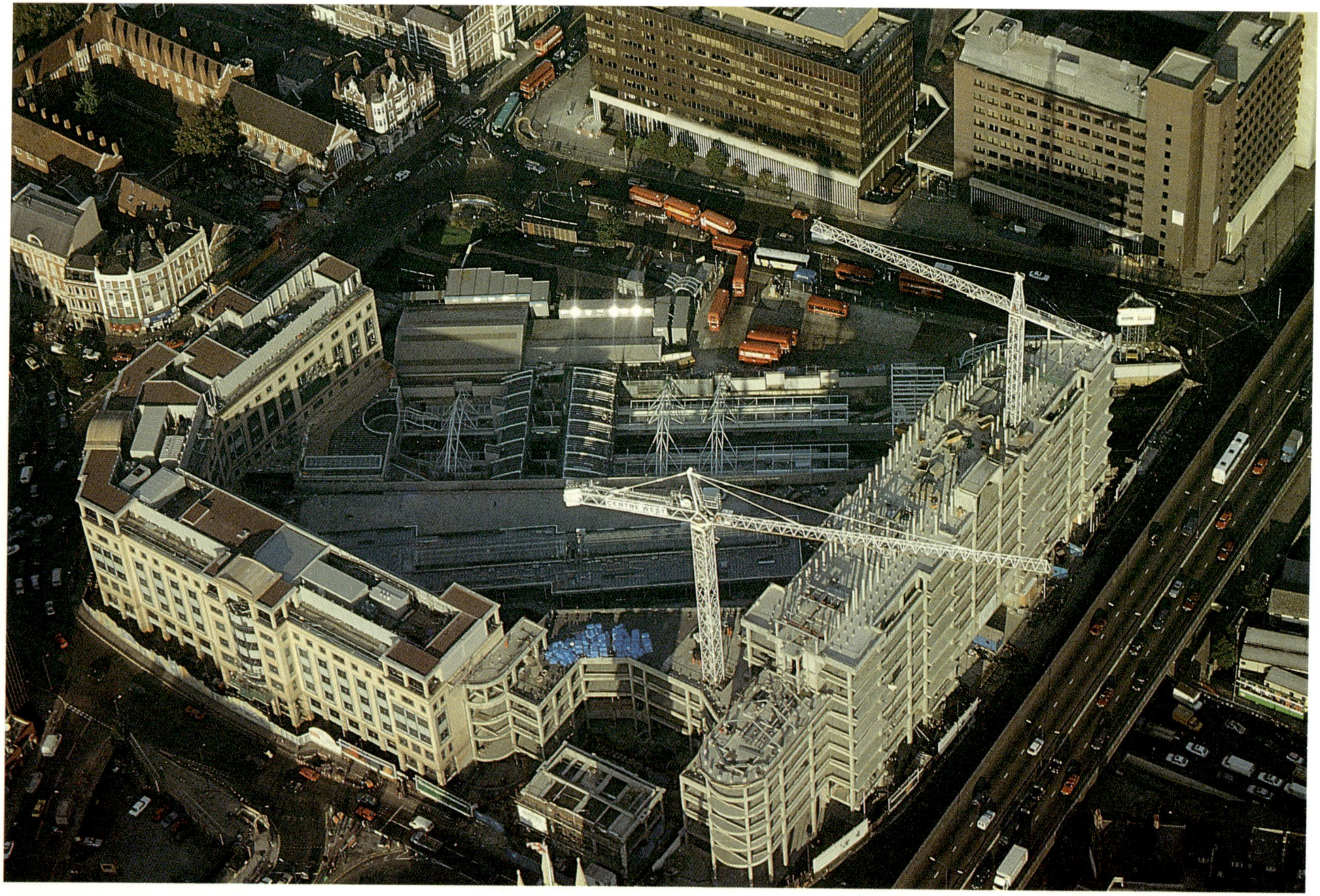

HAMMERSMITH

The hole in the ground that was Hammersmith has finally metamorphosed into Centre West, but the traffic jams continue.

WIMBLEDON

The Centre Court at Wimbledon is only used for the Championships. During the building of the new unsupported roof in 1991-92 not so much as a nail touched the hallowed turf.

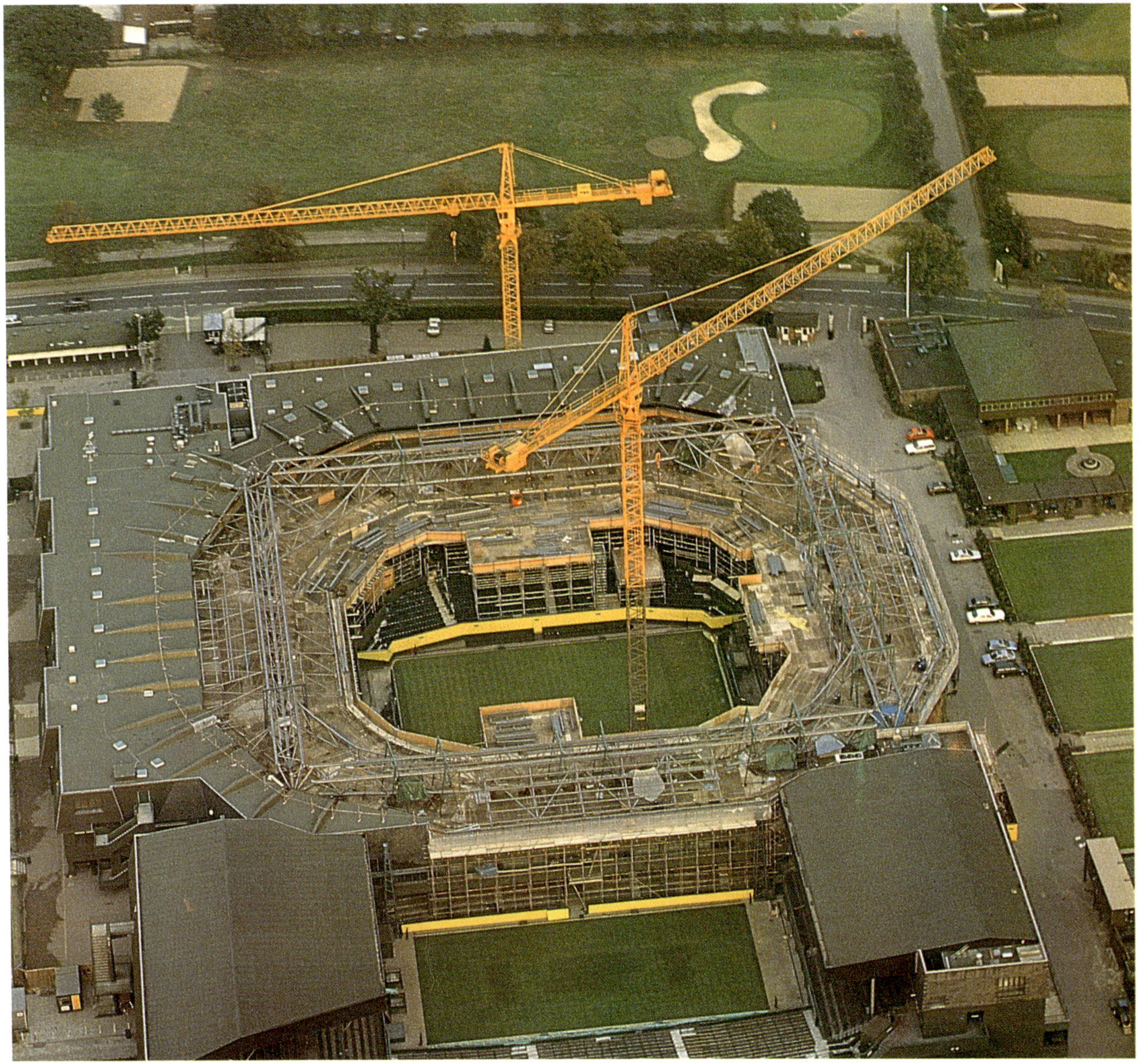

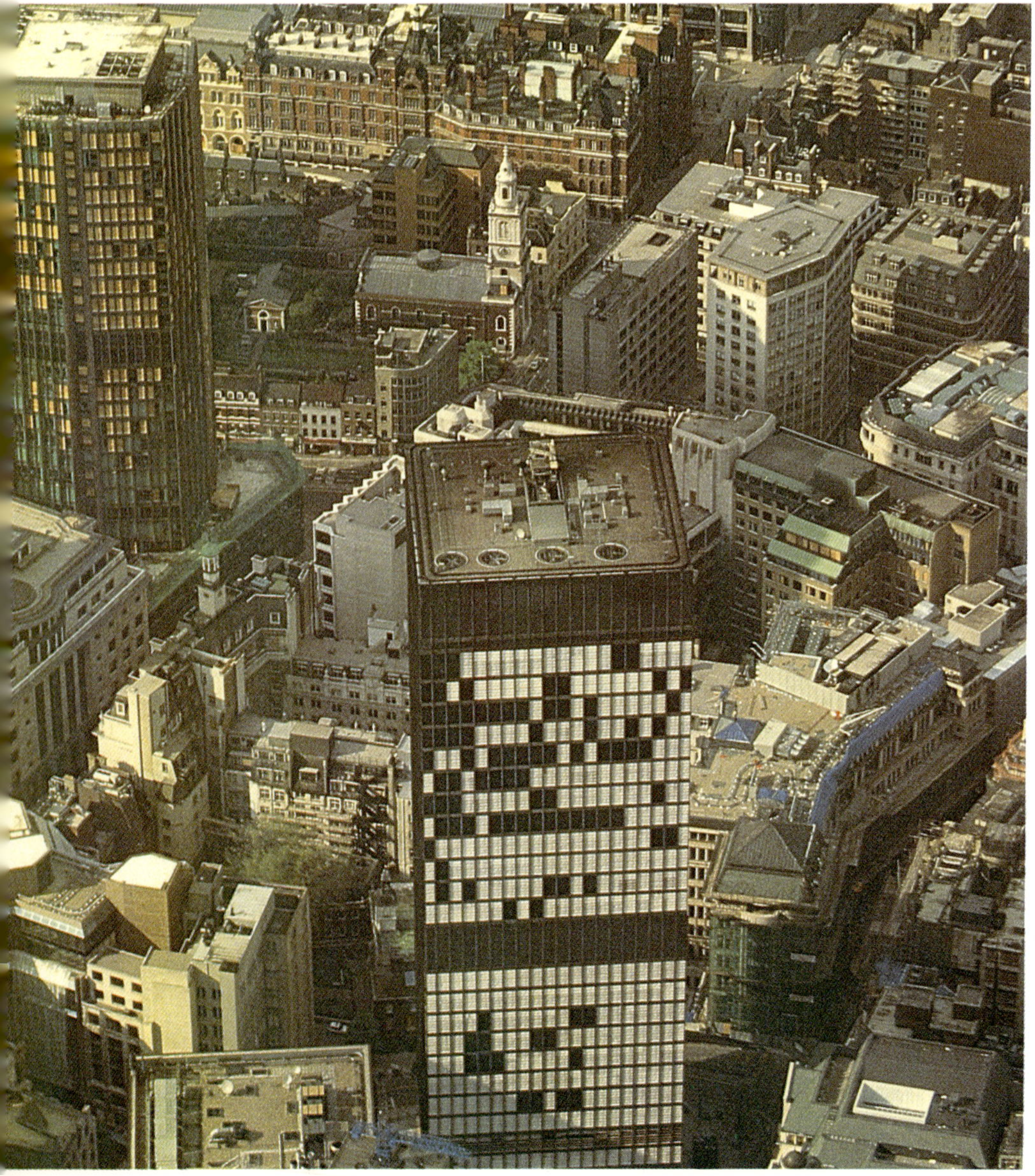

SUDDEN CHANGE

A terrorist bomb in St Mary Axe in April 1992 strips a modern building of its glass skin, and another on the same night destroyed a B&Q store at Staples Corner, damaging large parts of the flyover. Insurance claims totted up to £800 million, only for a repeat performance, on an even larger scale, to happen in the City a year later.

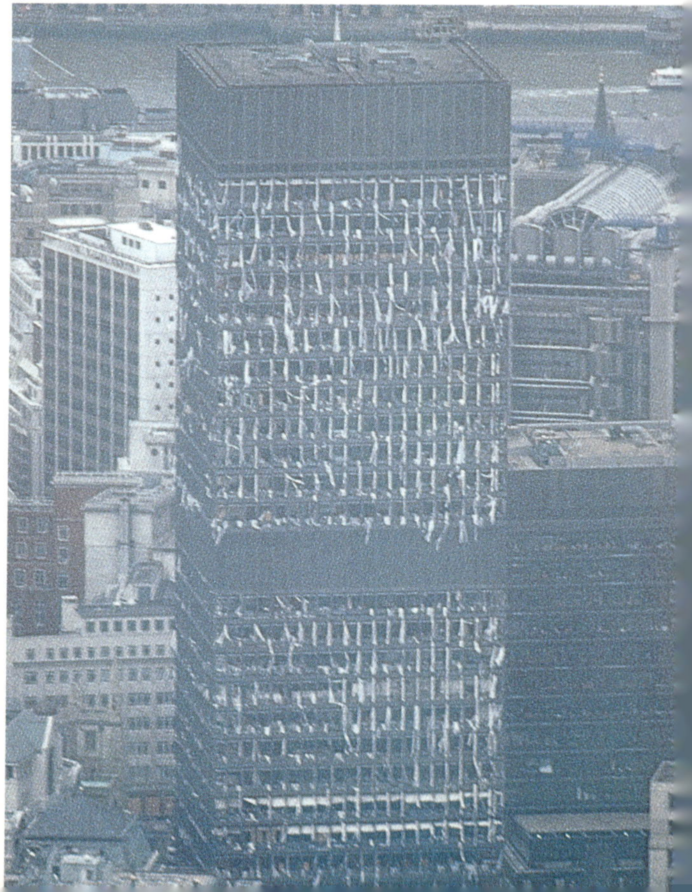

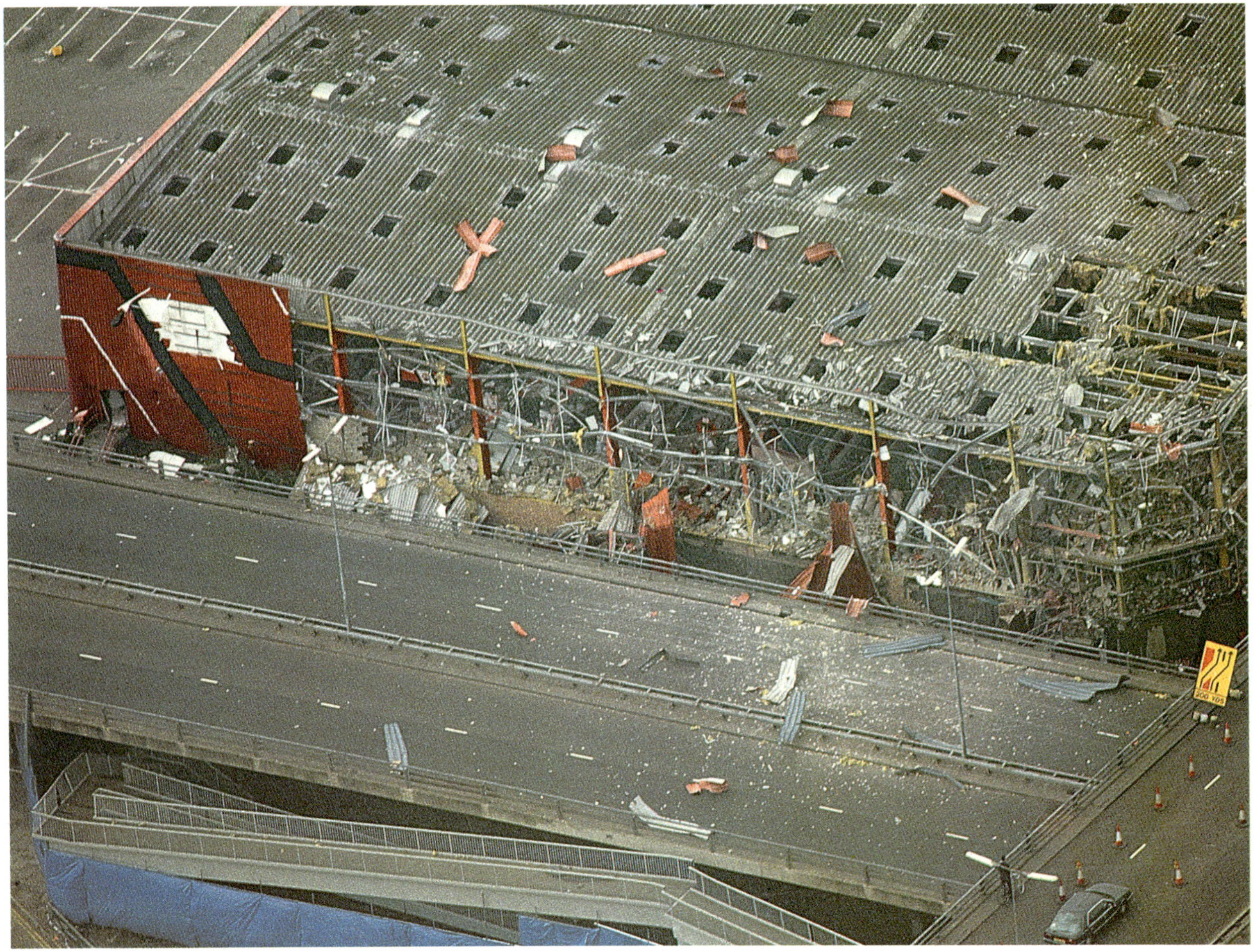

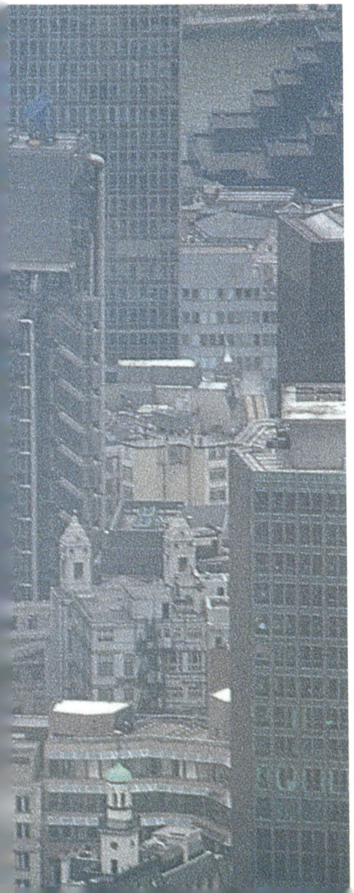

SECRET CITY

From the Flying Eye we get views of parts of London that no one else ever sees – even the occasional nude rooftop sunbather! And we see some places that the average Londoner may not even know exist.

For instance, above the grime and hustle of Baker Street there is a magical roof garden; and sitting on top of the Royal London Hospital is the Medevac Helicopter. The roof of the NatWest Tower advertises the company's logo to the skies, while a flight over Elstree reveals that all is not what you think at the Queen Vic and its familiar East End square.

Just off the M25 the outlines of the old Brooklands racetrack can still be made out. Epic flights in aviation history were made from here, but these days the planes are trapped in the Brooklands Museum without a runway. Elsewhere, even a grass strip is welcome for smaller planes.

On Hampstead Heath the muddy depths of the men's bathing pond are revealed, and Docklands disguises itself for a variety of film locations – parts of *Full Metal Jacket* set in Vietnam were filmed here by Stanley Kubrick, and it also provided the backdrops for *Lorenzo's Oil* and Harrison Ford's *Patriot Games*. For *The Long Good Friday*, starring Bob Hoskins and Helen Mirren, they even blew up a real pub!

MI6

Some of London's greatest secrets are well publicized, other less so. These are the new headquarters of MI6. You could hardly miss them, even on a dark night.

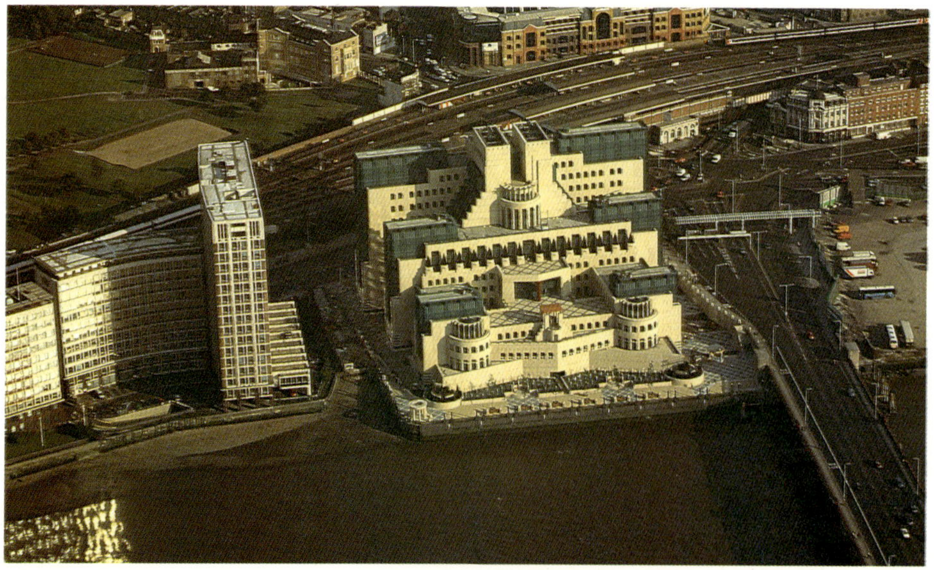

BAKER STREET

A huge and luxuriant garden high above a busy junction. You can't see *this* from the ground! Is this what Prince Charles means by 'greening the grey'?

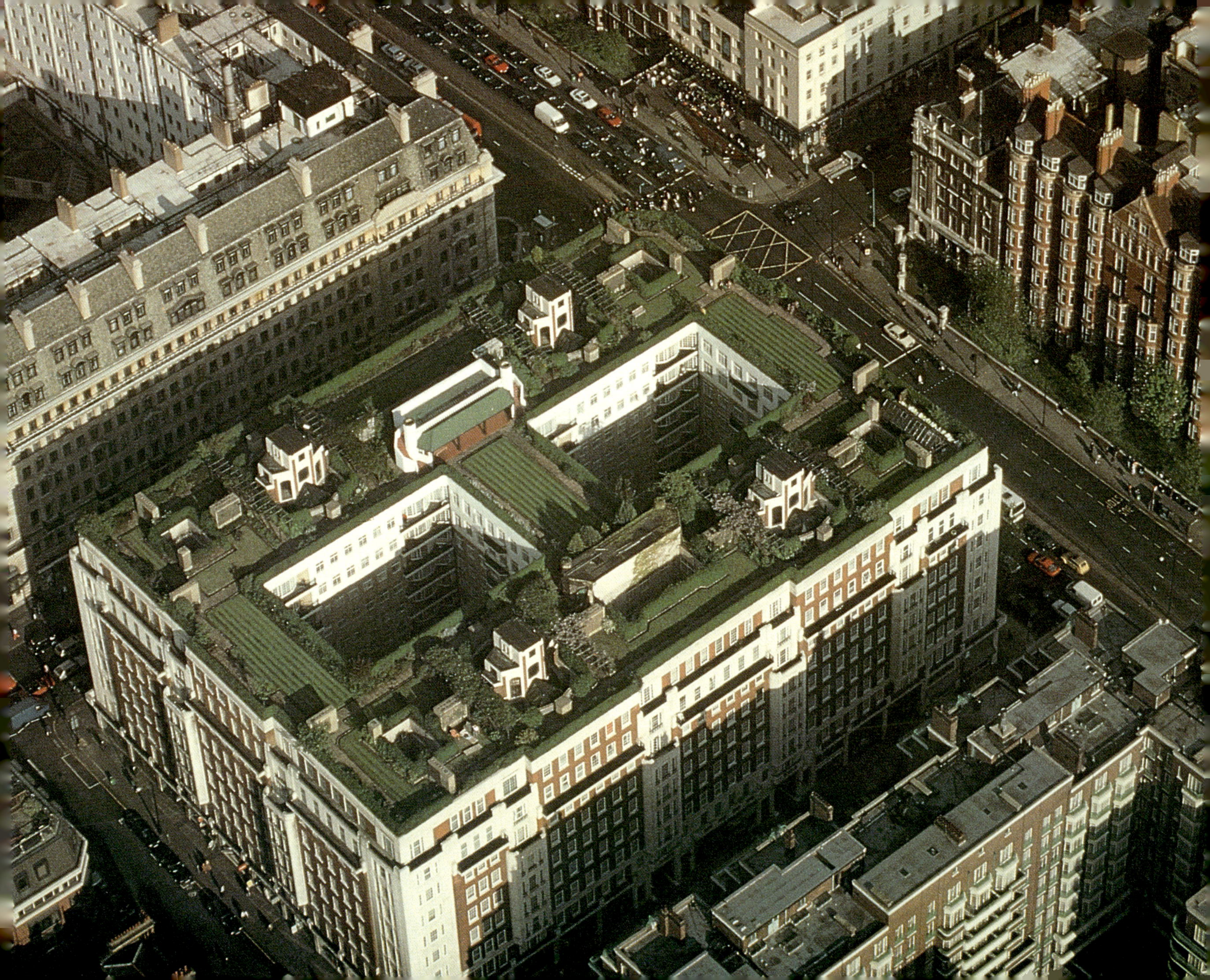

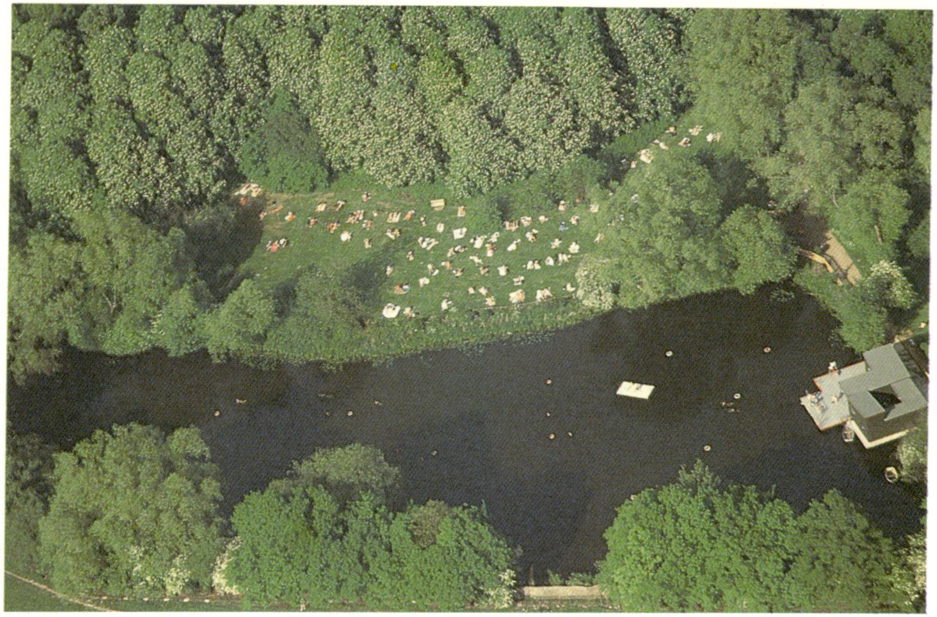

HAMPSTEAD HEATH

The Highgate Bathing Ponds, one for the men and one – shown here – for the women.

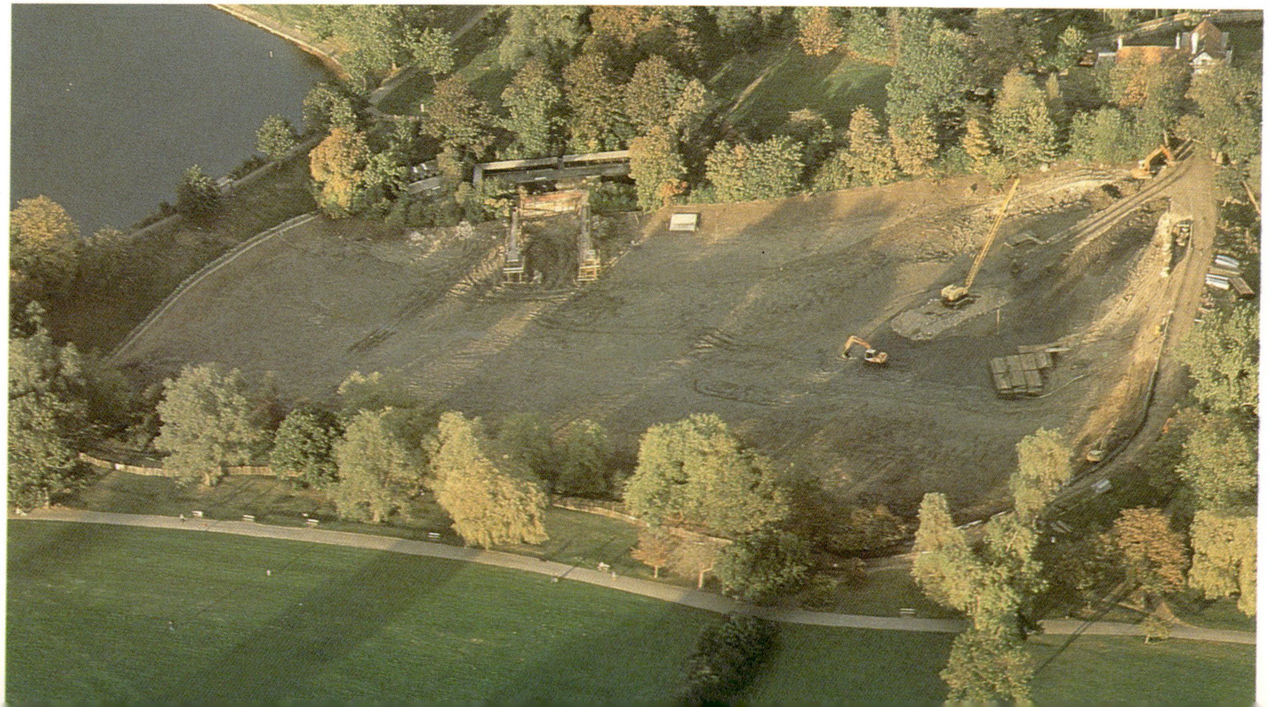

HAMPSTEAD HEATH

Plumbing the depths of Highgate men's bathing pond.

“I HAVE interesting memories of the Flying Eye – I went up with Hazel on a really hot summer afternoon a couple of years ago, together with a friend who had a video camera.

Hazel thought it would be fun if I did one of the traffic broadcasts, so she did the first one, just to set the scene, with the idea that I would do the next one half an hour later. By that time, though, I was feeling very ill indeed. I managed to do the report, but seconds later I was reaching for the dreaded paper bag – and the worst of it is that it's all recorded on video!

Because of that, I had my eyes closed for a large part of the time we were up there, and I don't actually remember seeing Hampstead Heath, which is one of my favourite parts of London. There is so much going on – in the past, in winter, I've skated on one of the ponds, and in summer I once walked across it when there was no water in it at all. But my favourite thing is to sail my boat there – it's a remote-controlled, scaled-down schooner, about a foot long, and my son Nicci, who's seven, and I have a wonderful time with it. The only trouble is that the remote control sometimes gets interfered with by cab radios, and it can end up going anywhere and crashing into ducks and things. Once it ran out of petrol right in the middle of the pond, and I had to wade in, with the water up to my chest, to get it back – which was ridiculous, because I had to drive home in my car, soaking wet and with no trousers on!

But apart from that, I have good memories of the Heath. There's nowhere like it to just sit and eat an icecream on a summer day and watch the world go by.”

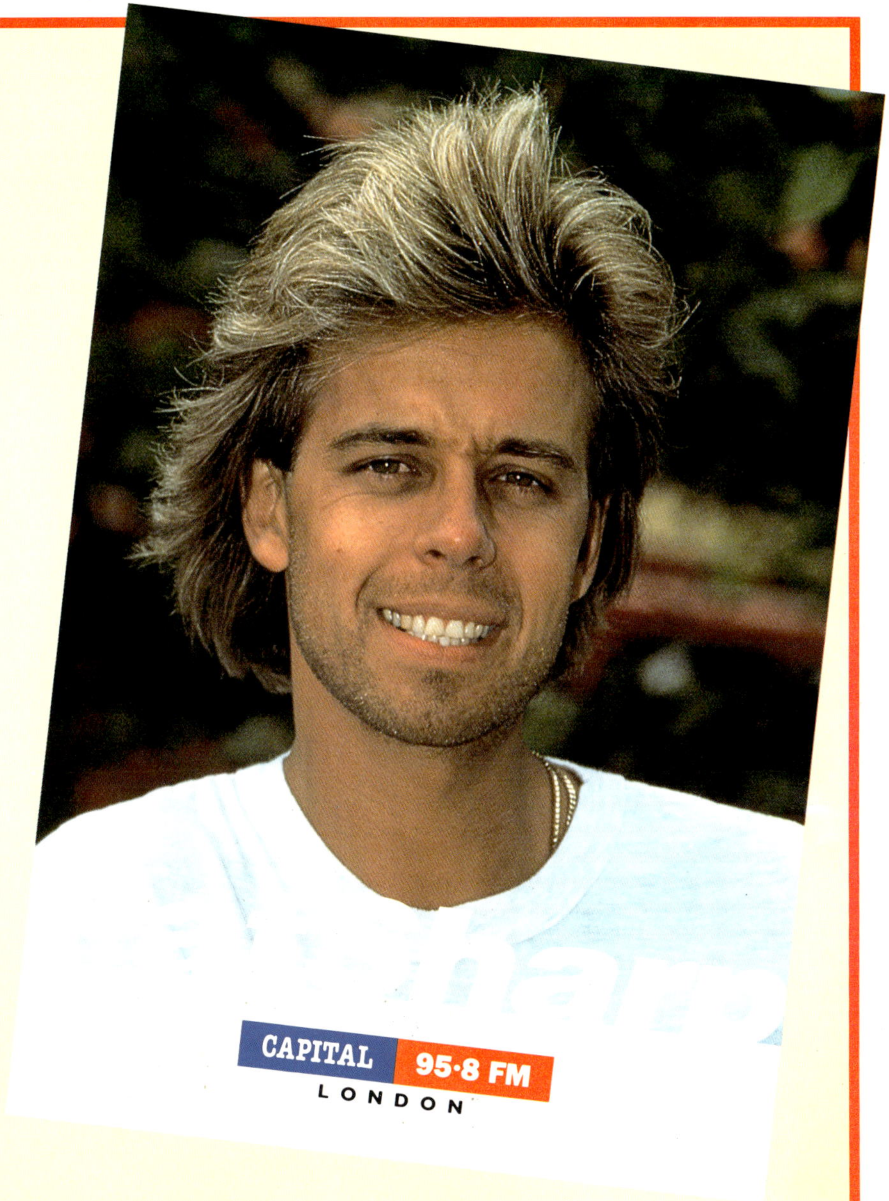

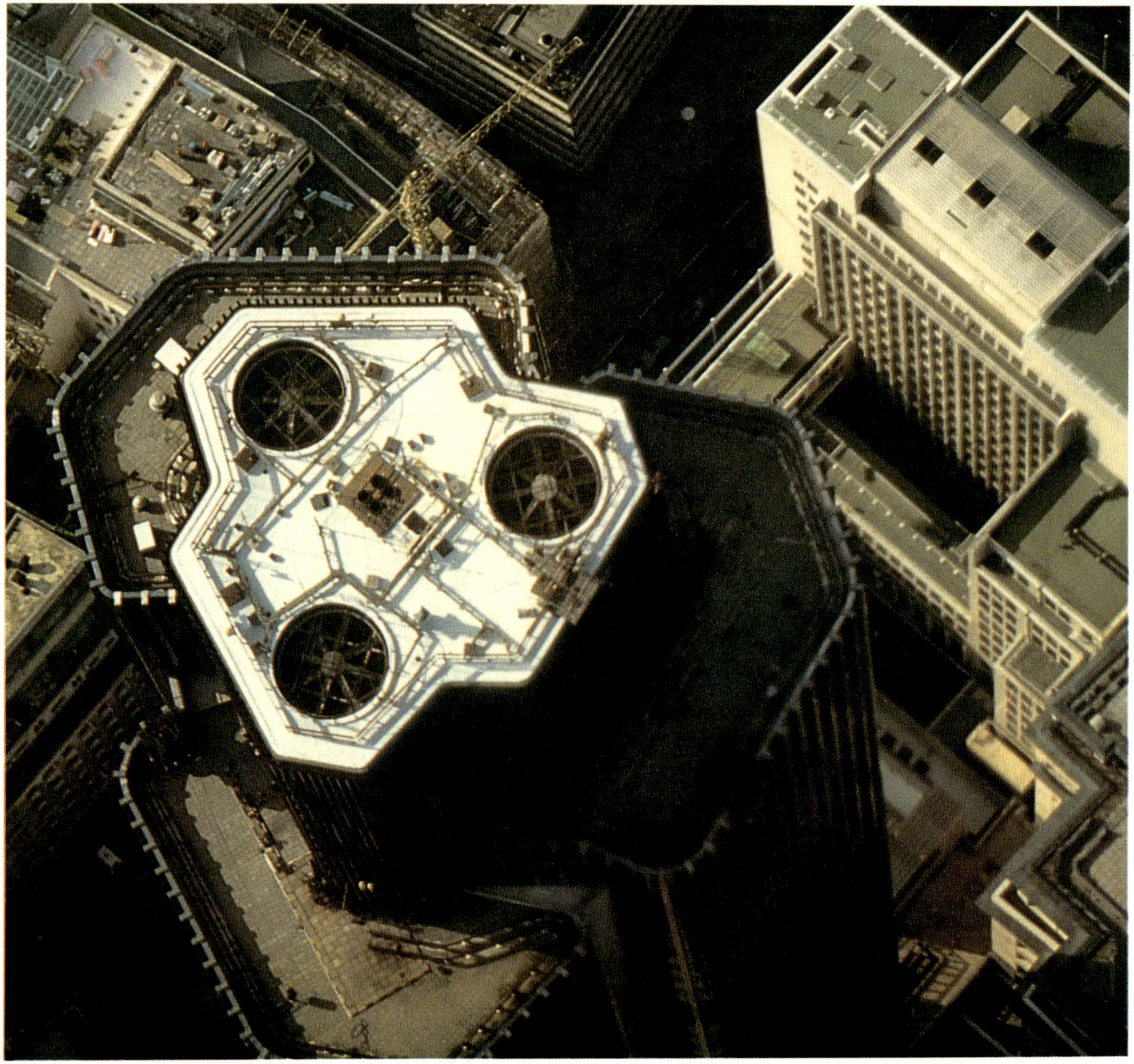

NATWEST TOWER

The logo revealed. Is this the largest trademark in London?

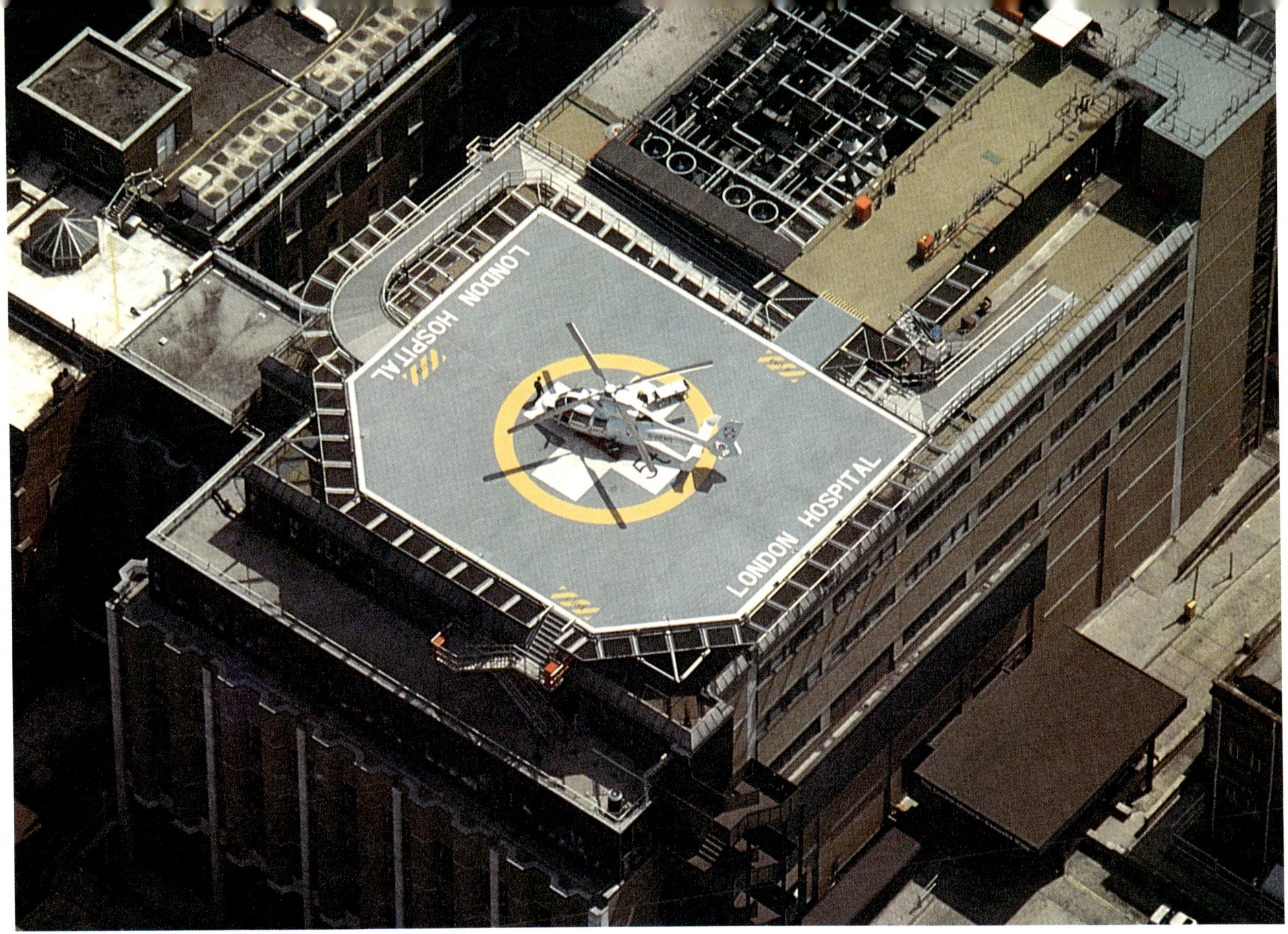

MEDEVAC HELICOPTER

Officially the Royal London Hospital/*Daily Express* Helicopter Emergency Medical Service, it was bought by the *Daily Express* and based on the roof of the Alexandra Wing of the Hospital. It operates within a radius of 50 nautical miles, a 20-minute flight.

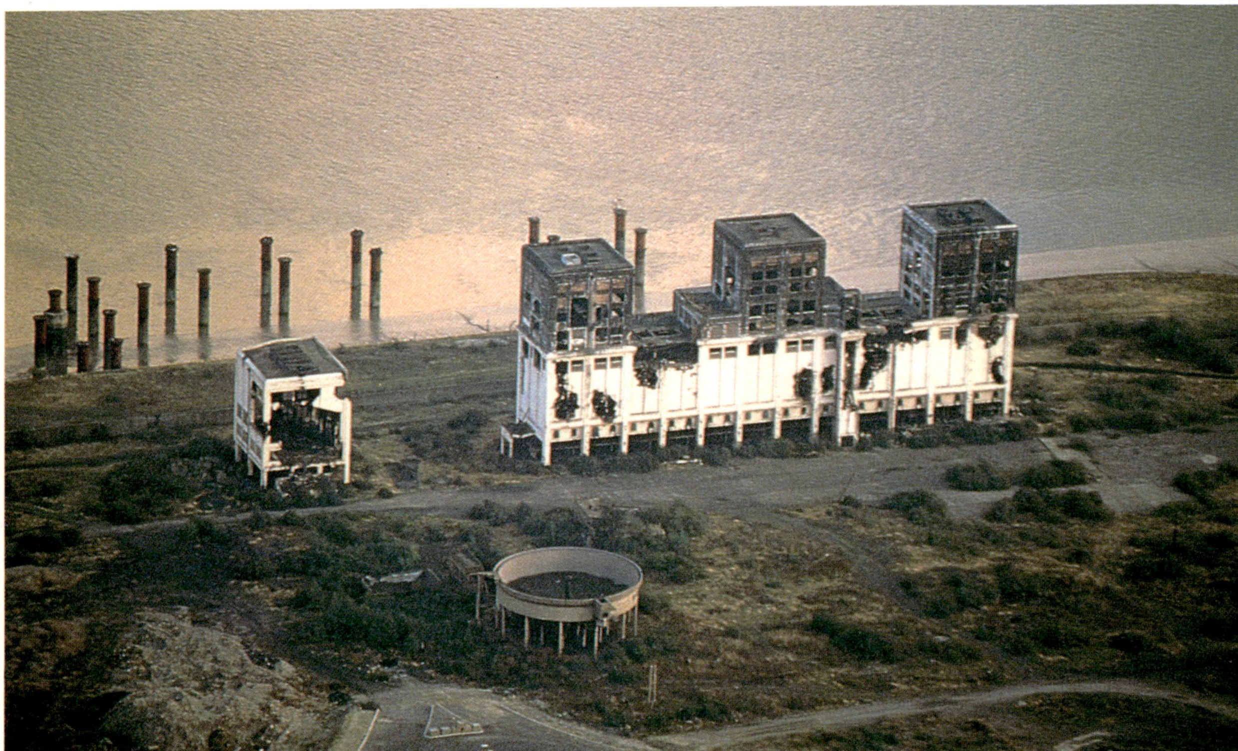

DOCKLANDS/VIETNAM!

A perfect film set for the action movie, courtesy of Rentawreck and the recession.

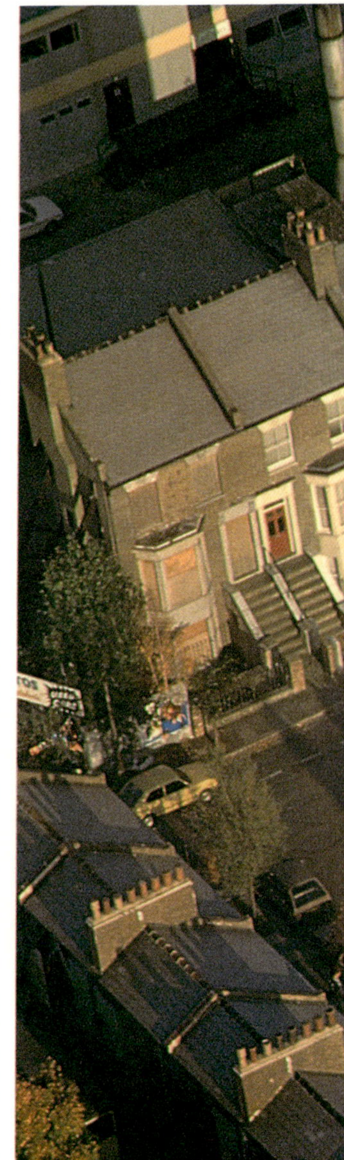

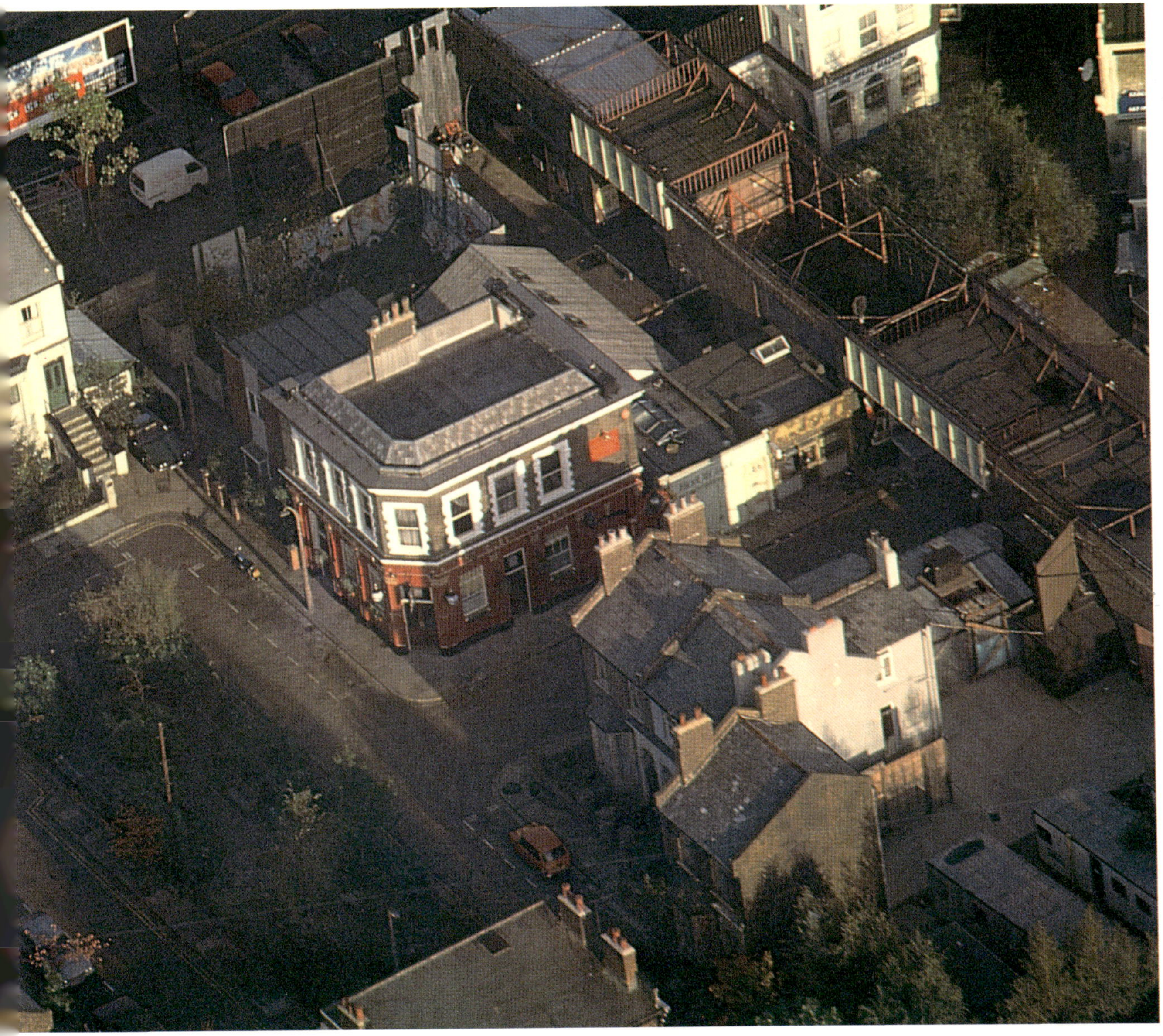

THE EAST END GOES TO ELSTREE

Not all is quite as it seems at the Queen Vic.

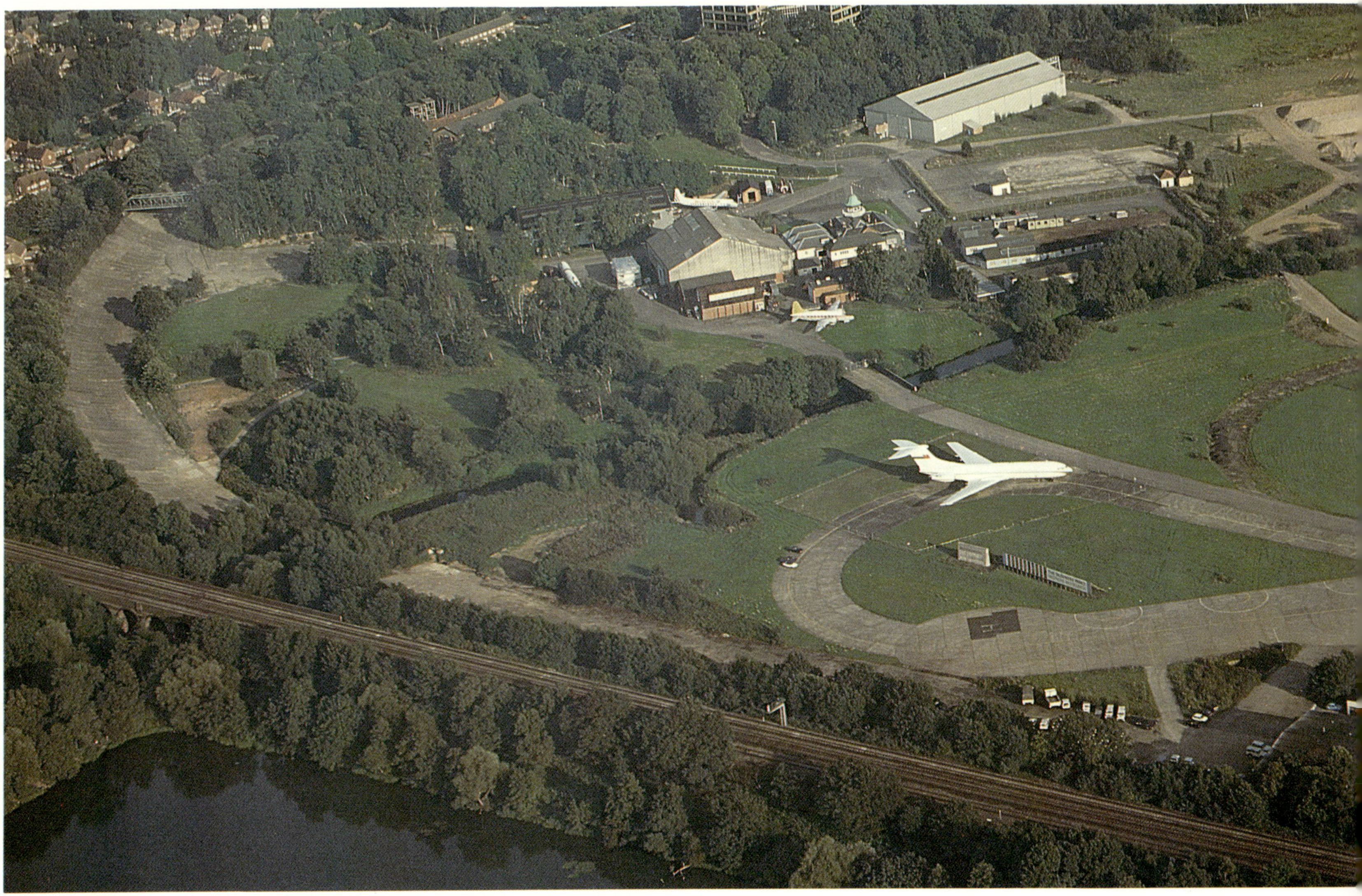

BROOKLANDS

You can still see part of the banked track that was the heart of British motor racing. The old runway has mostly disappeared beneath the Brooklands Museum; the marooned VC10, which was built here, was donated by the Sultan of Oman when he got a jumbo instead!

'I'VE ALWAYS lived near Brooklands, and right from being very young, I remember seeing planes going in and out of there. Of course, it's really a massive piece of British aviation history, as well as being one of the most important race tracks of its time, so I'm really glad they have got a museum there now.

I remember when I was a kid sitting with some friends on the wall of death and trying to imagine what it must have been like. We used to talk a lot about a guy called Percy Lambert, and this is a really weird story. Percy Lambert was in his car and went into the wall of death one day and just never came out. And there was no sign of him or his car! He was just never seen again – at least, that's the way the story goes. And I remember that when the place was British Aerospace there were often reports in the local papers of a ghostly car coming through the walls of one of the hangars! There was also the ghost of a cat, but I'm not really sure what that had to do with anything.

Just below the wall of death, where the sewage works is now, there used to be a tenth-century manor house owned by the Rede brothers – good old grandfather Bart, he was always one of my favourite ancestors. No, seriously, one of my uncles, I think it was an uncle, was a man called Jack Haslam, and he used to race regularly at Brooklands. And so of course did Billy Cotton Senior, the old band leader; he did a lap there once at 123.89mph and won loads of trophies and medals.

Of course, a lot of the places that I remember at Brooklands from when I was a kid have gone now – I think they are turning it into a building site again just at the moment, but if you look at the photo you can still see where the runway used to be and also some of the banking from the old race track.'

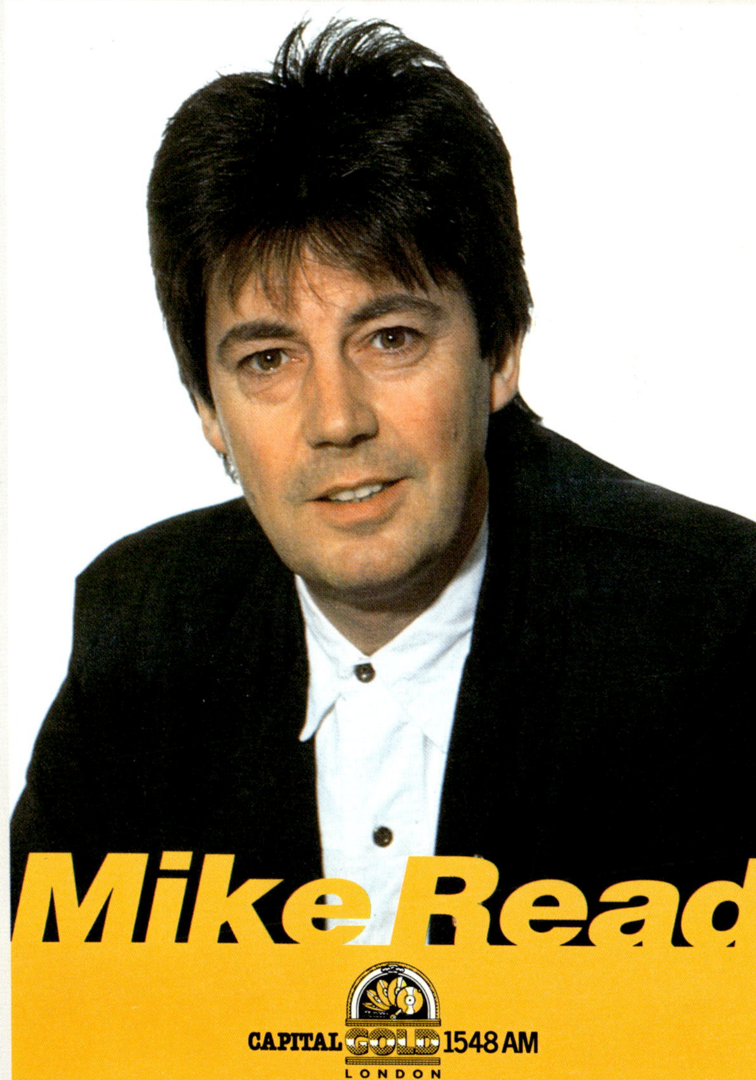

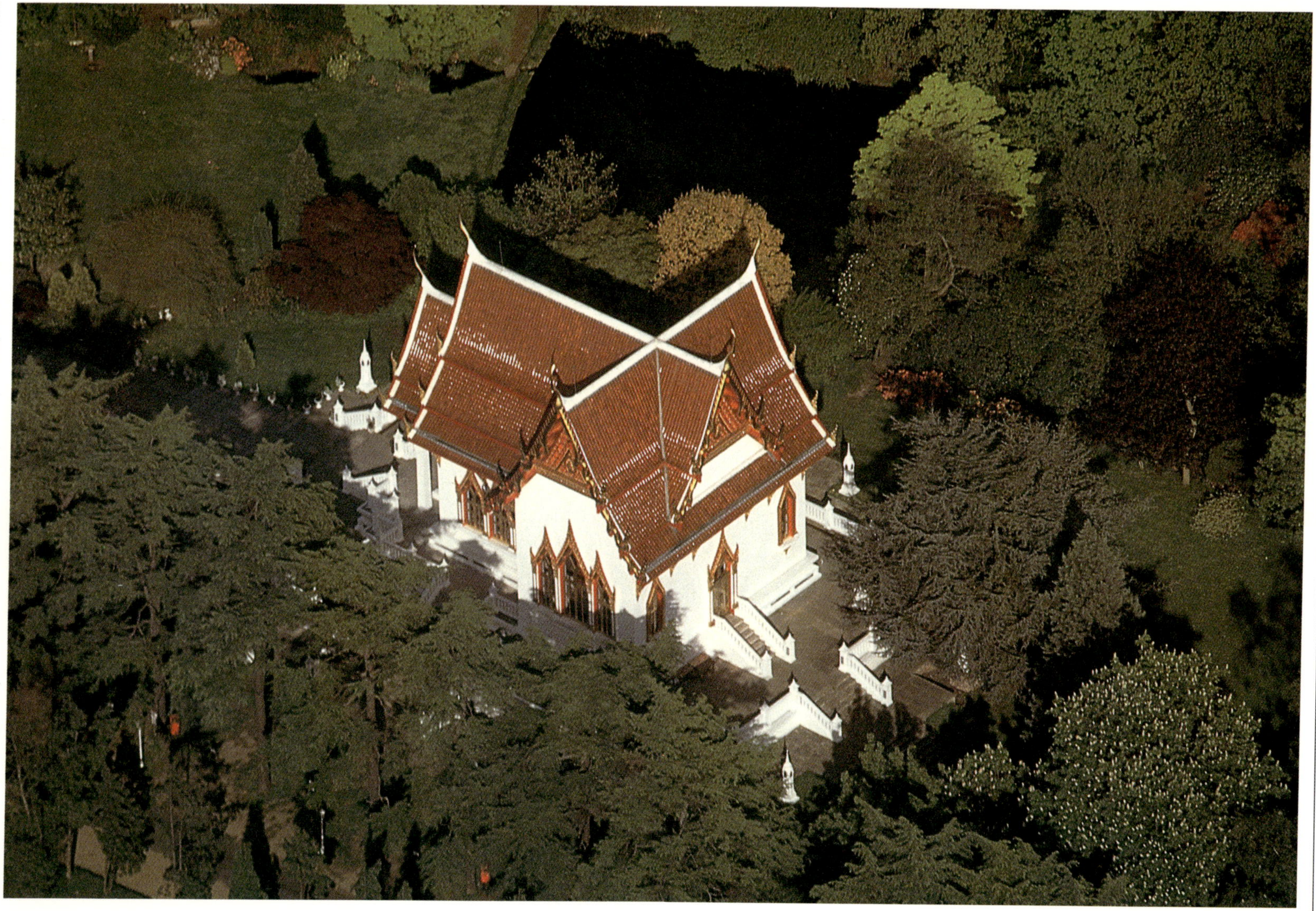

EASTERN PROMISE IN LONDON S.W.19

This miniature temple is hidden away in the Wimbledon trees.

WELCOME HOME

Definitely not Heathrow.

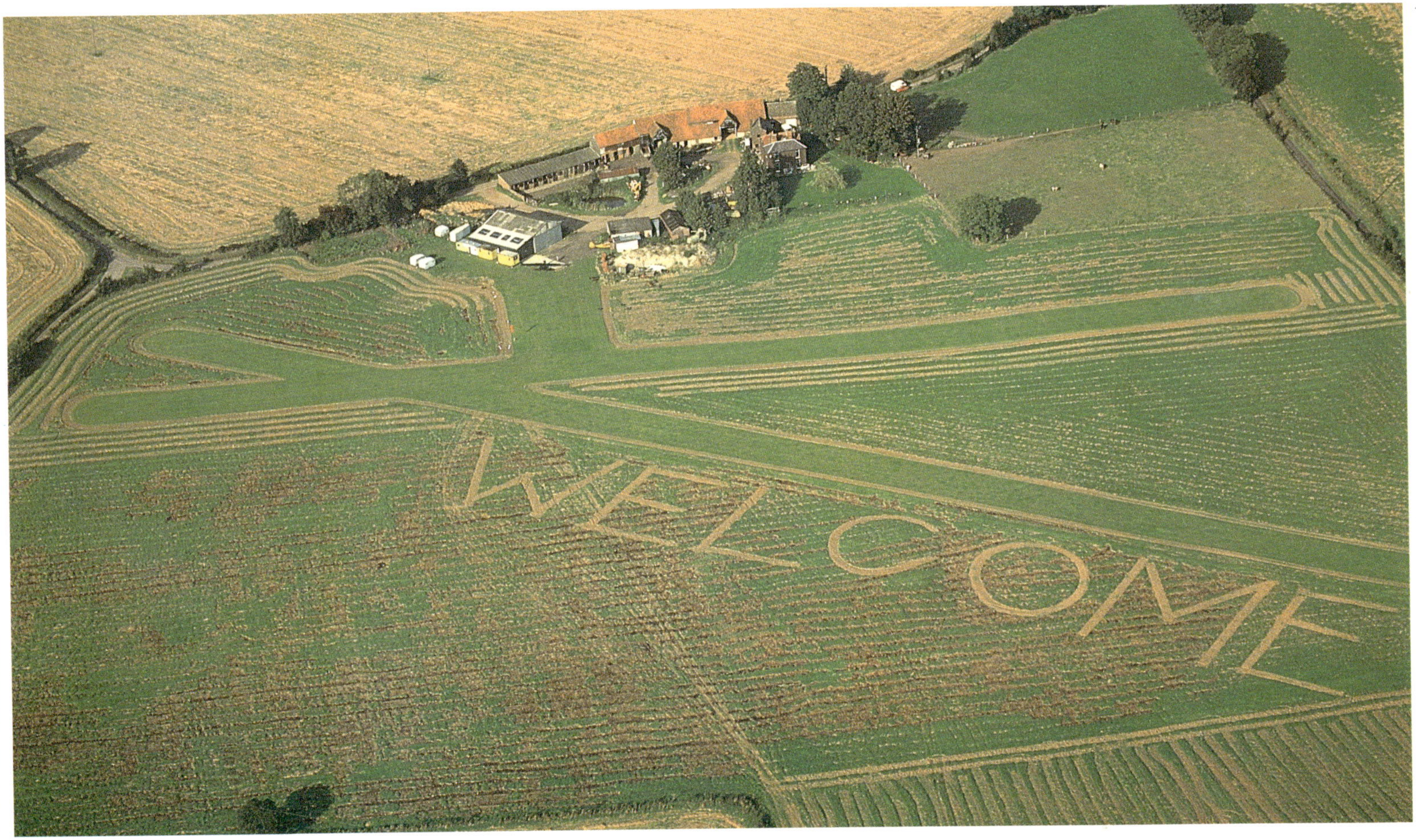

LONDON'S RIVER

The congested state of London's roads is all the more surprising when you consider the uncluttered nature of one of its main arteries, the Thames. It is apparent from our bird's eye view what an underused resource this is. Over the six years I have been broadcasting from the Flying Eye there has been an increase in river traffic, but it is only a drop in the ocean compared with what could be accommodated.

The building of Docklands and the Chelsea Harbour development have once again focused attention on the river. It may not be the most beautiful stretch of water, but it is fascinating – you can still see London barges gliding serenely along it, freight is towed here and there on large pallets, and the Woolwich Ferries chug from one side to the other. One summer we saw the Tall Ships come in and a sea plane flying out. Occasionally we spot a luxury yacht cruising through Docklands, the tankers and fishing boats make their way busily up and down, and, of course, the ever increasing flurry of river boats and taxis buzz between the revitalized piers. Taking life more sedately these days are the *Cutty Sark* at Greenwich and HMS *Belfast*, nestling in the lee of Tower Bridge.

It's not just the boats that make the river interesting, it's the buildings alongside them and the bridges: the majesty of Tower Bridge; Albert Bridge ablaze with light; Canary Wharf and its glittering reflections; the welcoming expanse of the runway at City Airport; and the protective humps of the Thames Barrier, ready to save London should the need, and the tide, arise.

Above all, there is the water itself, leaden grey on a cold winter's day, deep blue under the summer sun, or glittering silver in the dying light.

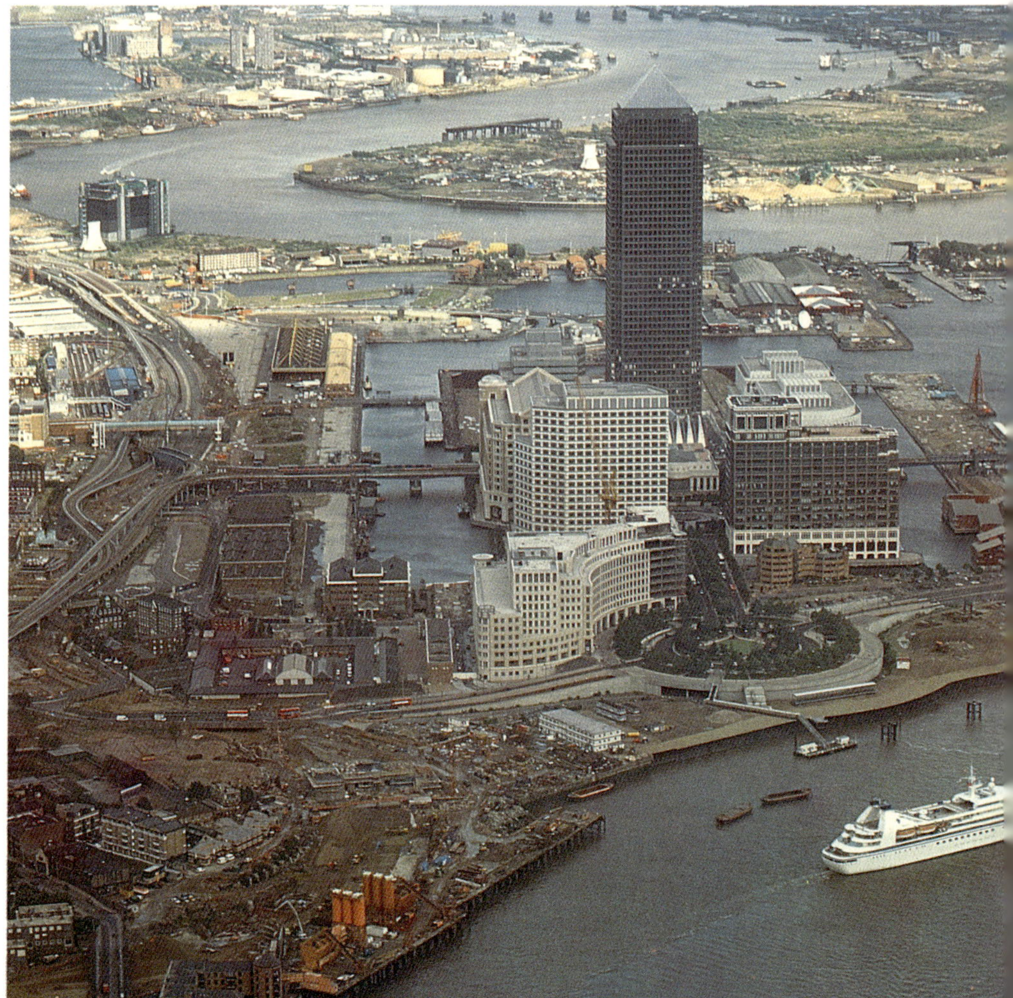

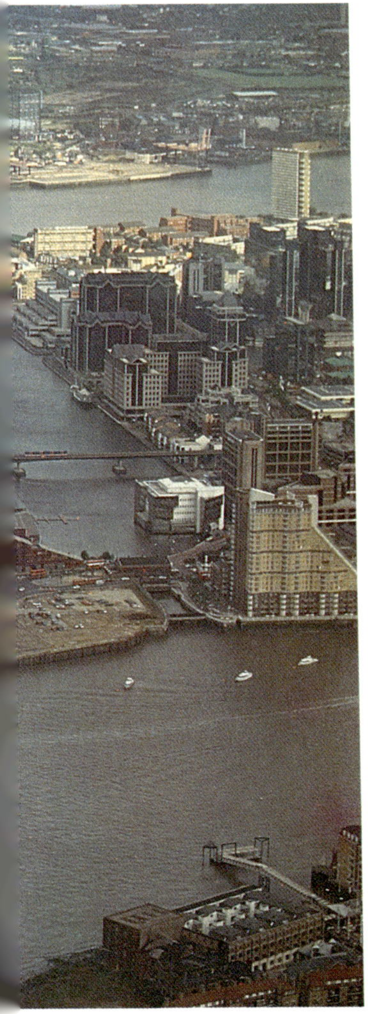

DOCKLANDS

The spectacular clutch of buildings, Canary Wharf at the centre, changes with the light, almost from black to white.

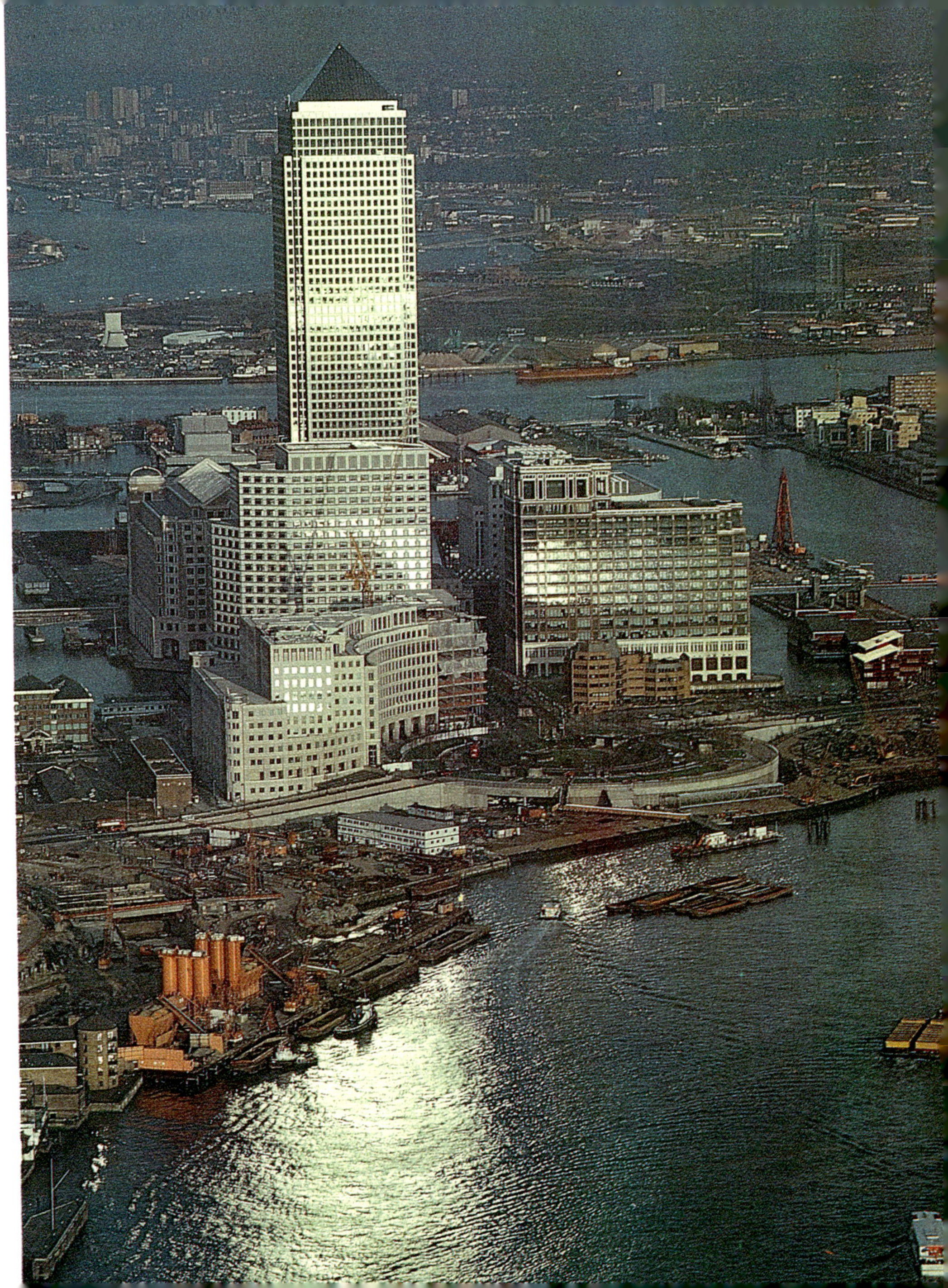

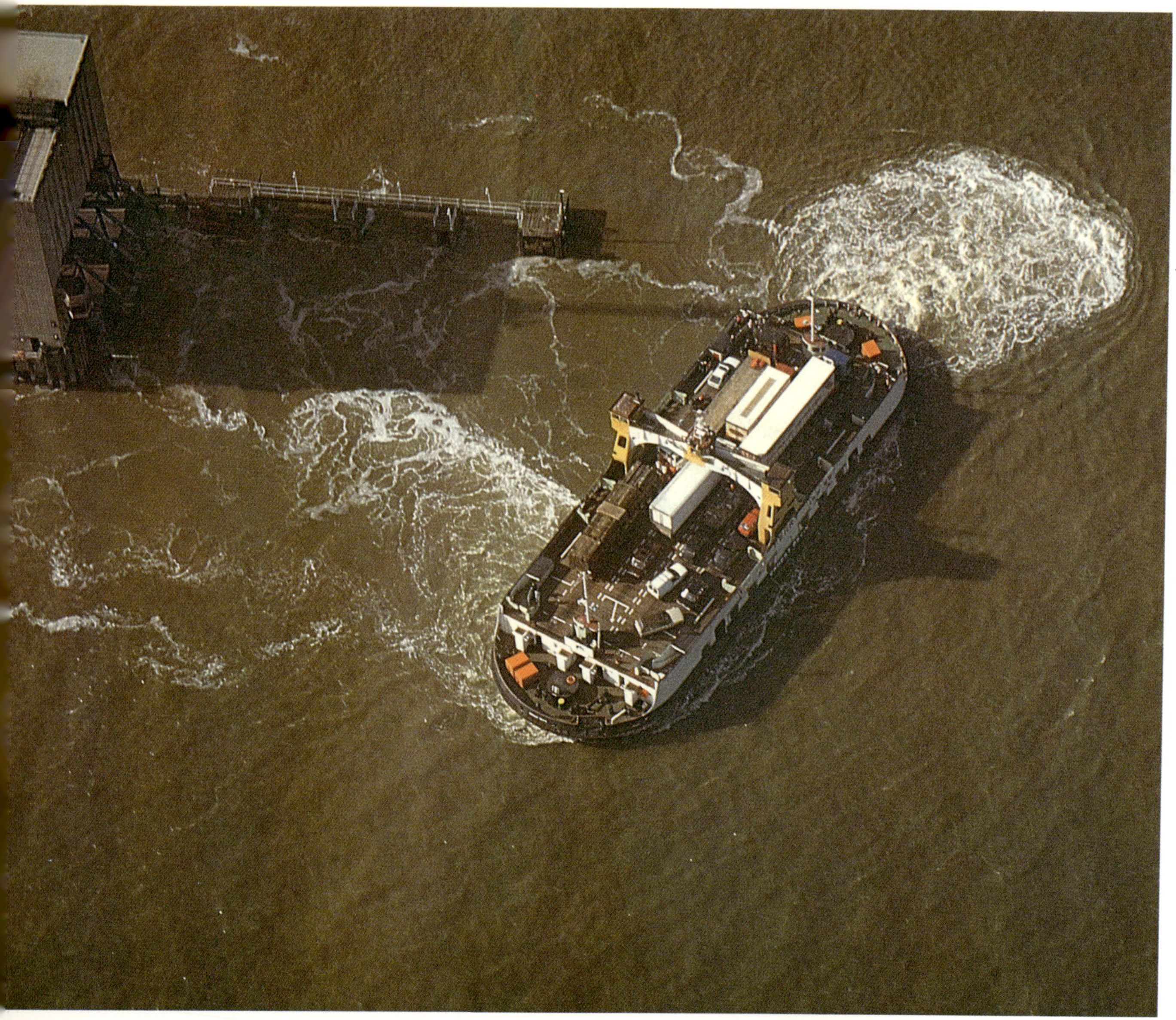

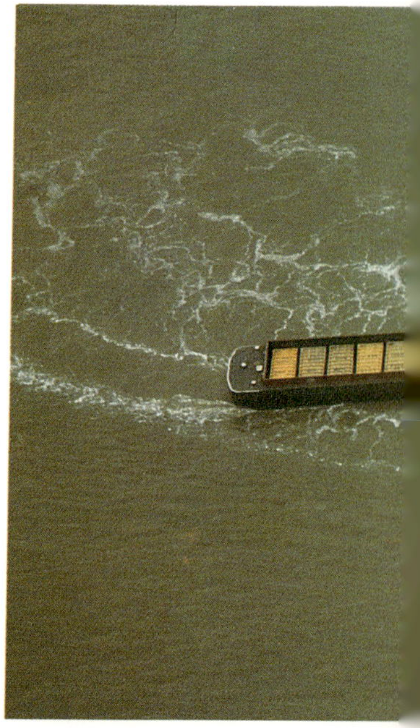

FERRY, BARGE AND RIVER BUS

Each year 50 million tonnes of cargo and a million tonnes of rubbish are transported along the Thames. The Woolwich Ferry can manoeuvre on a sixpence, and the bus is mysteriously parked in the depths of the vast barge alongside HMS *Belfast*.

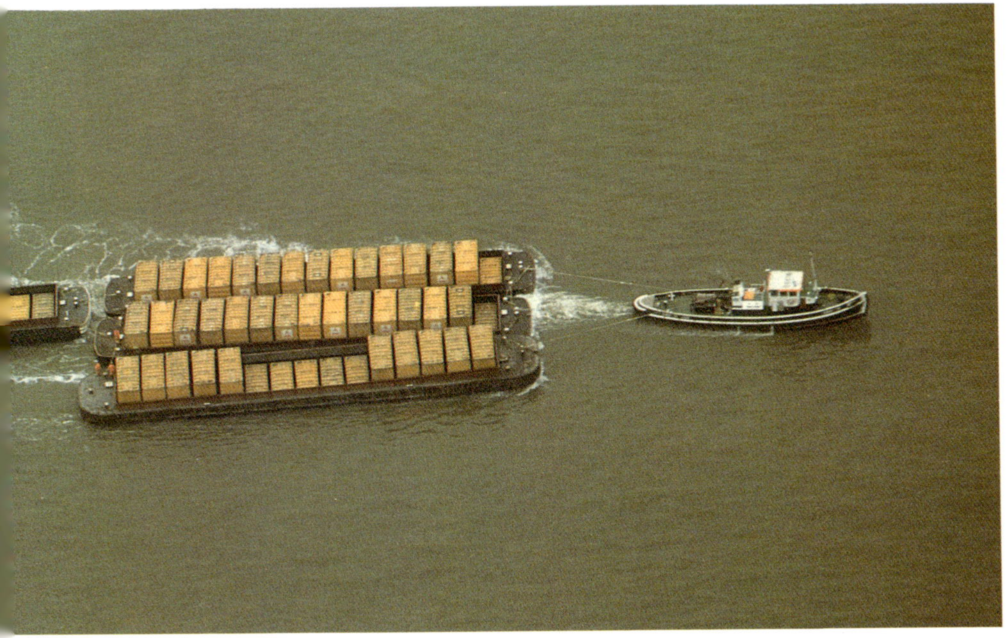

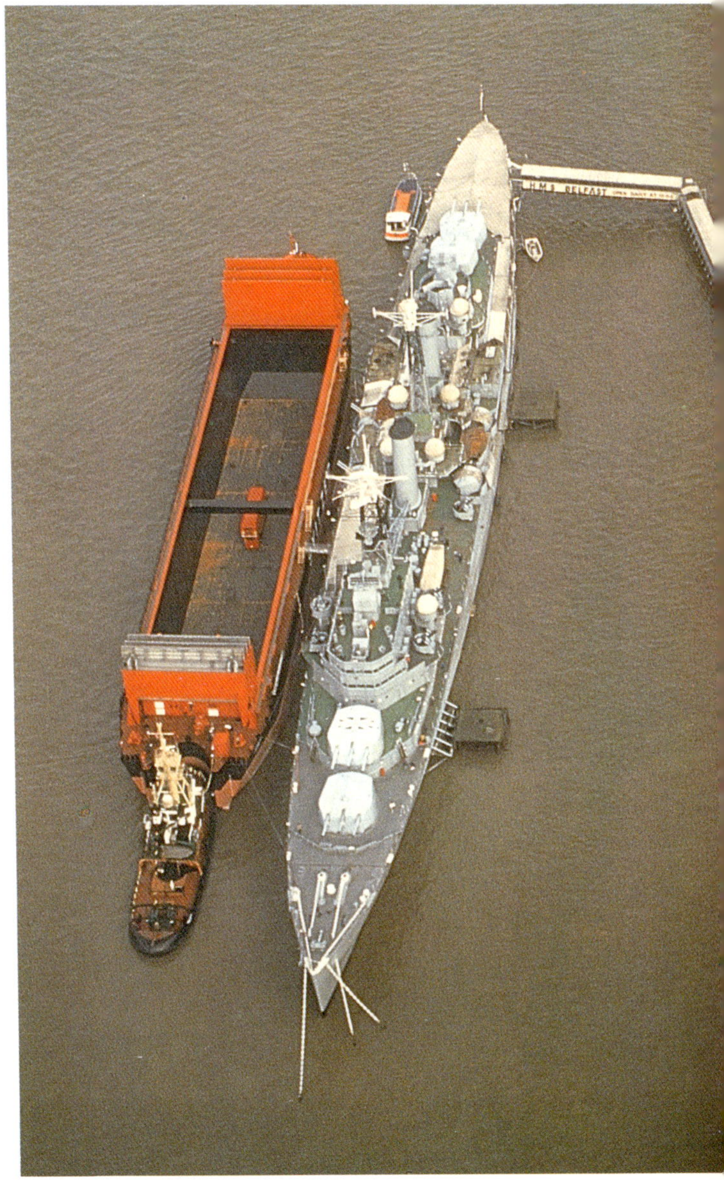
HMS BELFAST

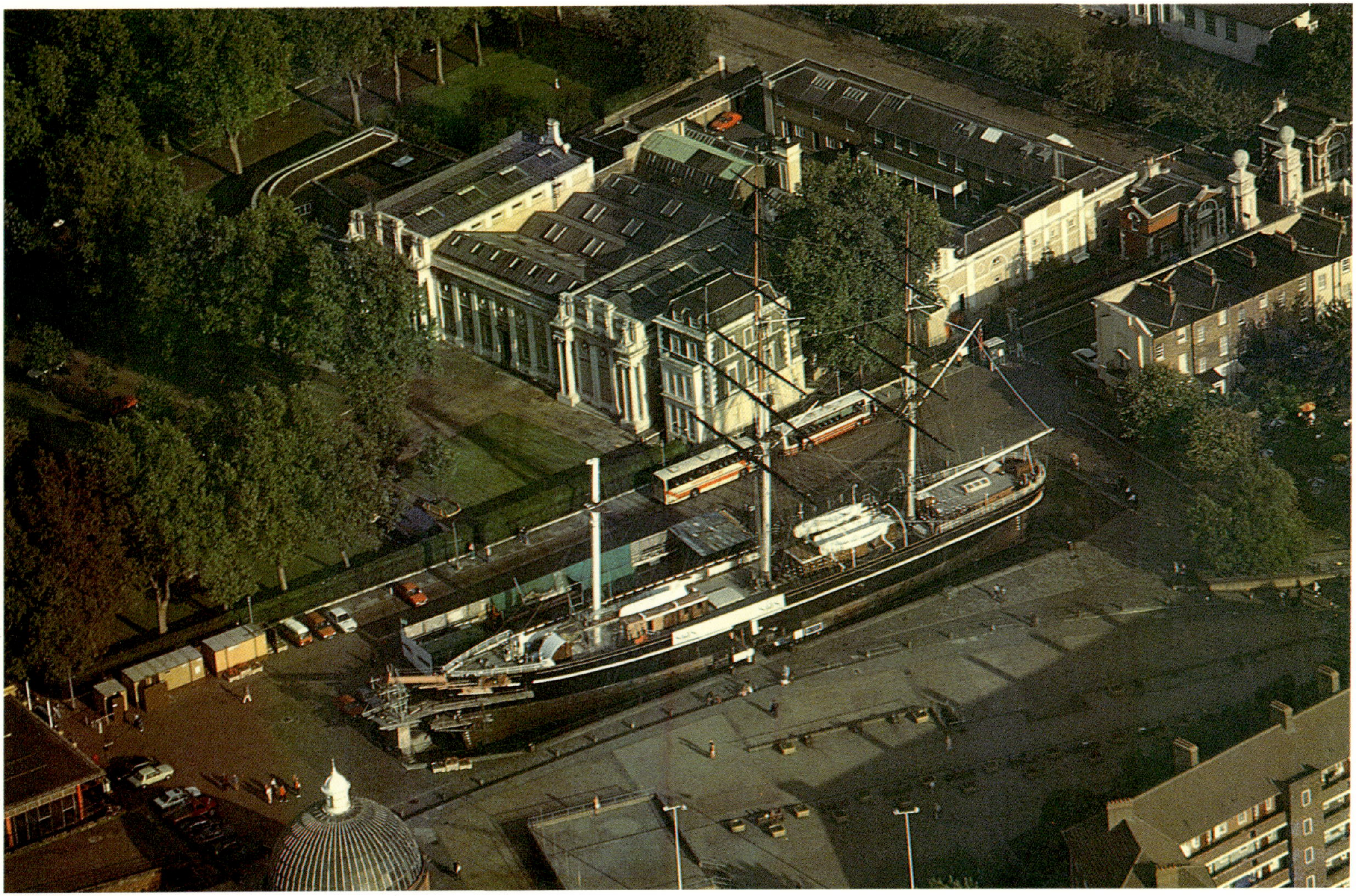

CUTTY SARK

High, dry and safe at Greenwich, this fine tea clipper was built on the Clyde in 1869. There were more than 10 miles of rope in the rigging, and the sail area was the size of eleven tennis courts.

‘THE PHOTOS of the Woolwich Ferry and *Cutty Sark* bring back a lot of happy memories for me – that area is where we used to dive out for a desperately needed drink when I was a teacher in New Cross. Actually, I very often had to do my marking in there as well, because for four very happy months I lived in a mini-van. I'm not quite sure how it happened – something to do with a fairly spectacular bust up with my then girlfriend, I think.

I was teaching English to a motley collection of very large West Indians, East Indians, Cypriots, Turks, Greeks, Italians, Irish and about four traditional English skinheads. Lessons were spent wrestling with the intellectual dilemmas posed by the full stop and with the more human dilemmas of who had set light to Thomson's hair and when they were going to put it out! As you can imagine, their domestic backgrounds were varied, to say the least, so the fact that ‘sir’ lived in a mini-van outside the school didn't bother them much. After an initial confrontation when two of them jacked the van up on bricks while I lay happily dozing inside, it all worked out very well. I even had my own curly headed little alarm clock called Johnson who used to knock on the windscreen at 7.30 every morning. I then used to dive into the school for a nice hot shower, and by the time all the other staff crawled in from all over southern England, grumbling about traffic jams and British Rail, I was as fresh as a daisy.

The ultimate achievement was getting the post office to bring my mail to me – after several weeks of hassle with the GPO head office, the first delivery was magic. There was this little scratching on the thick ice on the windscreen, and a little voice enquiring ‘Mr Tarrant?’ And as I slipped open the little mini-van window, there it was on the envelope . . .

C. J. Tarrant Esq.
161 GLO (my registration number)
Sprules Road
London SE4

In the end I gave it all up because my love life more or less came to a total standstill. Conversations like ‘shall we go back to your place?’, ‘well, actually we're in it,’ I could handle, and most of the ladies came to terms with the idea that ‘popping upstairs’ meant climbing over the seat into the back. No, what really seemed to put them off was waiting for a cup of coffee, sitting with a lighted blowtorch on their knees!’

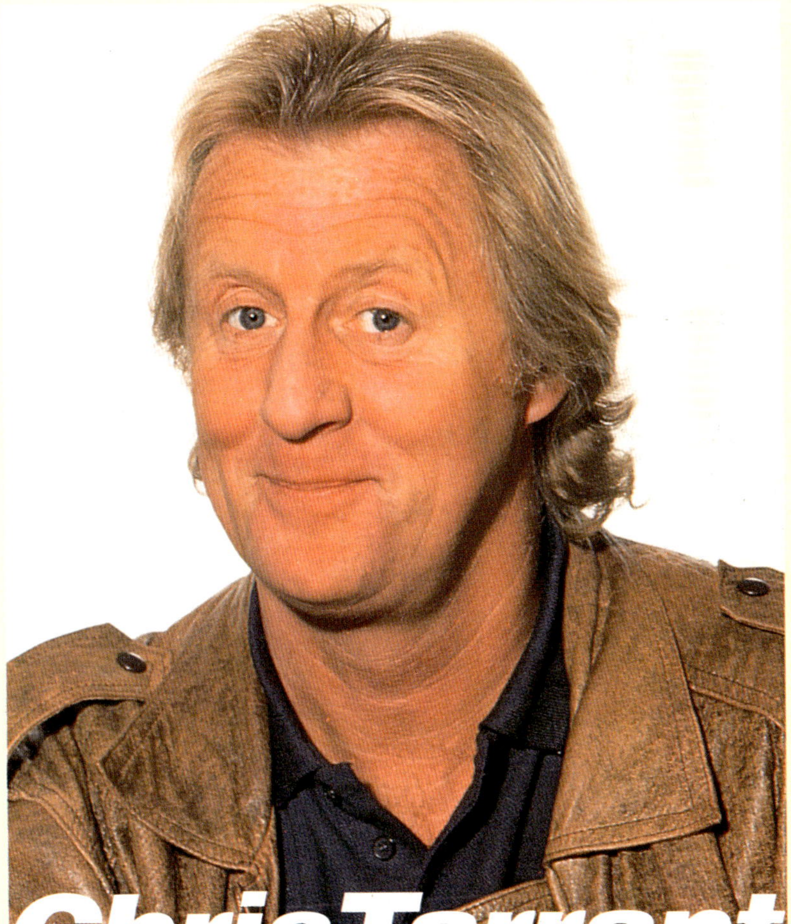

Chris Tarrant

CAPITAL 95·8 FM
LONDON

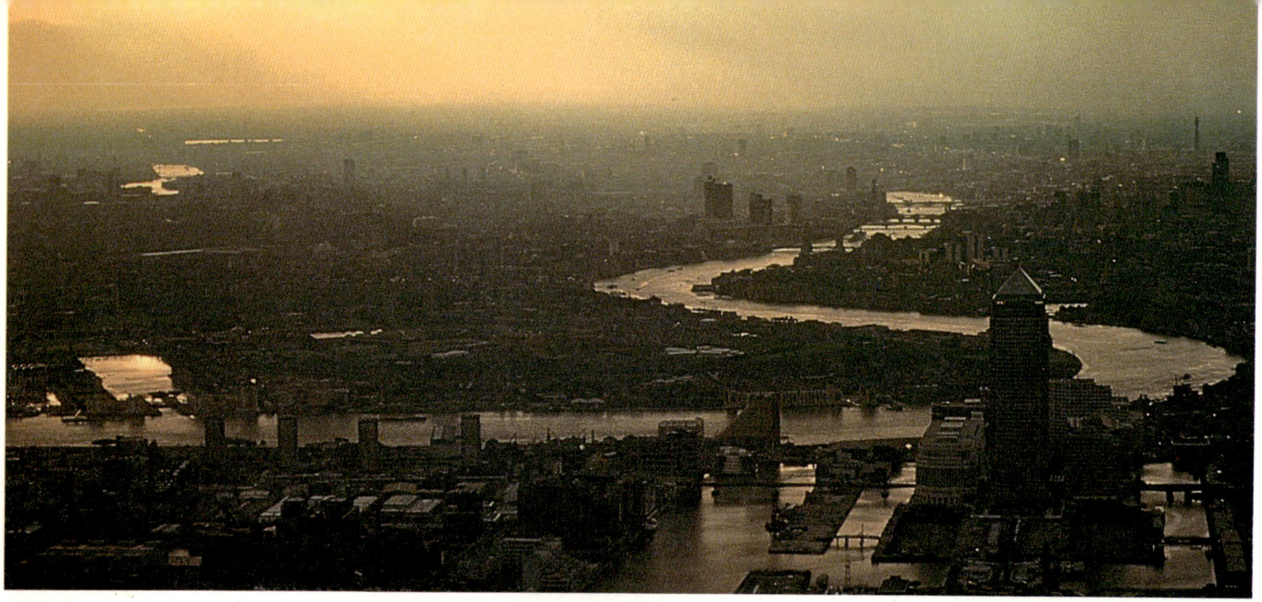

CHELSEA HARBOUR

A half-mile river frontage and a 75-berth marina in the heart of London. Michael Caine has a flat here – not a lot of people know that!

DUSK OVER THE THAMES

From our vantage point in the Flying Eye London sometimes seems nothing more than a wide, curving river, just as it was 4,000 years ago, when the Celtic settlers arrived. In this light, even Canary Wharf is almost invisible.

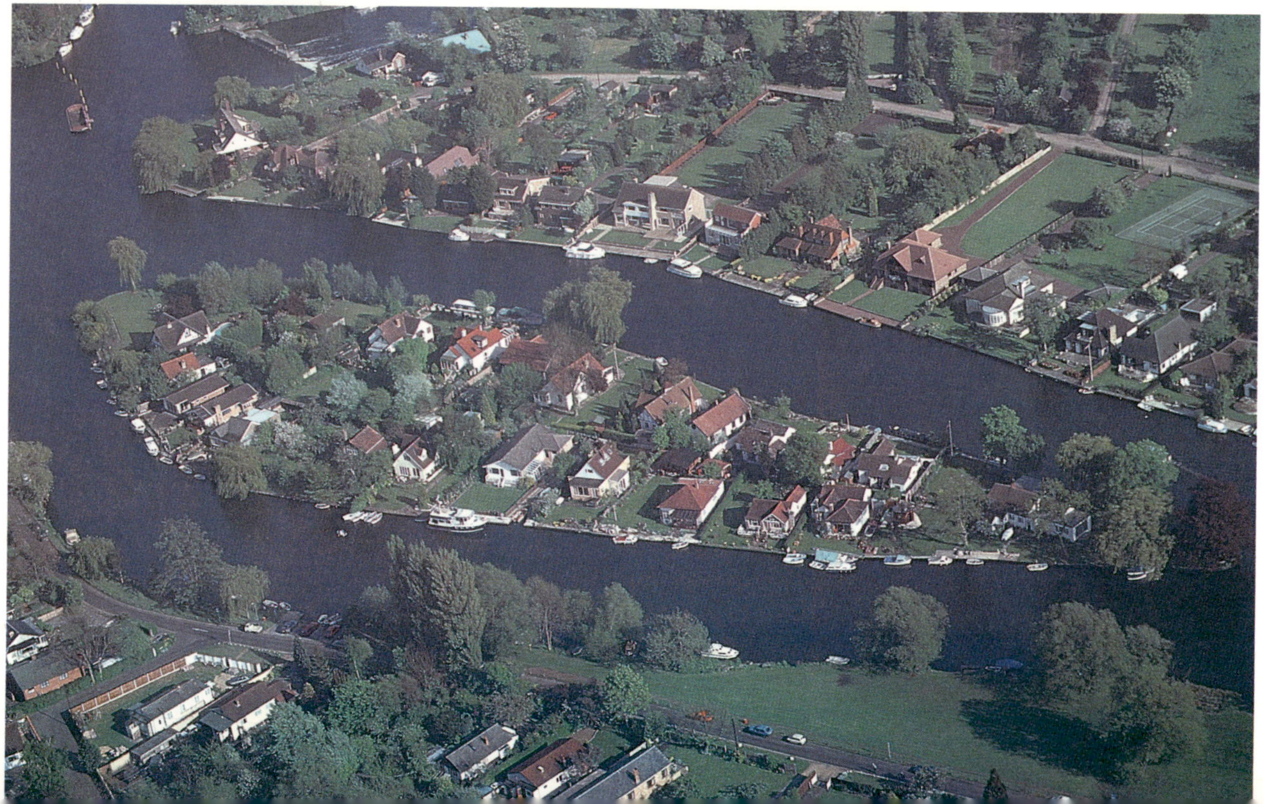

ISLAND BLISS

The Thames can be pretty and intimate, too. What better place to live than this miniature England?

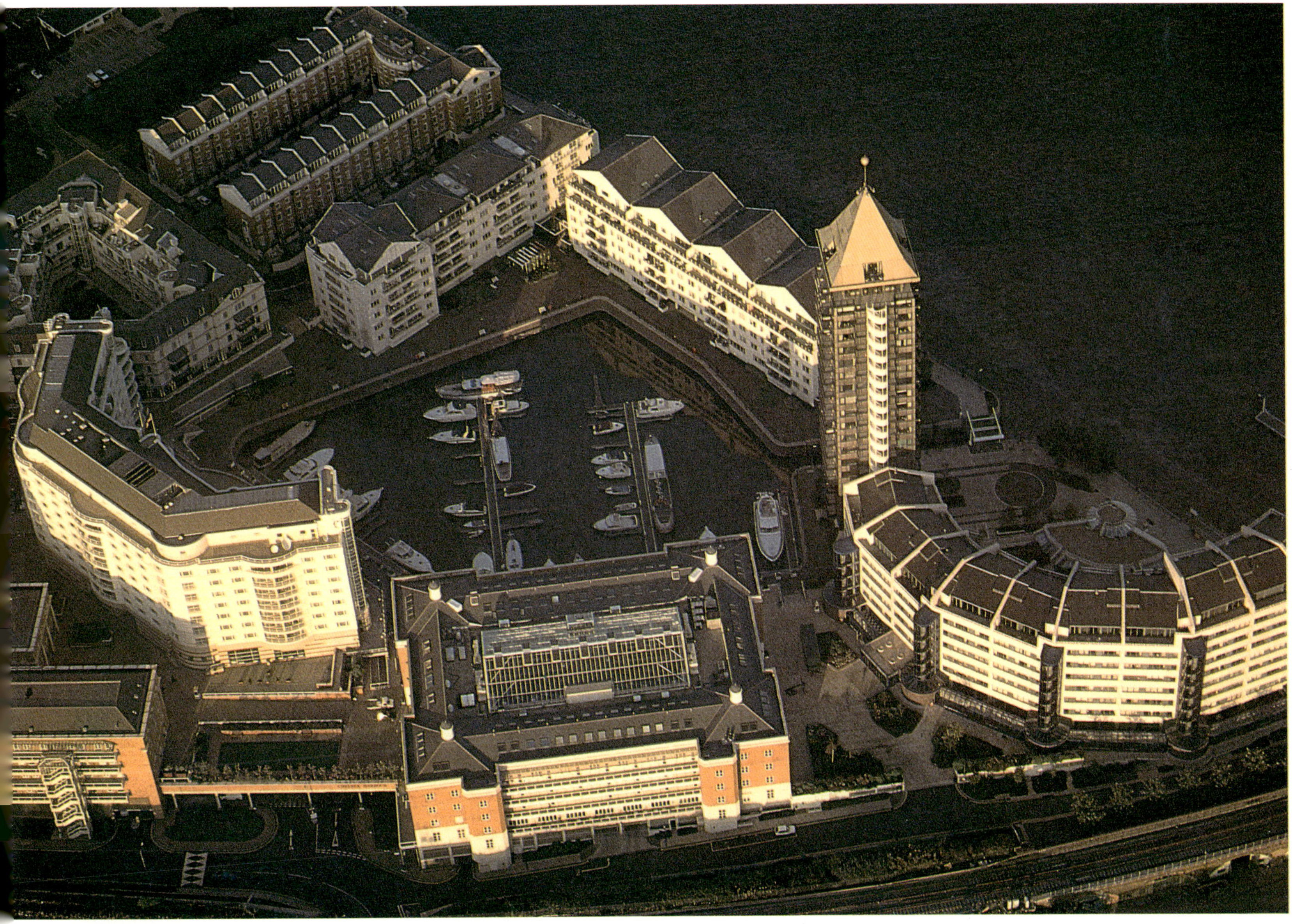

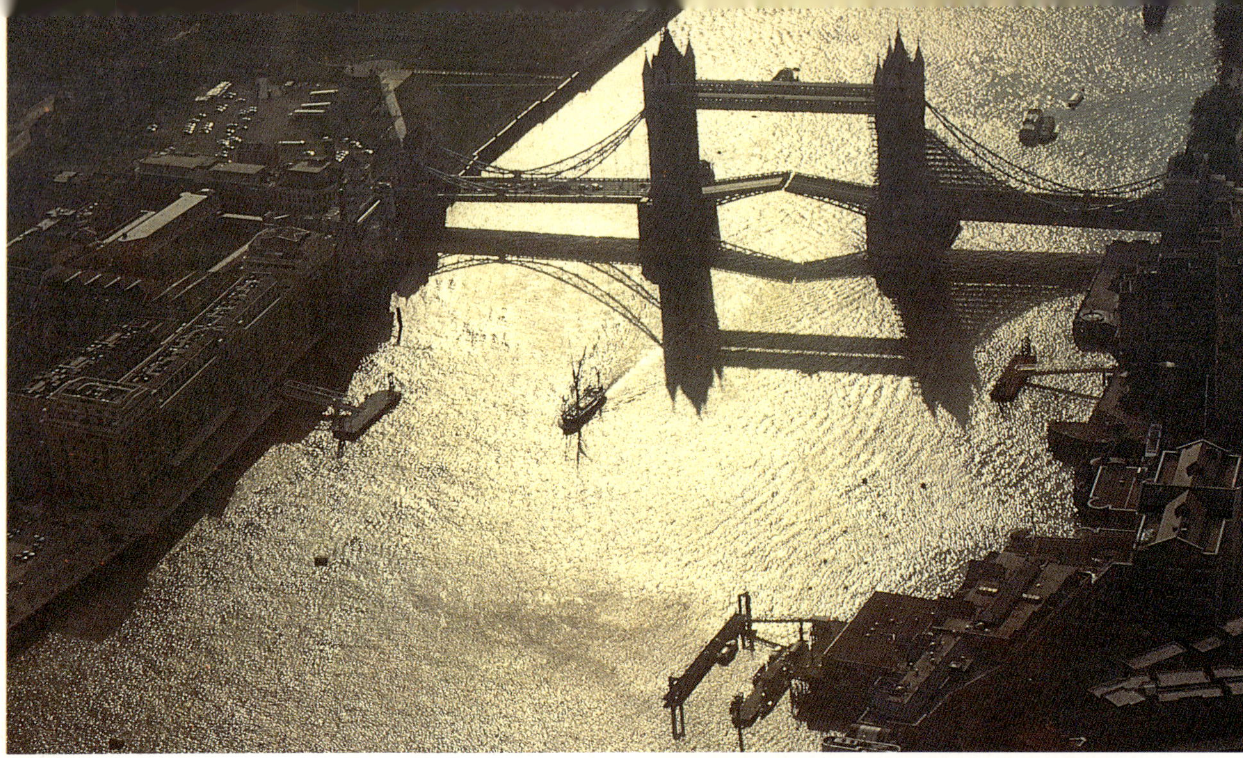

TOWER BRIDGE

The decks are just about to close after letting a vessel out of the Pool.

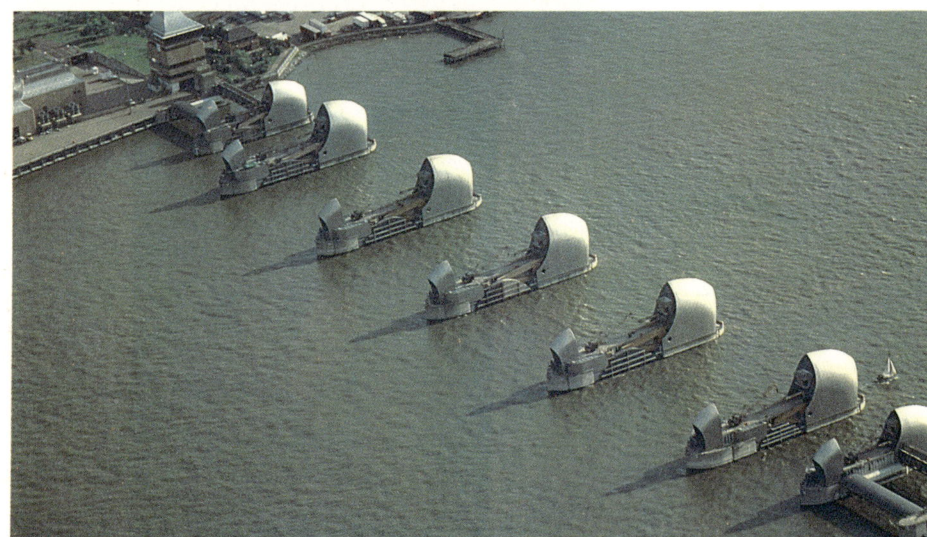

THAMES FLOOD BARRIER

Four massive main gates, each 65 feet high, and six smaller ones can shut off the river from a rising sea. The barrier has been raised in earnest thirteen times since it was built at a cost of £500 million in 1982.

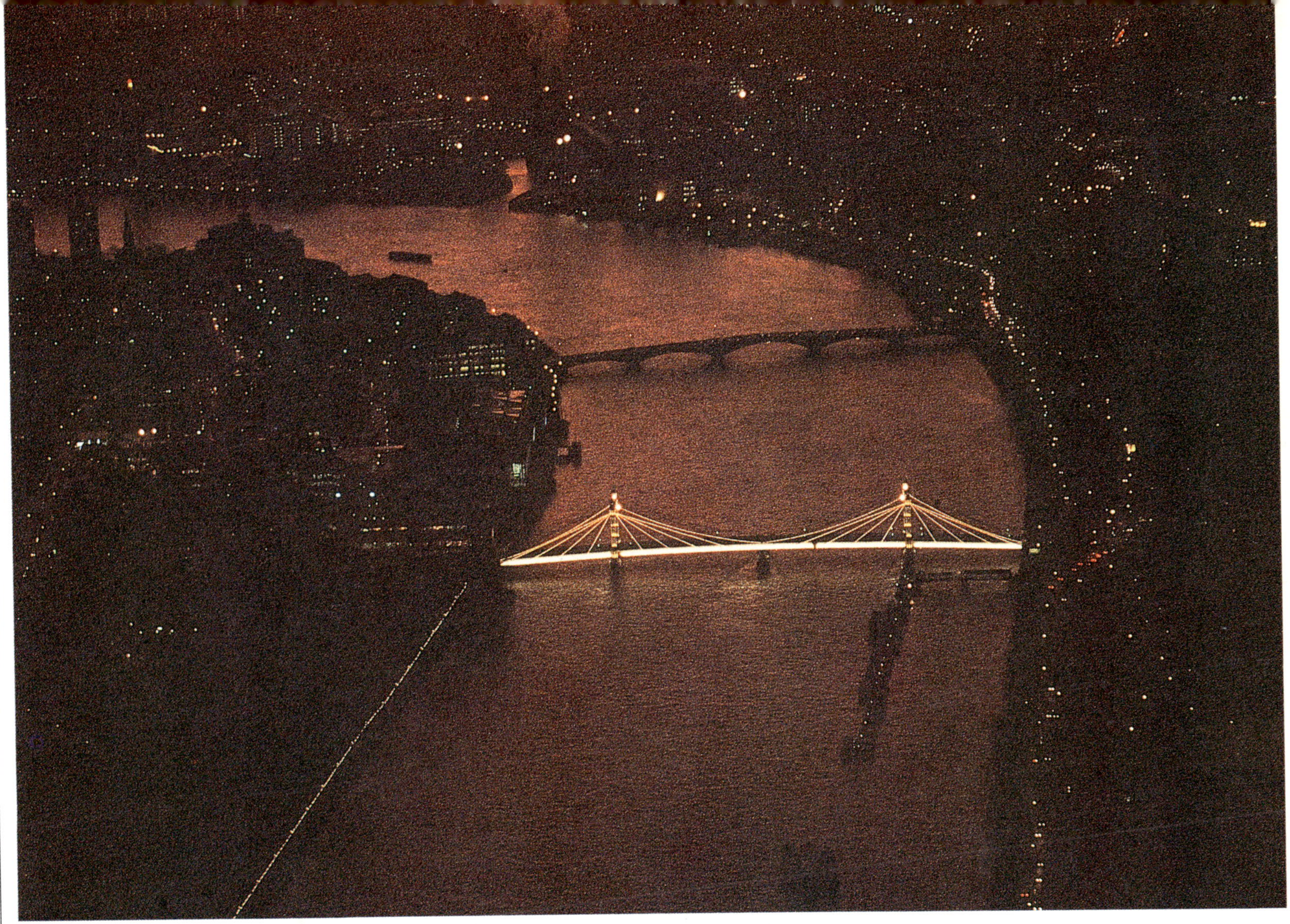

ALBERT BRIDGE

'All troops must break step when marching over this bridge.' Vibrations set up by marching feet can put a suspension bridge into a potentially fatal oscillation; no wonder it needs reinforcement to enable it to cope with today's road juggernauts.

Smoky City

Flying above London and looking down on it for long periods as we do means that we sometimes spot fire before anyone else, and both Russ and I have been able to report fires to the fire brigade earlier than they might otherwise have been.

Of course, not all the smoke above our city is accidental. From the Flying Eye we see with frightening clarity the air pollution that is becoming a major problem for so many Londoners. Quite often we take off from Elstree in sparkling sunlight to see the city in the distance choking under a yellowy-green blanket of smoke and dust. In 1993 stubble burning was banned, but every summer so far the smoke it creates combines with the fumes belched out all year round by various chimneys across London to produce a pall of pollution that smothers the capital. In the hot, windless days of summer it can be like flying around in pea soup.

Of the top ten worst polluted places in Britain eight are in London, and Londoners breathe the most polluted air in the country. According to the London Boroughs Association there were two severe pollution episodes in the last two years – at times pollution in London has reached levels recorded in Athens and Los Angeles, where air warnings are broadcast regularly. Thankfully we don't have the smogs of years gone by, but it's obvious that the grandeur of the city's sunsets are not nature's work alone.

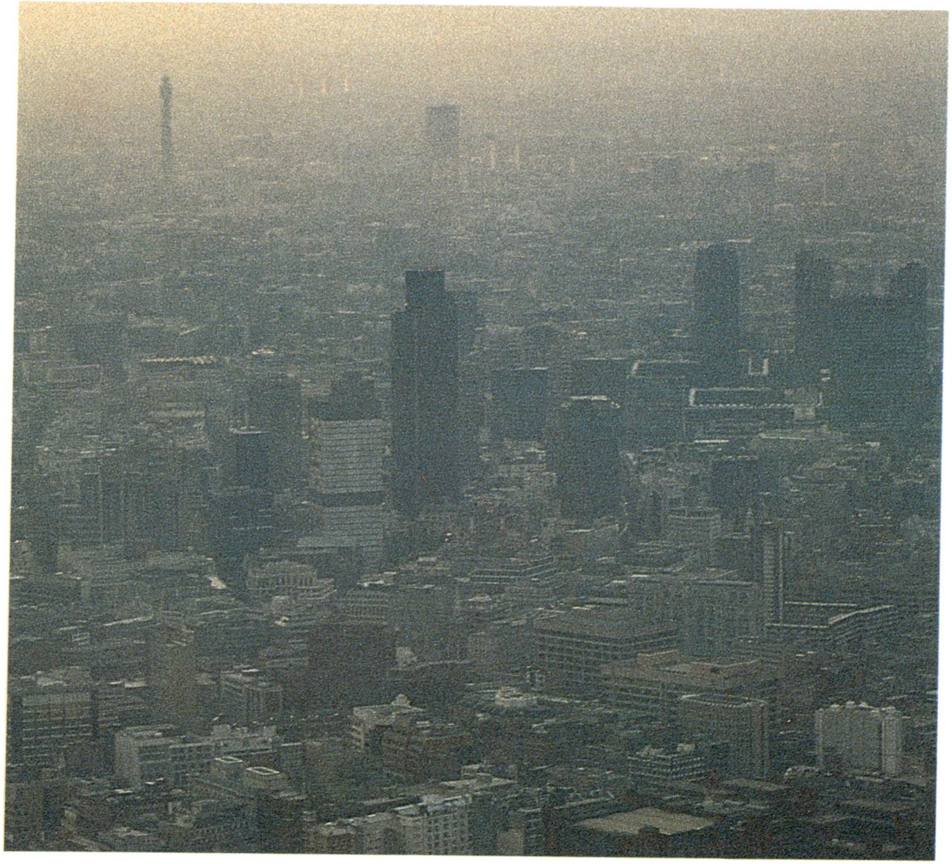

SMOKY CITY

One of the best times to see London from the air is at sunset. The pollution, which is all too evident from the air, provides some spectacular evening skies. More local causes, such as the building fire and stubble burning add to the effect.

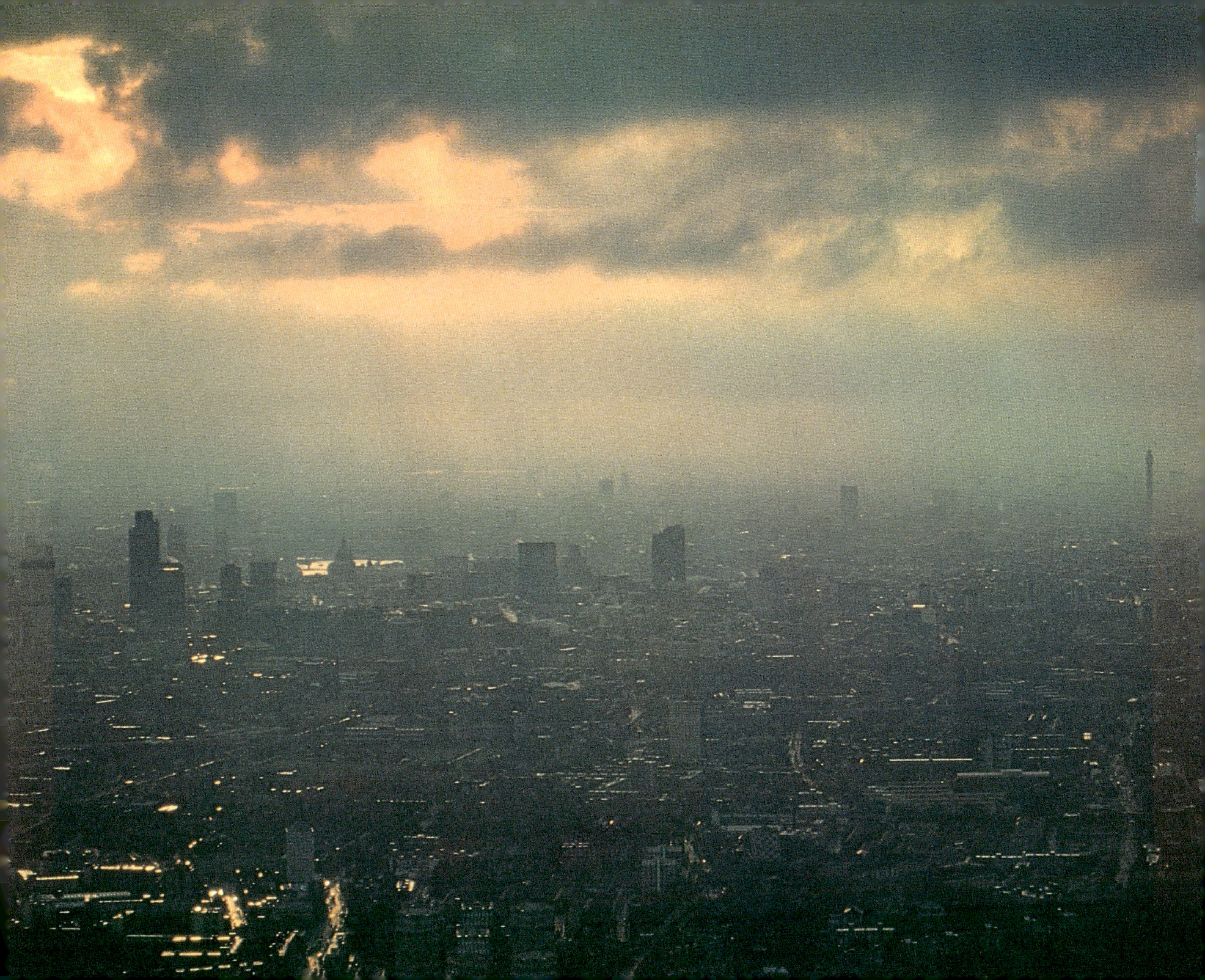

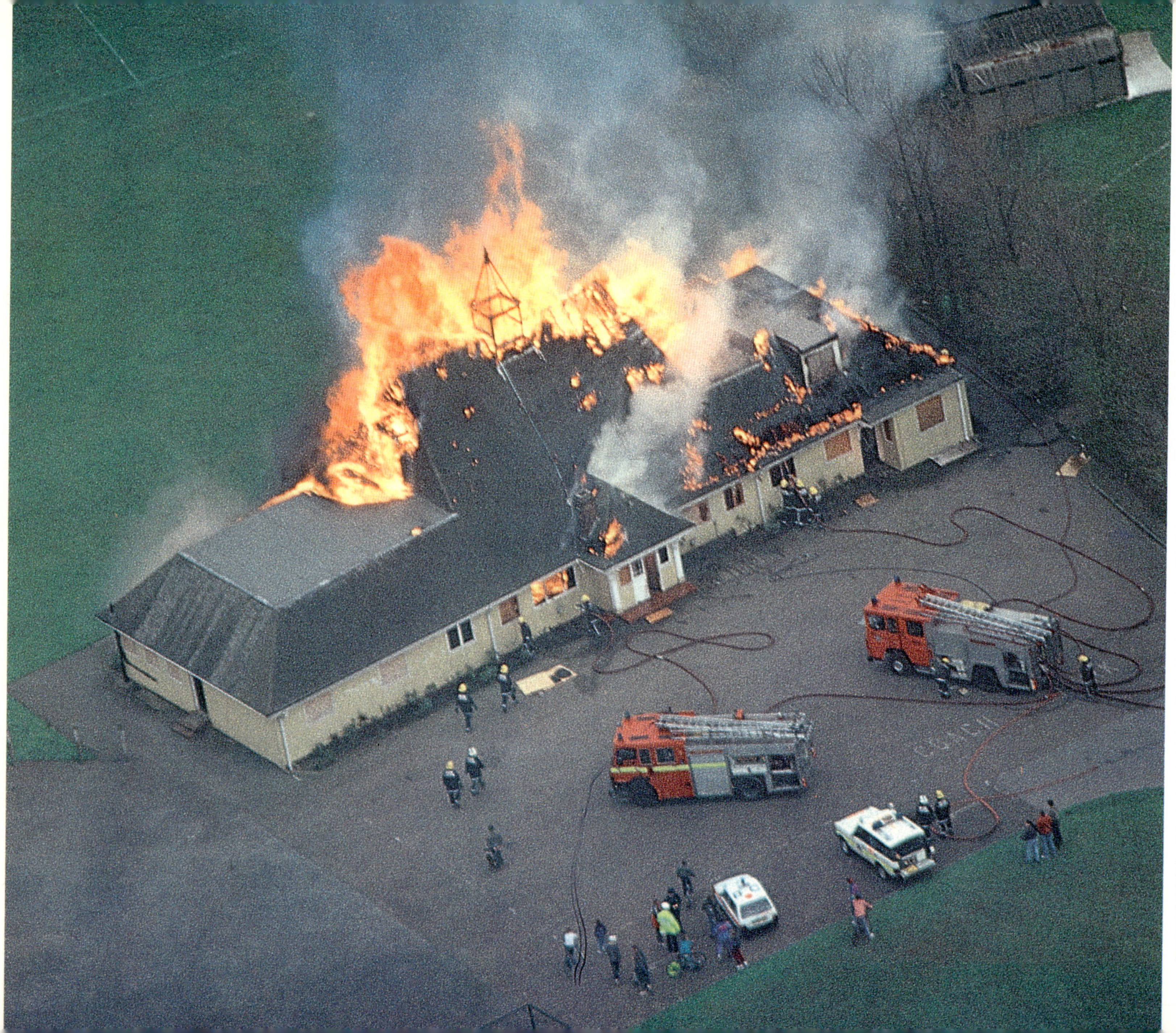

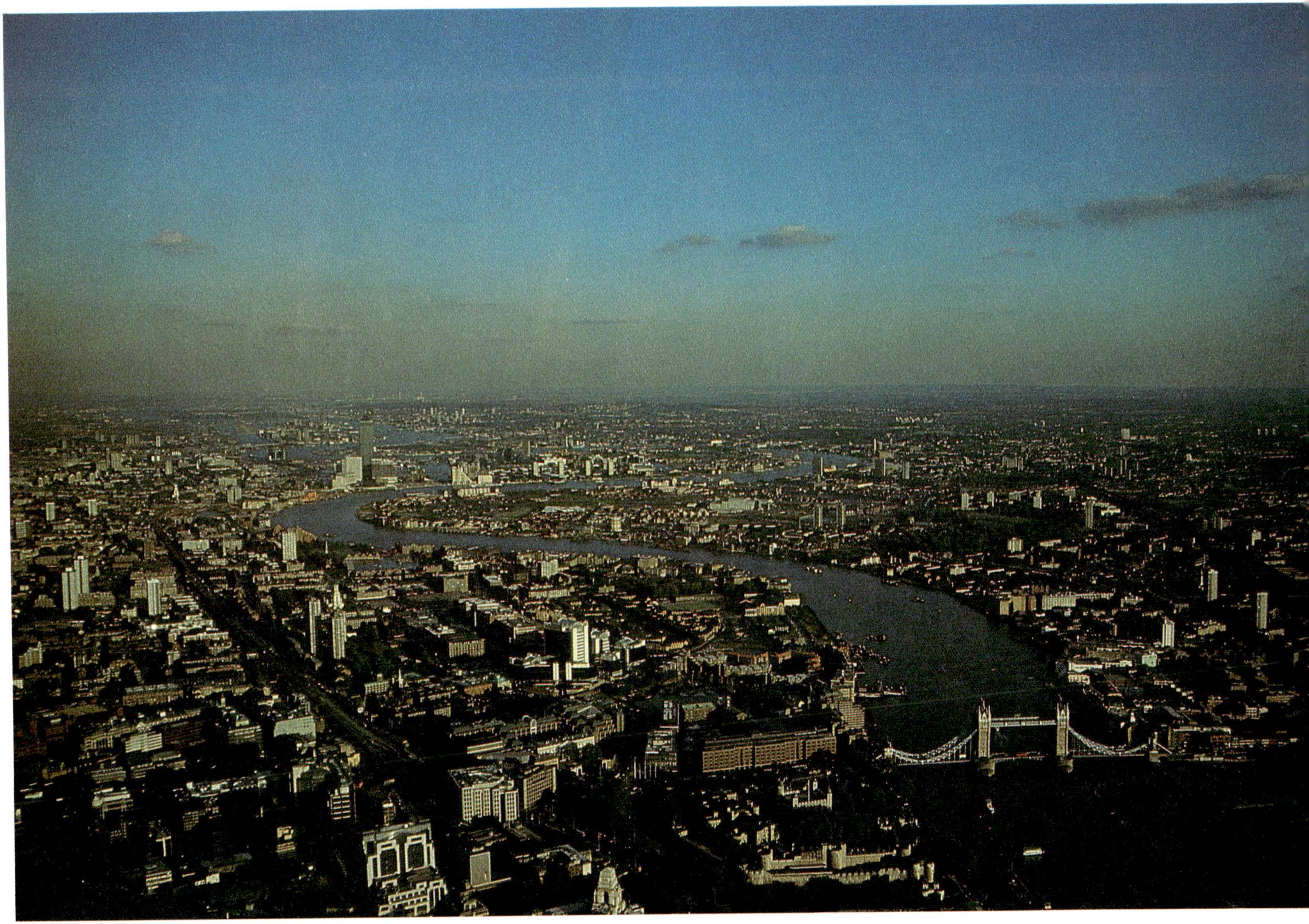

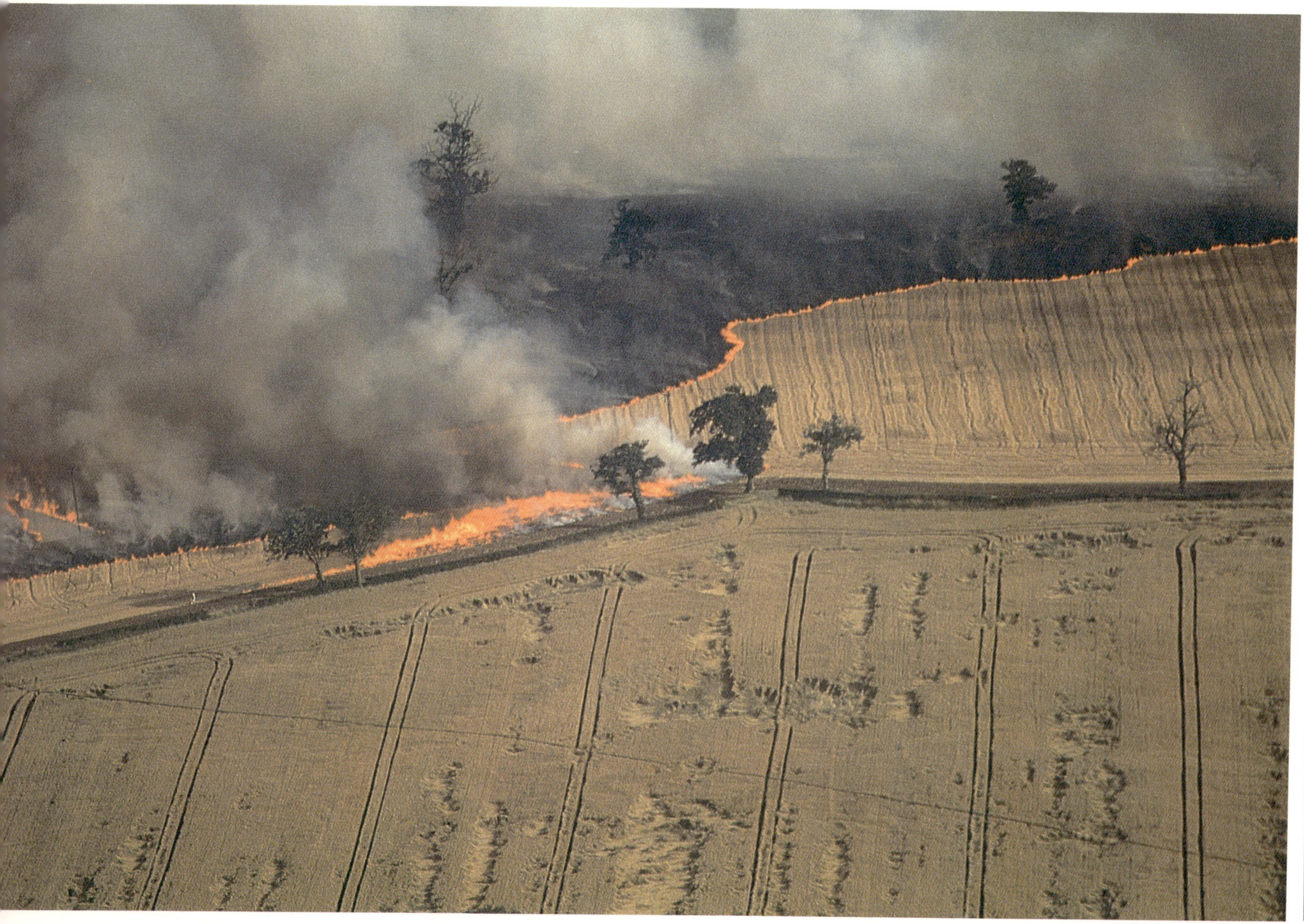

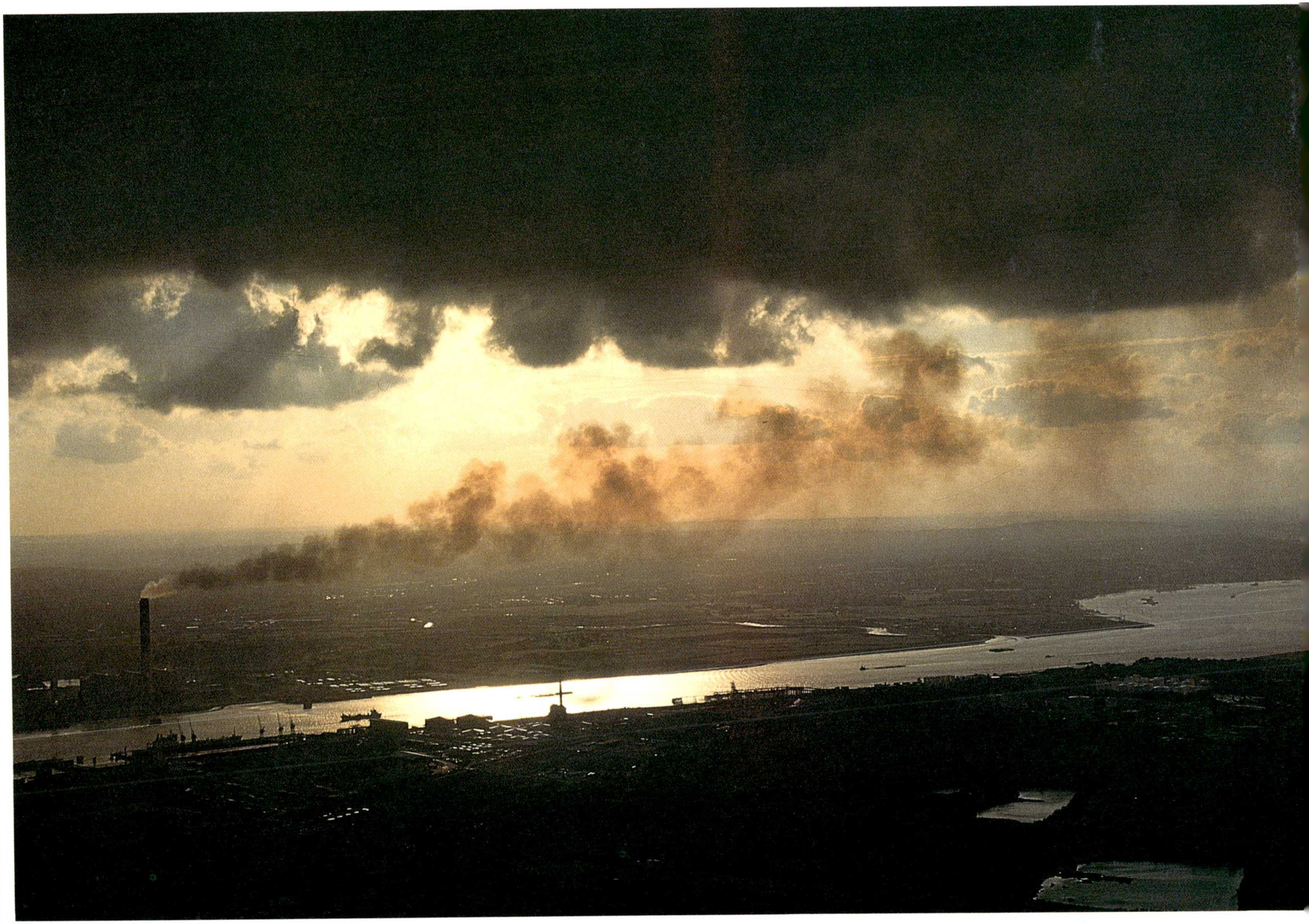

‘IF YOU WERE to ask me ‘Fox, do you love London?’ I would have to answer ‘Is the Pope Catholic?! Yes I do. I was born in London, grew up in London, went away for a few years to university, then abroad to Germany and the States, then to the Midlands to try to get into radio, and finally back home to London. Thank you God! I know it has problems – doesn’t any big city? – but this is London. All those thousands of years of history, all the power, all the excitement, all the fun, all that life in one place. Wow! But sometimes I feel I’ve got to step back to appreciate it all and get my breath back. And that’s when I leap into the chopper and fly! Look at it – it’s incredible. As far as the eye can see, it’s *all* London. To fly around this amazing city at sunrise or sunset on a clear midsummer day must surely rate as one of the world’s most spectacular sights. Like a real life Emerald city. Except when I click my red slippers (black bike boots for my Harley Davidson, actually!) the dream won’t end – it will all be there tomorrow to wonder at again.’

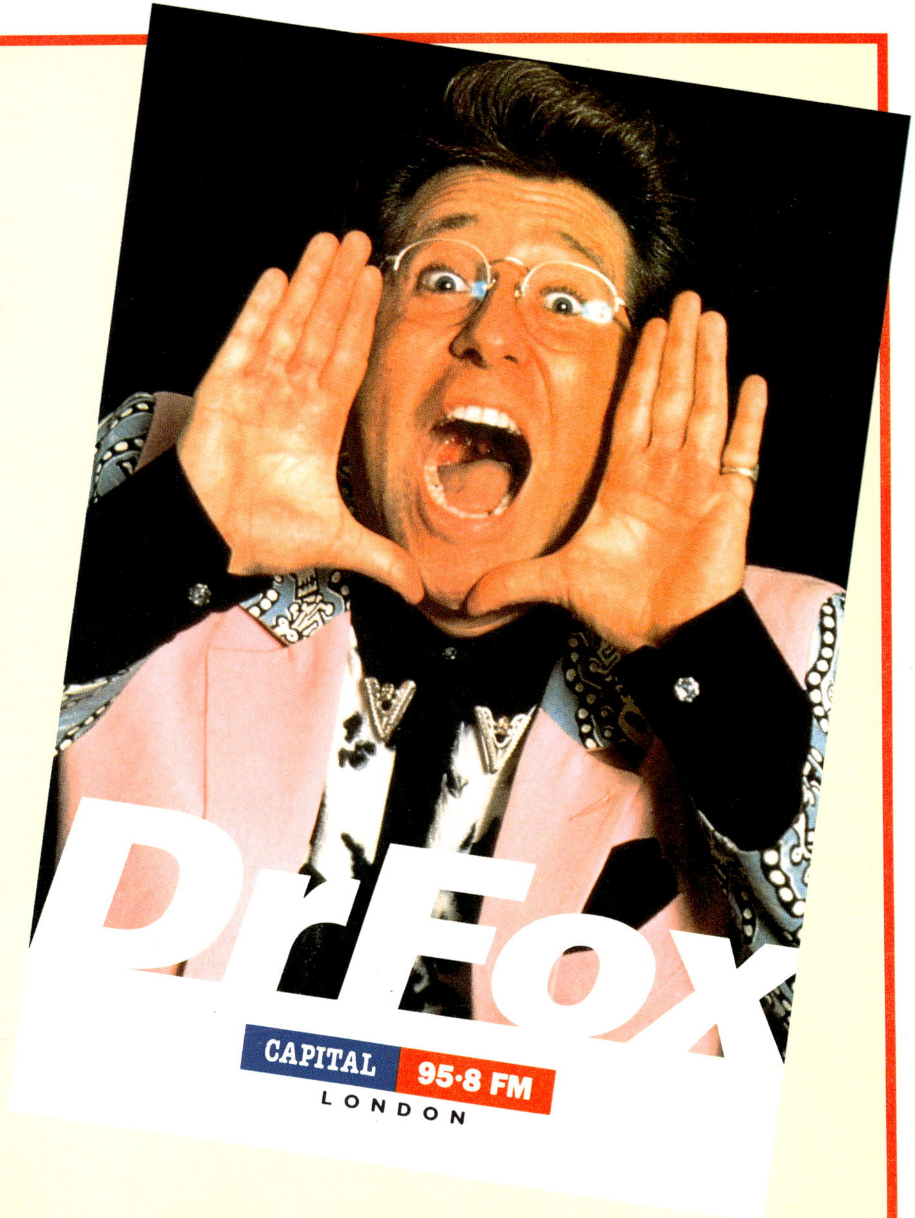

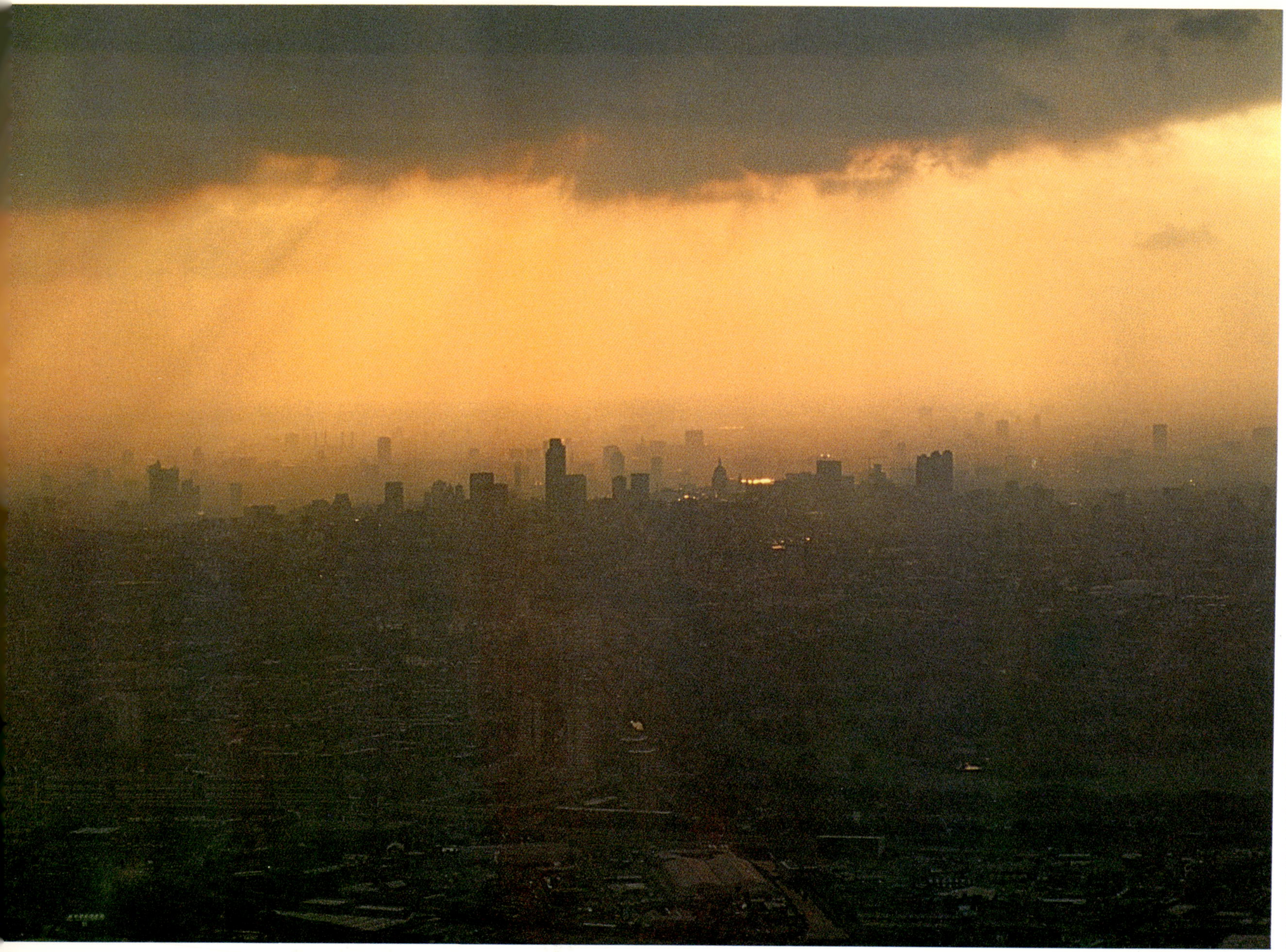

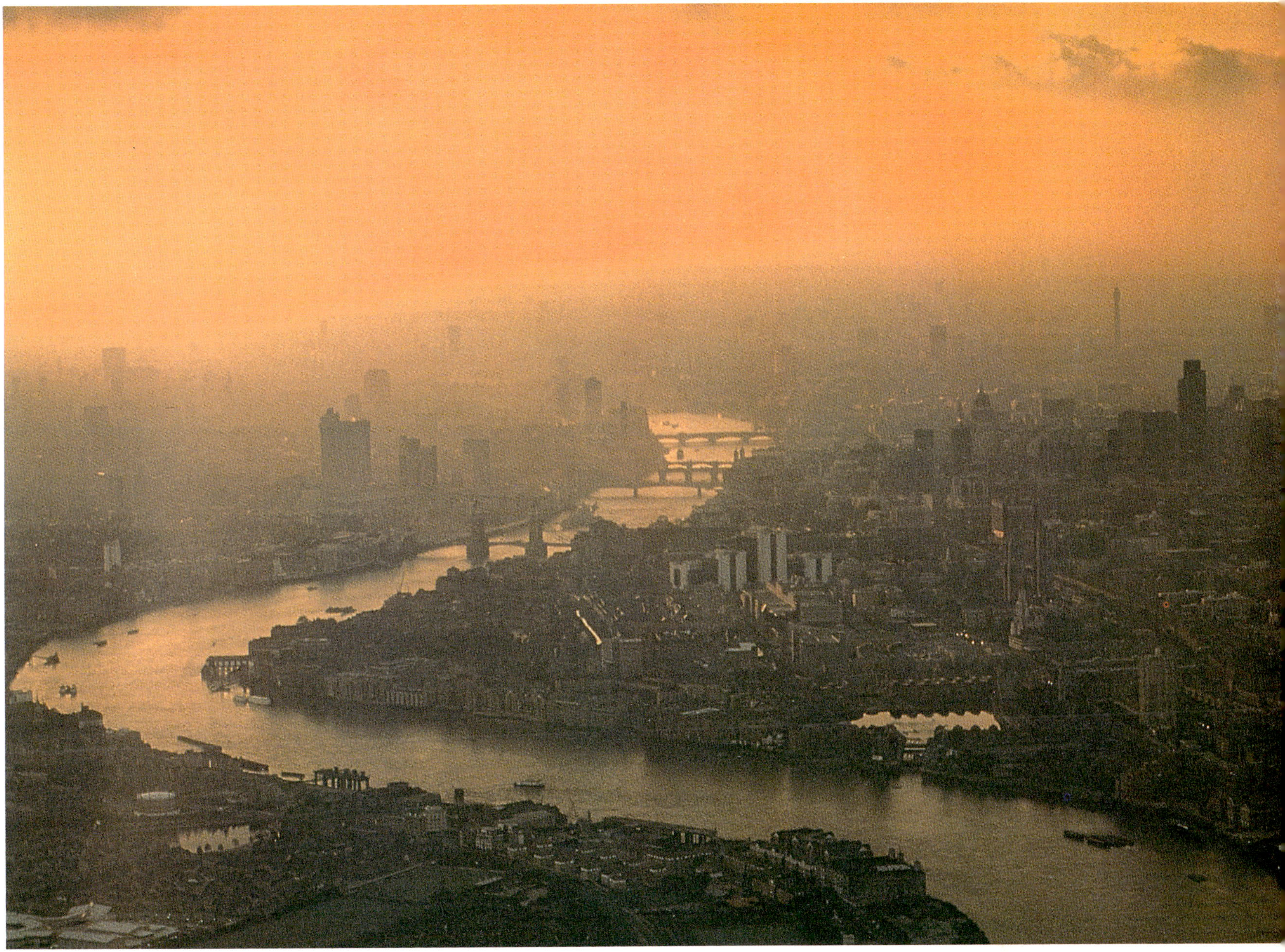

London Lights

I began flying with the Eye in October 1987, and just when I started to recognize all the roads, the clocks went back and we were suddenly plunged into darkness. Once you get used to it, it is not as much of a problem as it sounds. There is so much traffic on the roads that the headlights and brake lights together with the street lights illuminate everything quite clearly, and you soon get used to recognizing the patterns of the lights. In some ways, it's easier at night to spot the jams because you can see the telltale glowing red snake of brake lights from quite a distance.

Of course, one road that isn't completely lit up is the M25, and I do remember one occasion when a serious accident had closed a stretch near Maple Cross, and the police had diverted all traffic off both carriageways. We came flying along, following the lights of the motorway traffic, when all of a sudden we got to the junction that had been closed and the motorway disappeared – with no traffic it became invisible in the dark.

Each winter I am surprised by just how bright London is at night. Typically the sun goes down and the city fades to grey. Then the first lights start to flicker on. Normally Piccadilly Circus is the first thing to catch your eye, a bright spot of colour in the dusk. Gradually, the big office buildings begin to glow, and Harrods illuminates itself like a fairy-tale castle. Before Canary Wharf came along one

HYDE PARK CORNER

Once again, the mighty roar of London's traffic has ground to a well-lit halt.

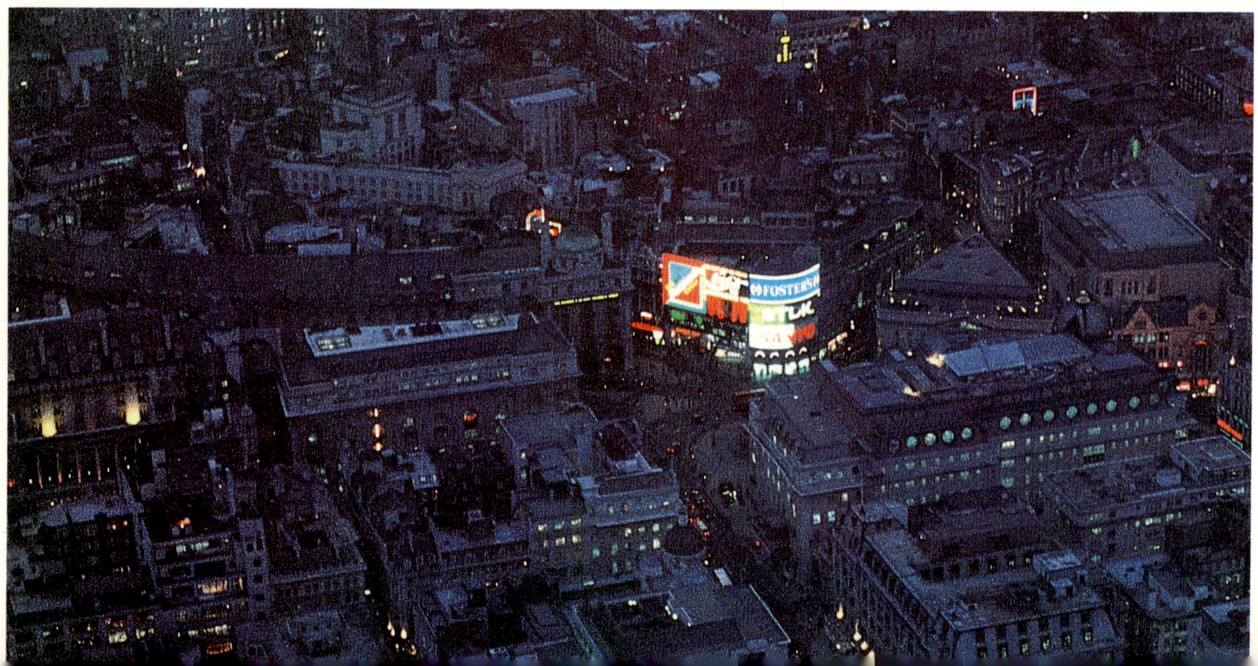

PICCADILLY CIRCUS

The vivid light show continues. Rumour has it that Westminster City Council would like the neon toned down – surely not?

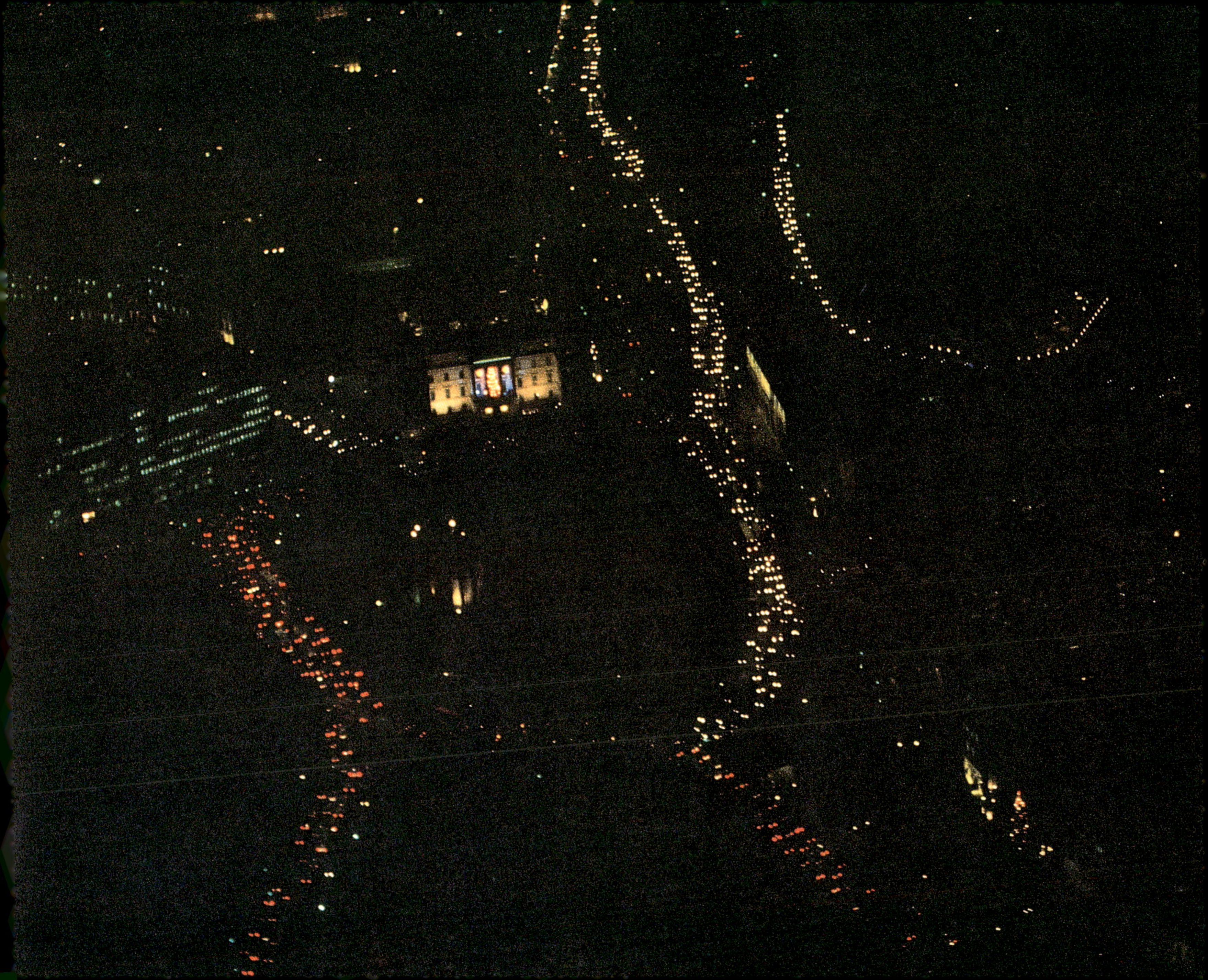

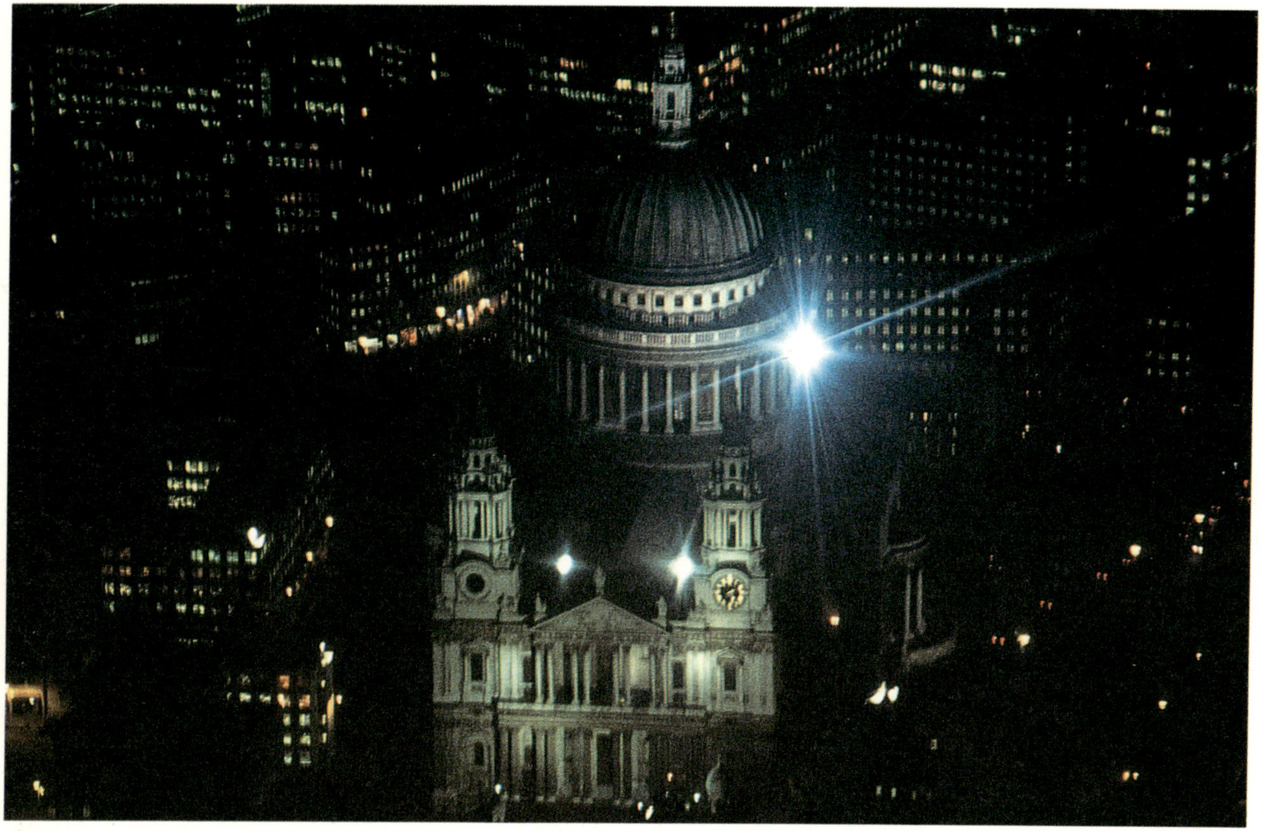

ST PAUL'S AND LLOYDS

God and Mammon dominate the City at night, when the Lloyds building completely outshines its daytime self.

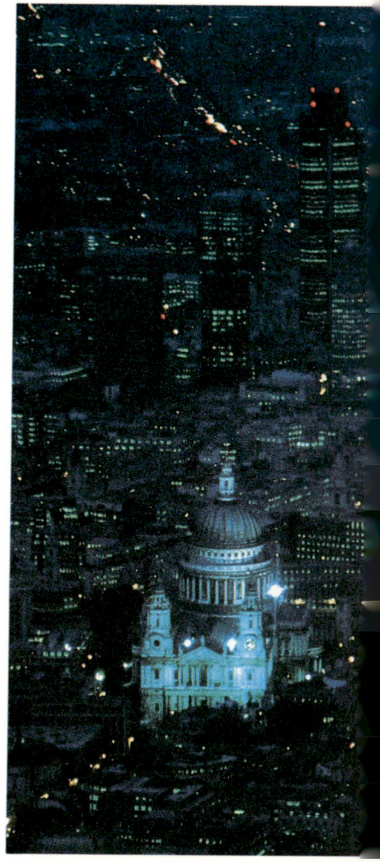

of the first changes to the night skyline was the Lloyds building. It may be a rather odd looking structure in the light of day, but at night it is beautiful, its splash of blue and white light complemented by the brooding bulk and red lights of the NatWest Tower.

Some buildings look completely different at night – even Centre Point looks quite nice. Tolworth Tower on the A3 looks like a miniature Eiffel Tower, and Embankment Place, the monumental extravaganza built on top of Charing Cross Station, always reminds me of an elephant lying on its back with its legs in the air – but maybe you need a rather wild imagination for that one!

By day Canary Wharf dominates the capital's skyline, but at night it's not particularly impressive. In fact, I remember when it was being built that it was sometimes quite disconcerting to find it looming up out of the dark at us. However, all of that changed at New Year 1992, when the top ten floors of unoccupied offices were turned into a vast light show, and for two weeks London was treated to a wonderful laser display every night,

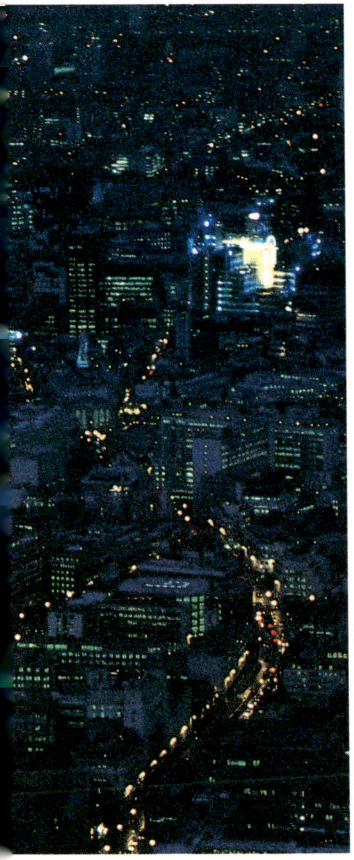

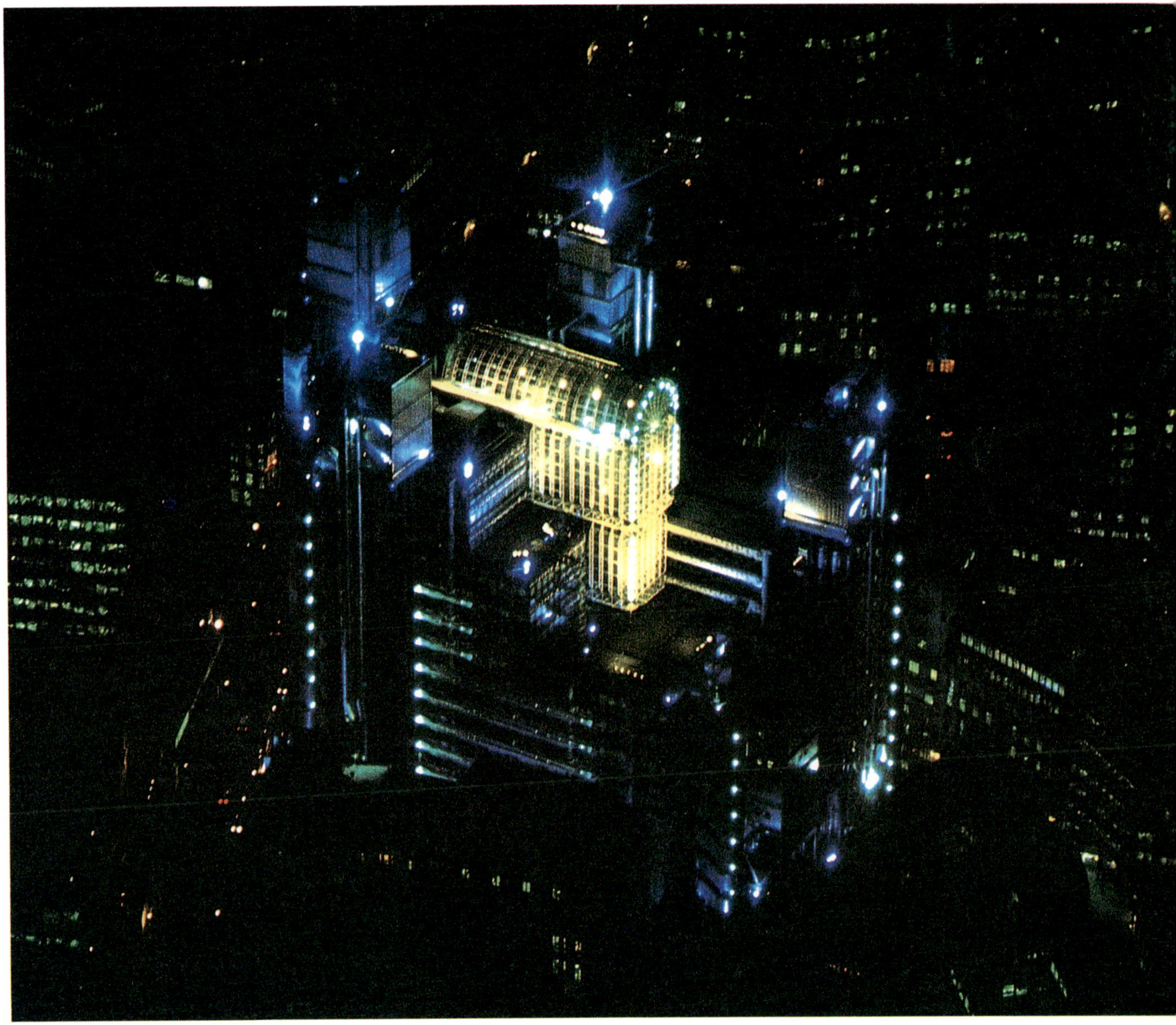

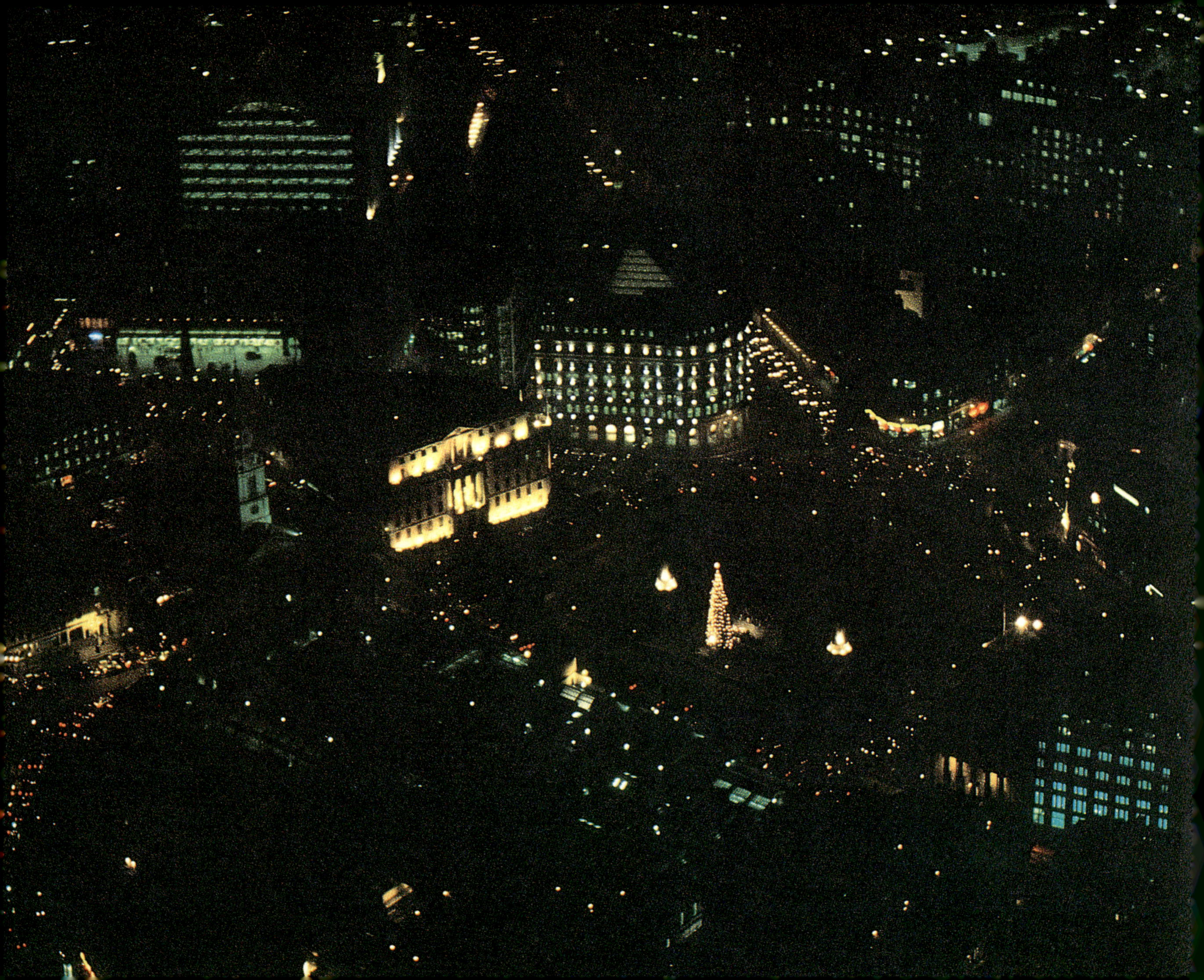

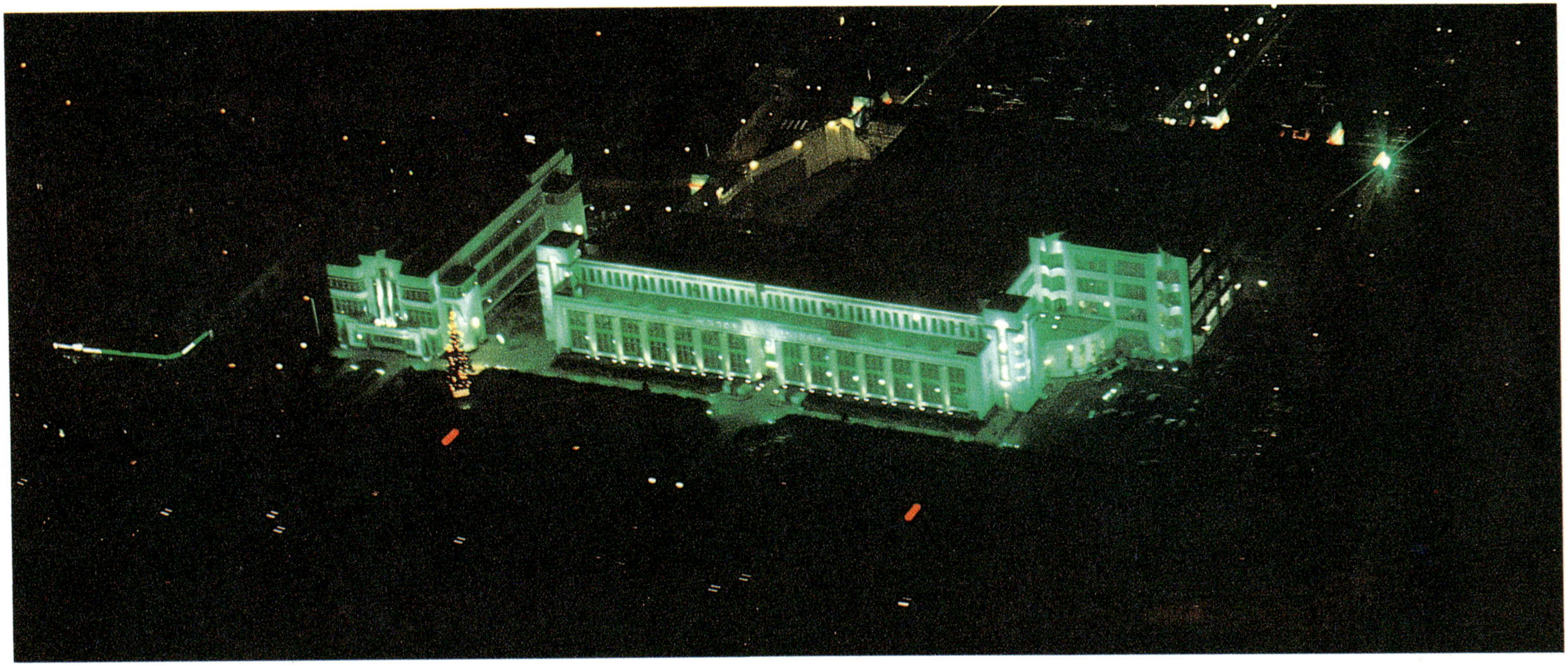

CHRISTMAS GLITTER
The tree at Trafalgar Square has been given to the City of Westminster each year since 1947 by the people of Oslo in thanks for Britain's help to Norway during the Second World War. The 1992 tree was 75 feet high and decorated with 500 white bulbs in the traditional Norwegian style. Christmas also comes to the lovely old Hoover building out to the west.

which was good news for the drivers who were sitting in the inevitable queue at the Blackwall Tunnel – they got a grandstand view.

Of course, Christmas is the time when the lights really come into their own, not just along Oxford Street and Regent Street, but in lots of smaller town centres, which glow in a dazzle of festive frivolity. Most of the large construction cranes get in on the act, too, dangling illuminated reindeers and Santa Clauses hundreds of feet in the air. And I always feel that Christmas is really underway when the giant tree in Trafalgar Square is illuminated.

Most years I have flown on Christmas Eve. Usually, it's very quiet as far as traffic is concerned, and in fact one year the roads were so quiet that I even had time to write a poem and read it out on air.

It can be a bit disheartening sitting up there with not much to do, knowing that everyone is already getting stuck into the Christmas spirit, and we normally take up a little treat of our own. One year it was bacon sandwiches, kept warm by the heater, and another time a thoughtful passenger provided mince pies and a small bottle of champagne. We loosened the cork, intending to pop it on air during one of the broadcasts just before we landed. Unfortunately, it erupted prematurely, spraying us and the plane – we landed smelling like a brewery but without a drop passing our lips. The mince pies were good though, and after all, there aren't many jobs where you can begin your Christmas celebrations a thousand feet above the lights of London.

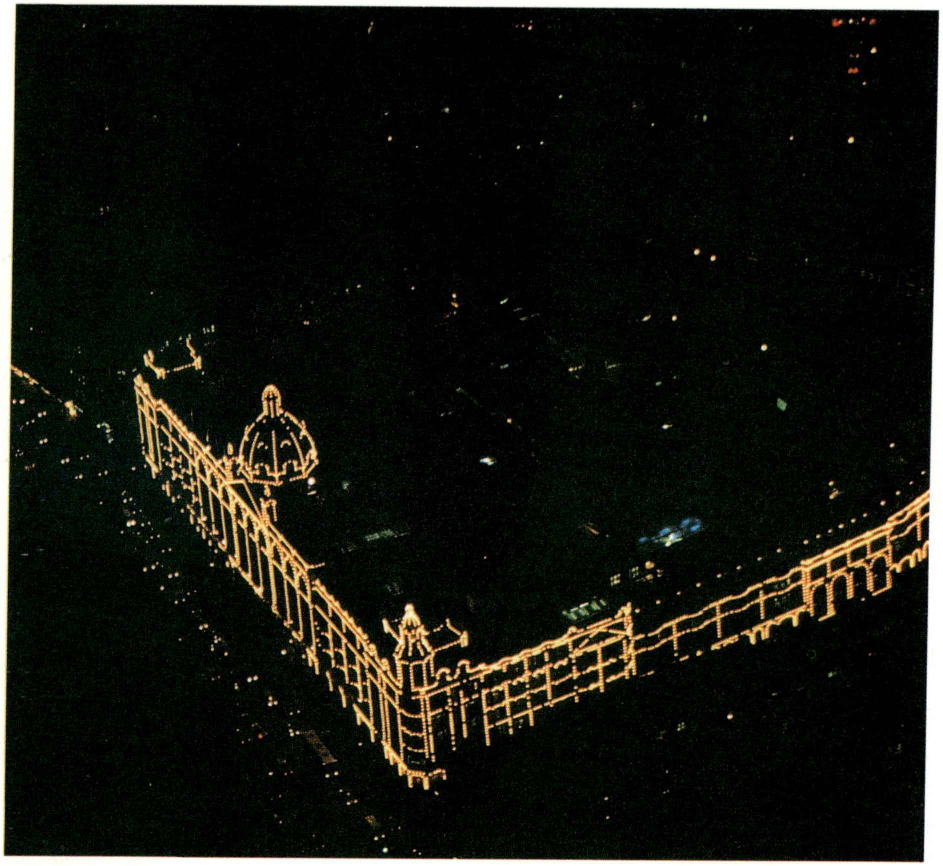

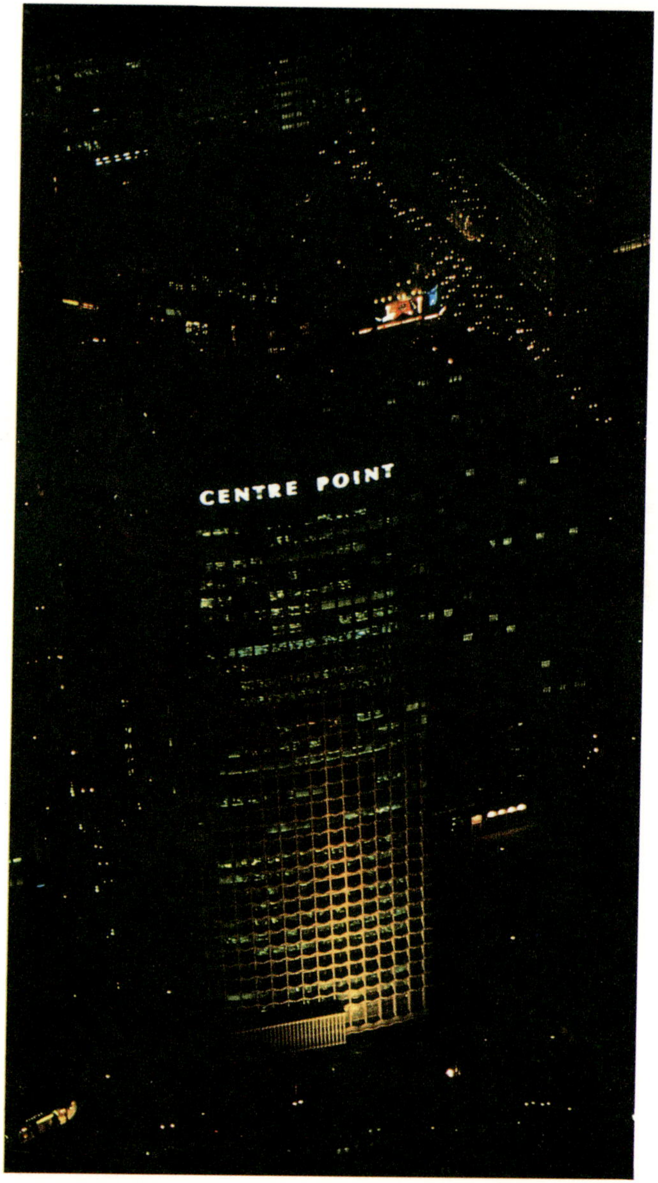

NIGHTSPOTS

Like Lloyds, some of London's bigger buildings take on a new life at night: Harrods, all neatly outlined by 11,500 bulbs – just as well it produces 70 per cent of its own electricity; Centre Point – refused Listed Building status in 1992, despite a plea by English Heritage that it is a 'famous landmark'; Capital Radio's night-time rythm and blues and Charing Cross.

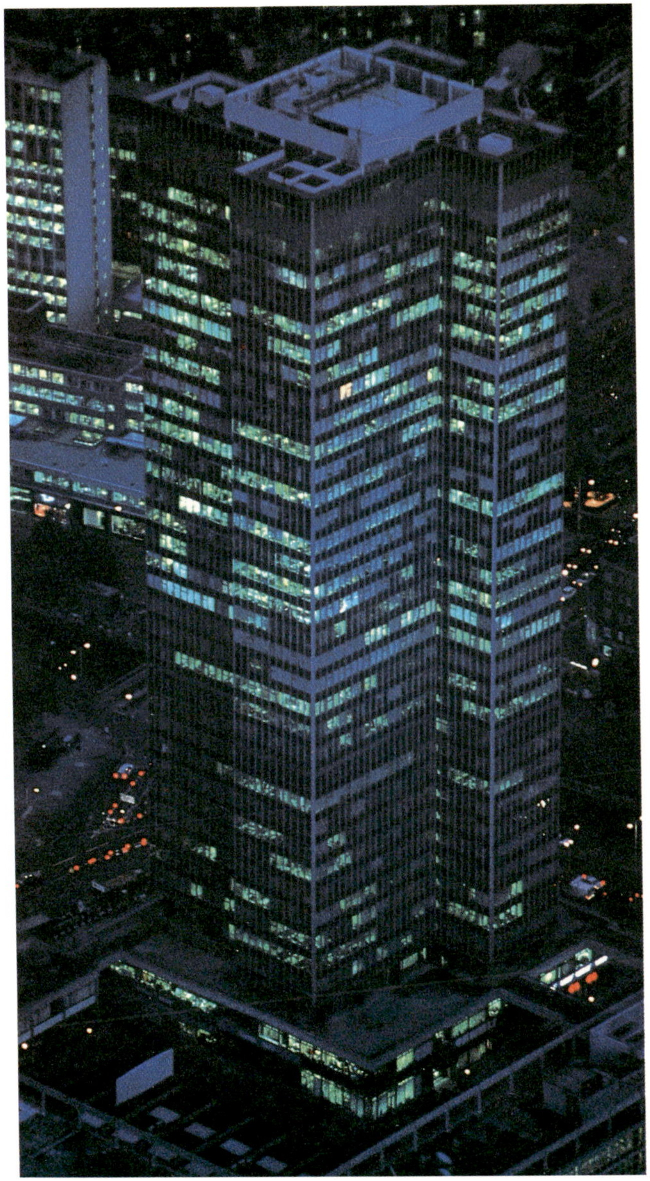

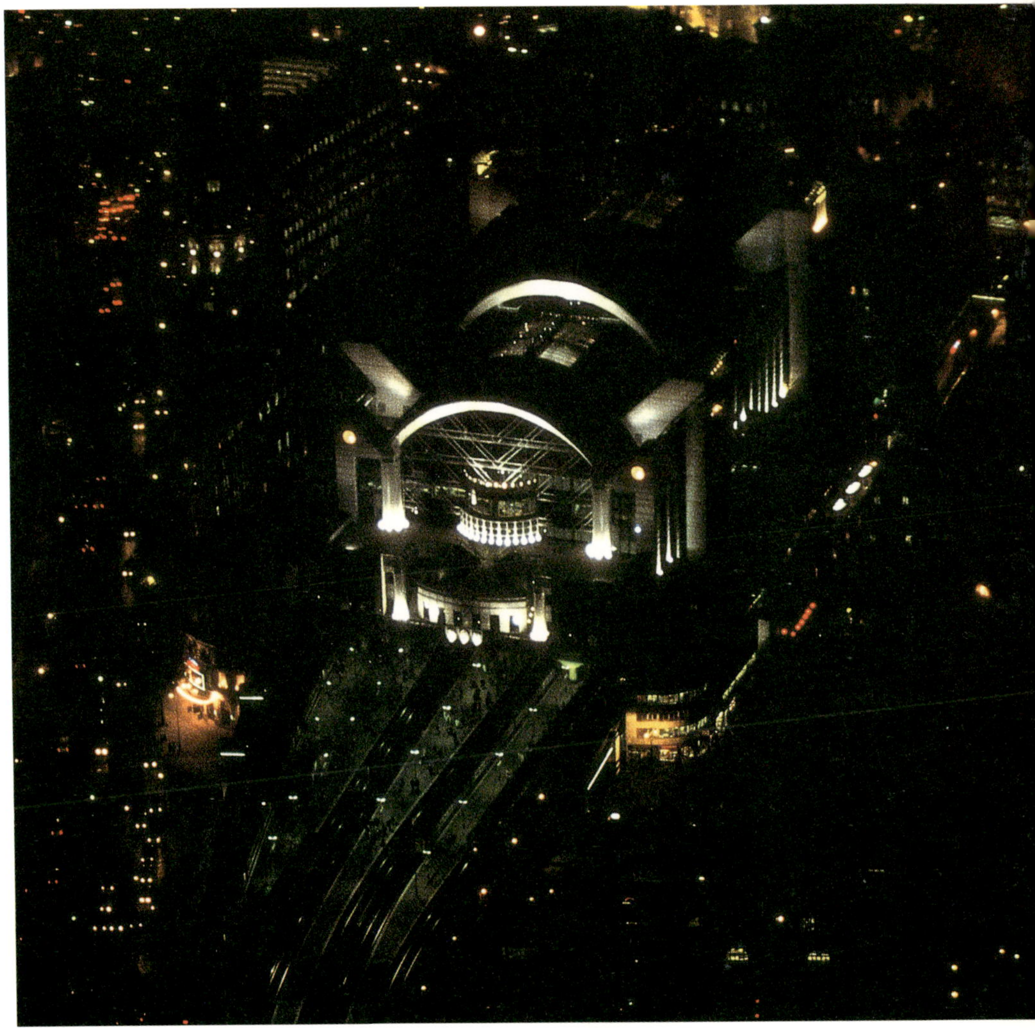

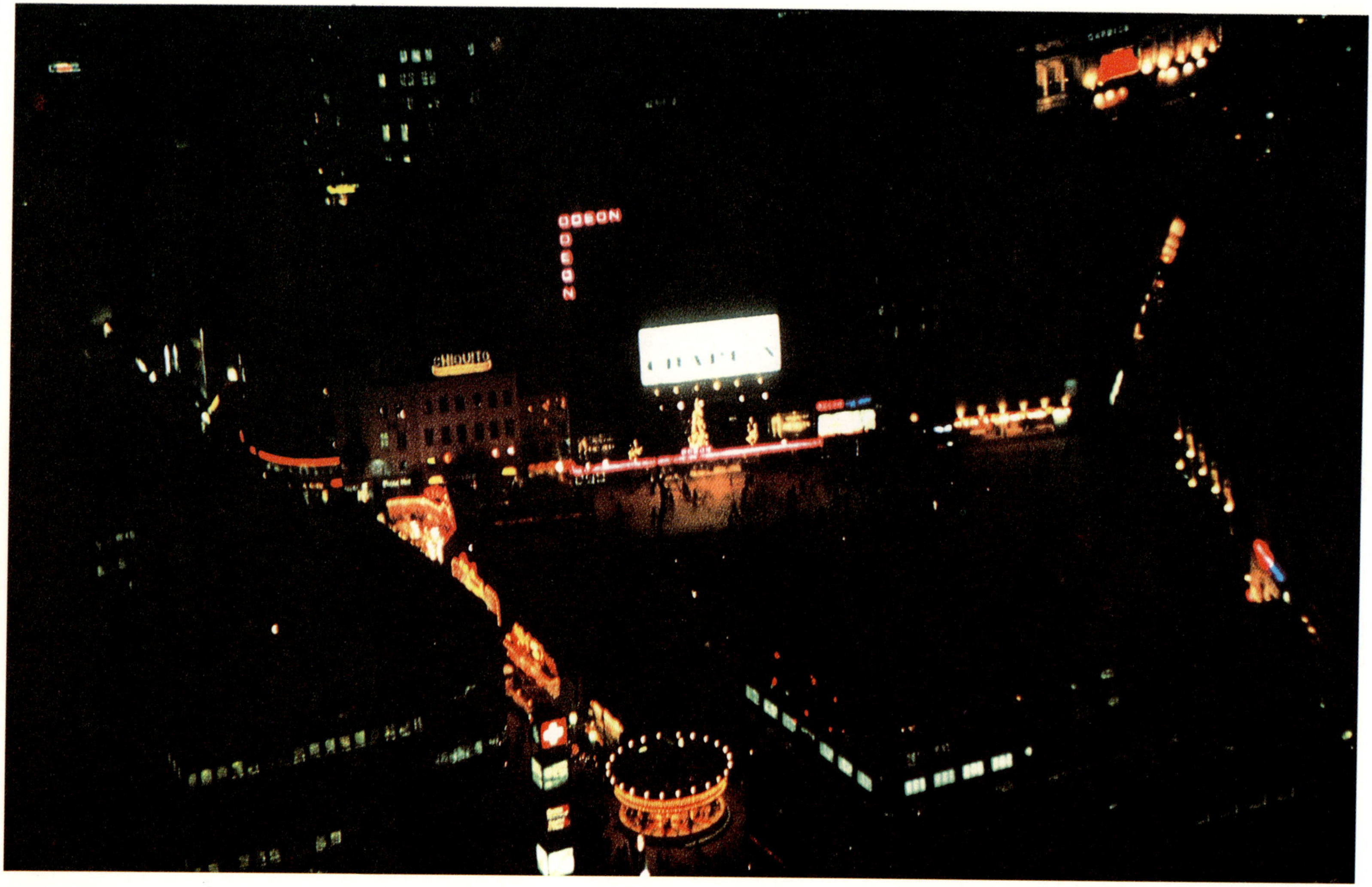

LEICESTER SQUARE

Tonight, Richard Attenborough's *Chaplin* at the Odeon. Tonight and every night, Charlie Chaplin's statue in the Square, a permanent reminder of one of the greatest of British comedians.

COUNTY HALL

The most imposing building on the South Bank is now Japanese owned and due to be converted into a luxury hotel.

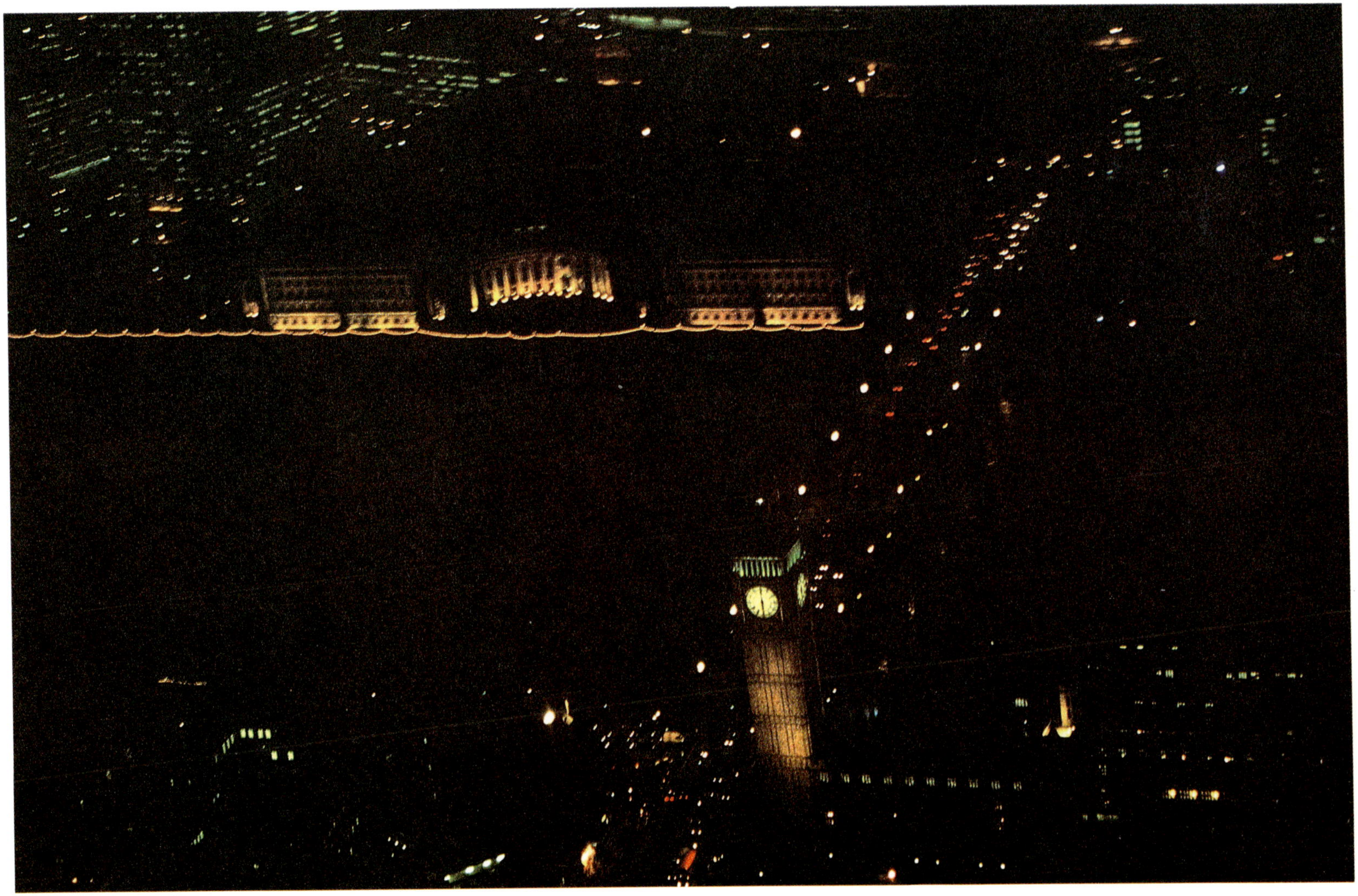

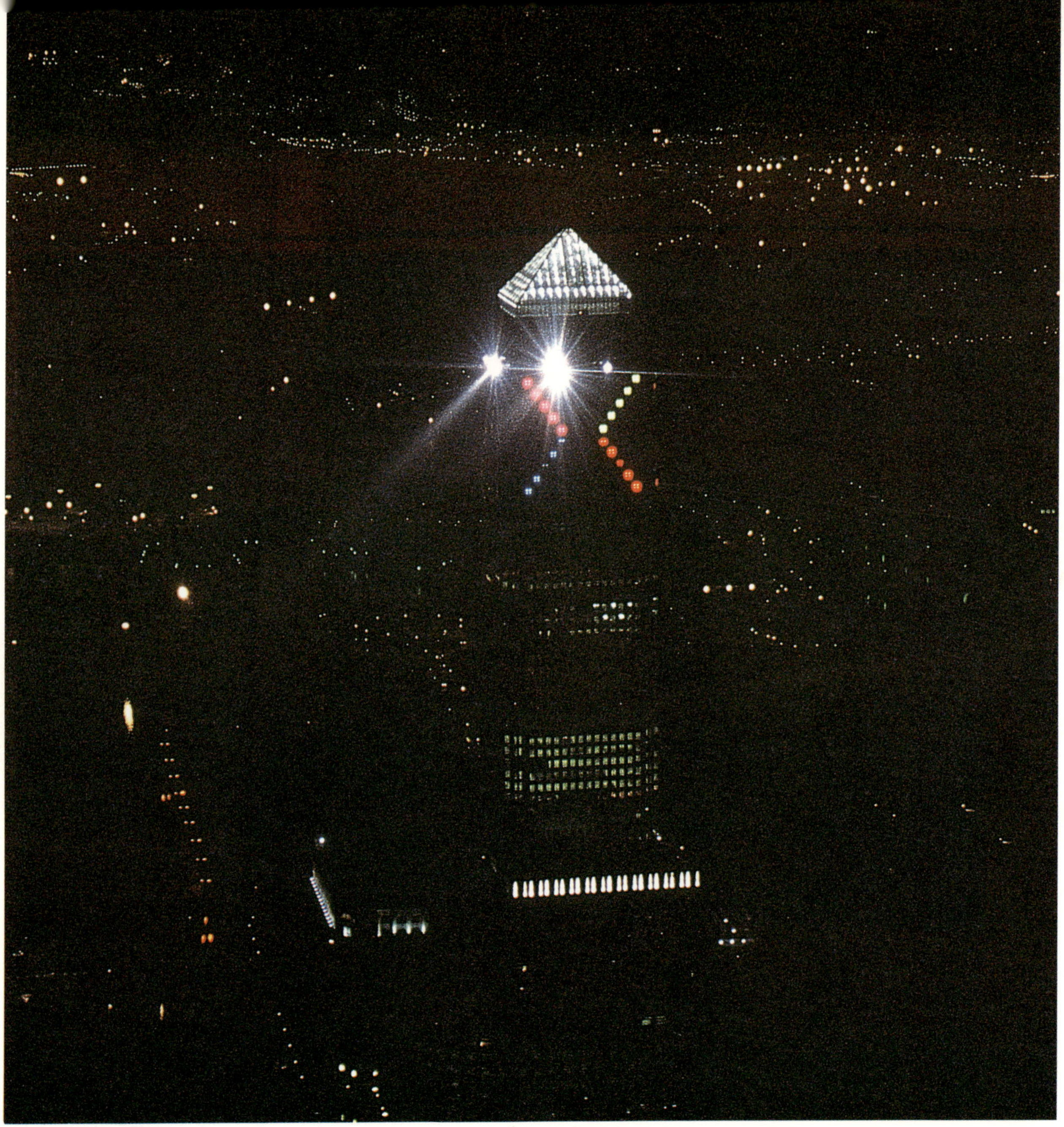

LIGHTSPOTS

Canary Wharf showing off its lasers; south London's idea of the Eiffel Tower at Tolworth; and the bright approach lights on the City Airport runway.

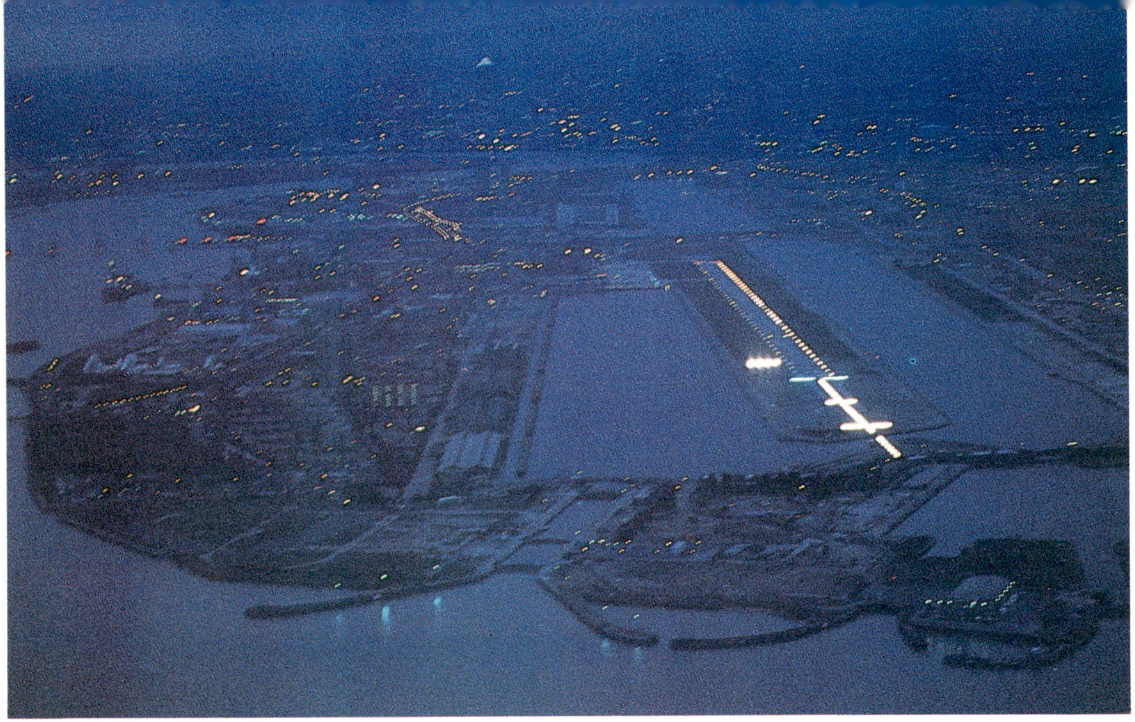

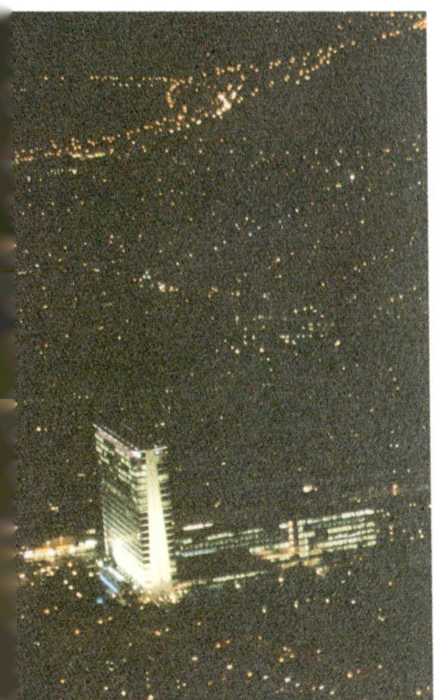

NIGHT DESCENDING

Moon rising and lights lighting as London changes for another Capital night.

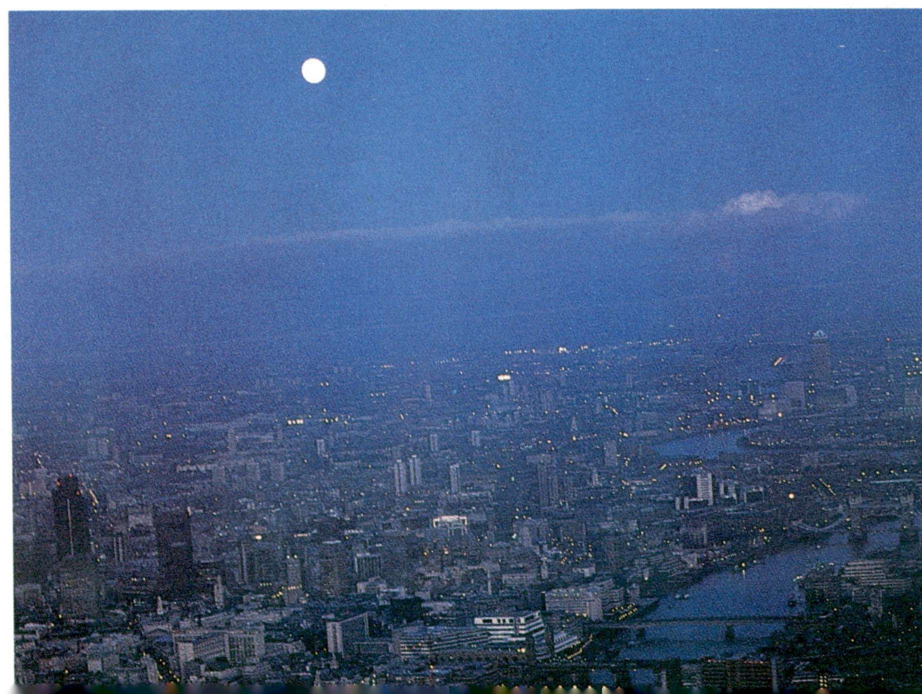

LONDON AT PLAY

London is always busy. Especially in summer there are lots of people gathering together to do something. And the next best thing to being there and participating in whatever it is, is to be up in the Flying Eye, watching it happen from a great height. The exciting thing about seeing large events from a thousand feet in the air is that you can really get to grips with the scale of things.

For instance, although there is nothing that can quite match the hustle and excitement of dancing along behind the floats at the Notting Hill Carnival, when you're down at street level you can't see any further than the nearest person's head, the nearest wall or the nearest float. Only from our viewpoint can you really capture the amazing size of it all and appreciate just how many people are happily milling around Ladbroke Grove and any number of streets radiating from it.

Summer is a great time for visiting – families flock to Thorpe Park, Chessington, Hampton Court and London Zoo. Chelsea puts on its floral finery for the flower show, and posh frocks are donned by the lucky few heading for the Queen's Garden Parties.

Then, of course, there are the great sporting events. A full house basking in the sunshine at Lords or the Oval;

GARDEN PARTY
Three times a year up to 9,000 guests are invited to stroll across the lawns at Buckingham Palace, have tea and greet their royal hosts. It is, naturally, assumed that those invited will attend: you need reply to your invitation only if you can't go.

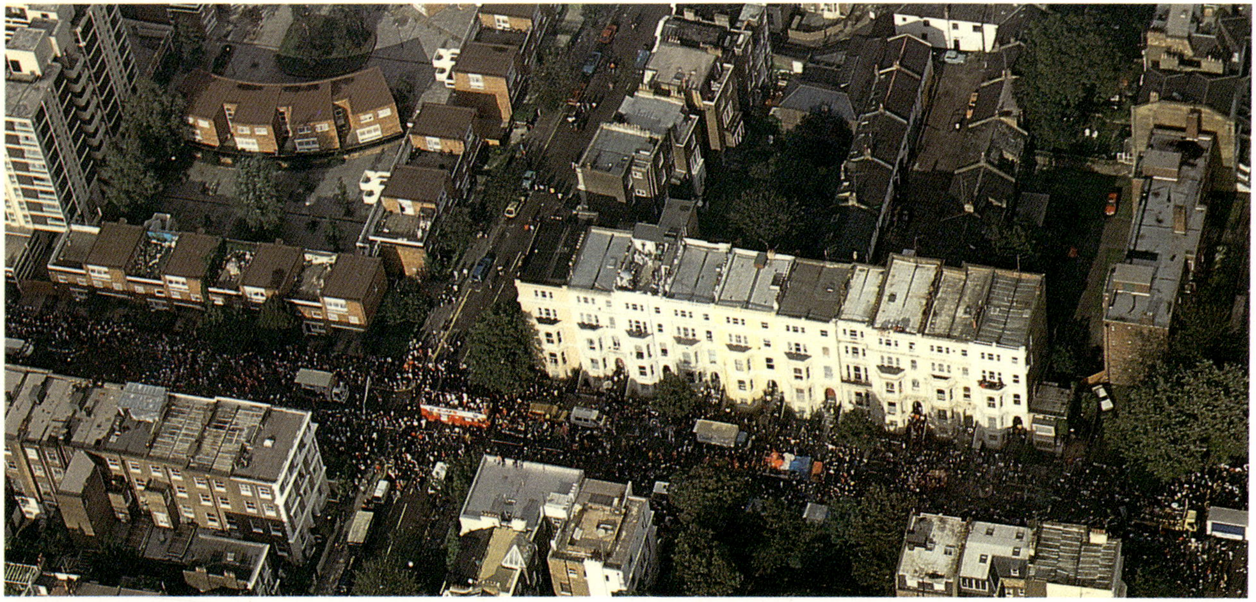

NOTTING HILL CARNIVAL
Now the largest street festival in Europe, the Carnival attracts one and a half million people over the two days of the August Bank Holiday. Not bad for an event that began with just one steel band.

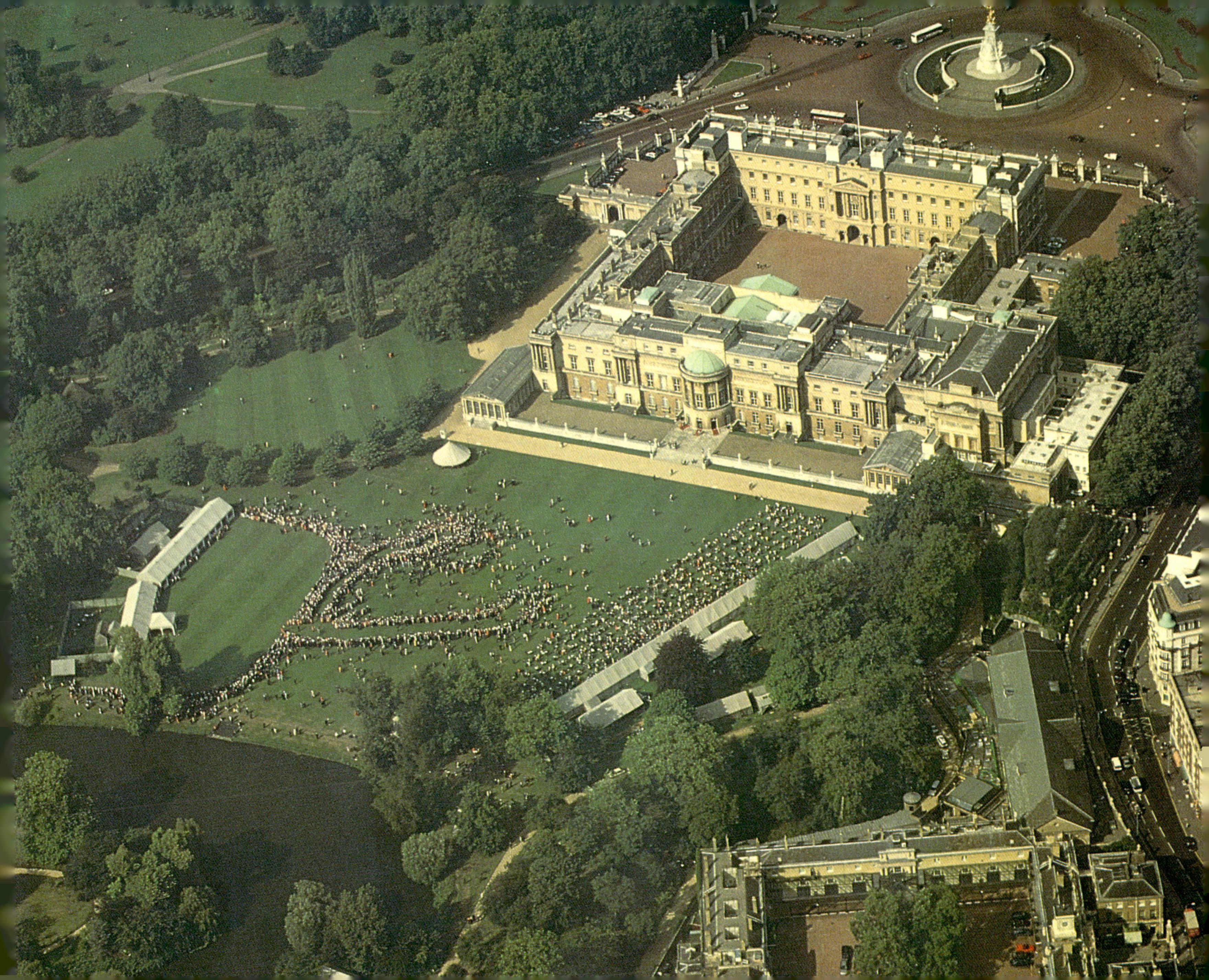

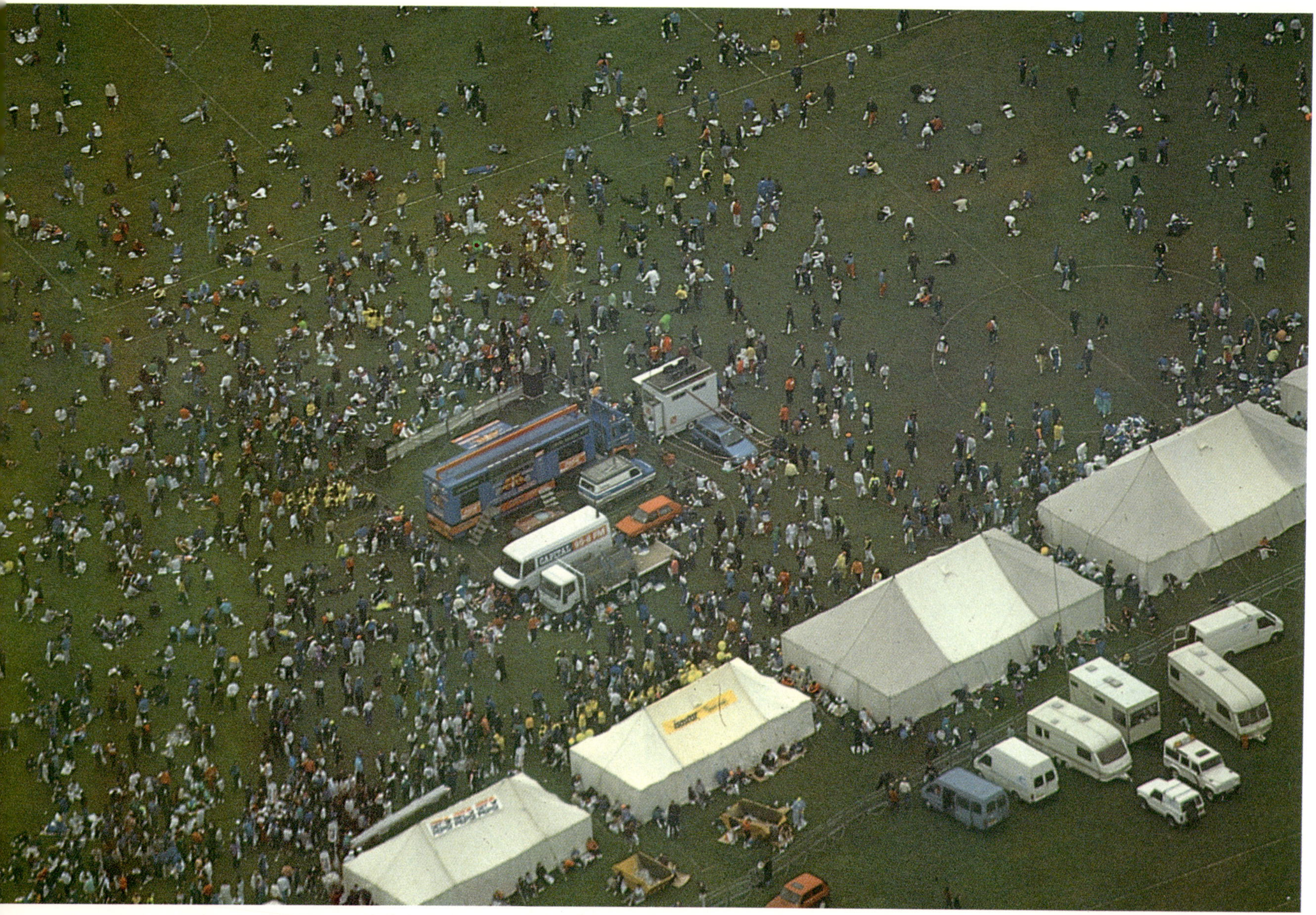

at Wembley we watch the North Circular grind to a halt as fans flood in for a football match or a concert; and we may not have a ticket for Centre Court, but we do have a unique angle on Wimbledon. It's very frustrating staying just far enough away to avoid disrupting the tennis, while just below Agassi, or perhaps Bates, is battling away. To get into the spirit of things, we sometimes take up our very own punnet of strawberries, and we have one great advantage – at least if it rains we don't need an umbrella.

The events season kicks off with what is perhaps the greatest spectacle of them all, the London Marathon. We can't see the agonies and the ecstasies of individual competitors, but the extraordinary view of 35,000 runners setting off across Blackheath, pounding through London's streets and finally staggering across Westminster Bridge to the finish line – now that's a sight not to be forgotten, even if it does seem traditionally to take place under gloomy grey skies.

These are the occasions that punctuate London life, the red-ringed days on the city's calendar, and as often as not, somewhere above it all will be the buzzing blue and red shape of the Flying Eye, spotting queues, reporting the traffic news and getting a grandstand view at the same time.

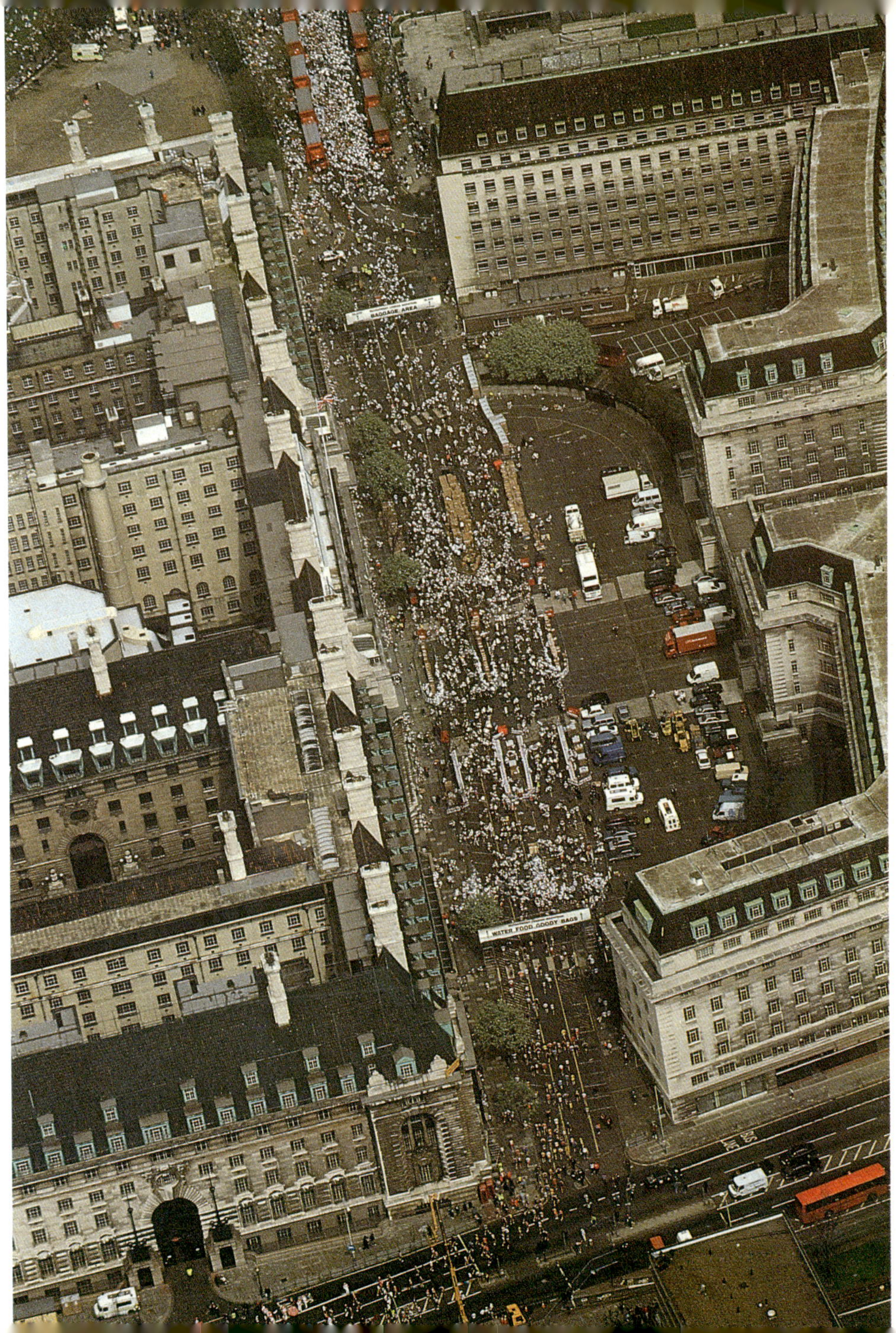

THE MARATHON

The 1993 Nutrasweet London Marathon: 35,000 runners, 150 portable toilets, 550 stretchers and the Capital FM mobile roadshow.

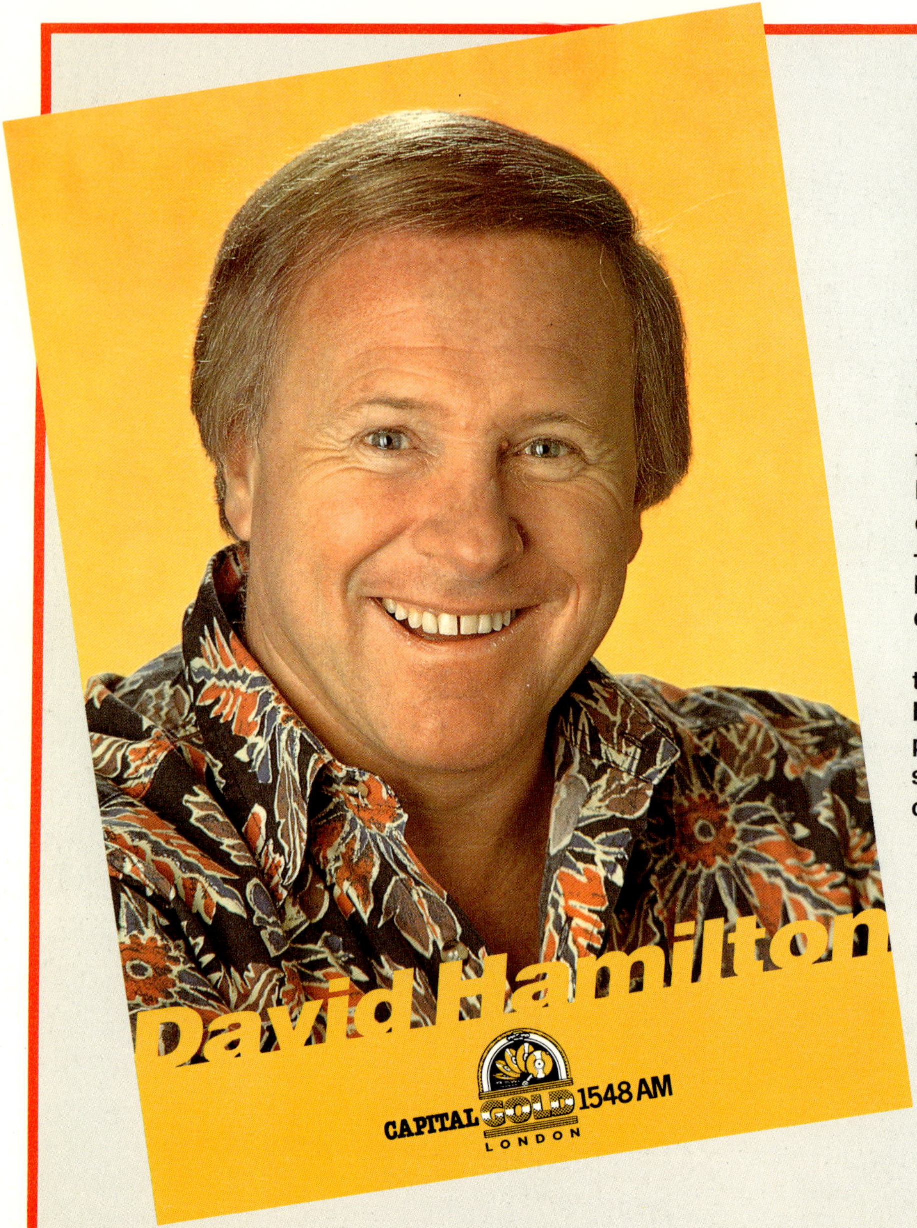

‘WHAT COULD BE more English than Wimbledon tennis fortnight? Every year I get hooked on the Championships, not to mention the strawberries and cream! But there's nothing more frustrating than having a seat on Centre Court, with the rain trickling down your neck, and watching the grass grow – and I've done that a few times, I can tell you.

Wimbledon has always played a big part in my life. When I was young I lived in a flat only about half a mile from the courts. Of course, every year it's very disruptive for the locals, who find that just popping down to the local shop for a newspaper can take forever because of all the extra traffic. Now many of them have hit back by leaving the country for two weeks and renting out their houses to the top tennis stars for thousands of pounds – not a bad little earner! Failing that, they can make a quick buck or three by charging motorists who want to park in their driveways. It's almost as good as having shares in NCP.

I play down at the David Lloyd Club in Raynes Park, and now that we have an increasing number of indoor tennis centres I honestly believe that we shall see more top British players, possibly even champions, in the future. I've loved tennis ever since I was a kid – I even got close to playing at Wimbledon once – at Parsons Green to be exact!’

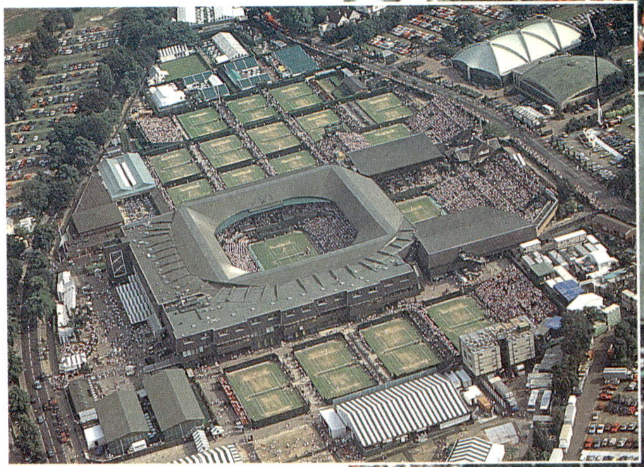

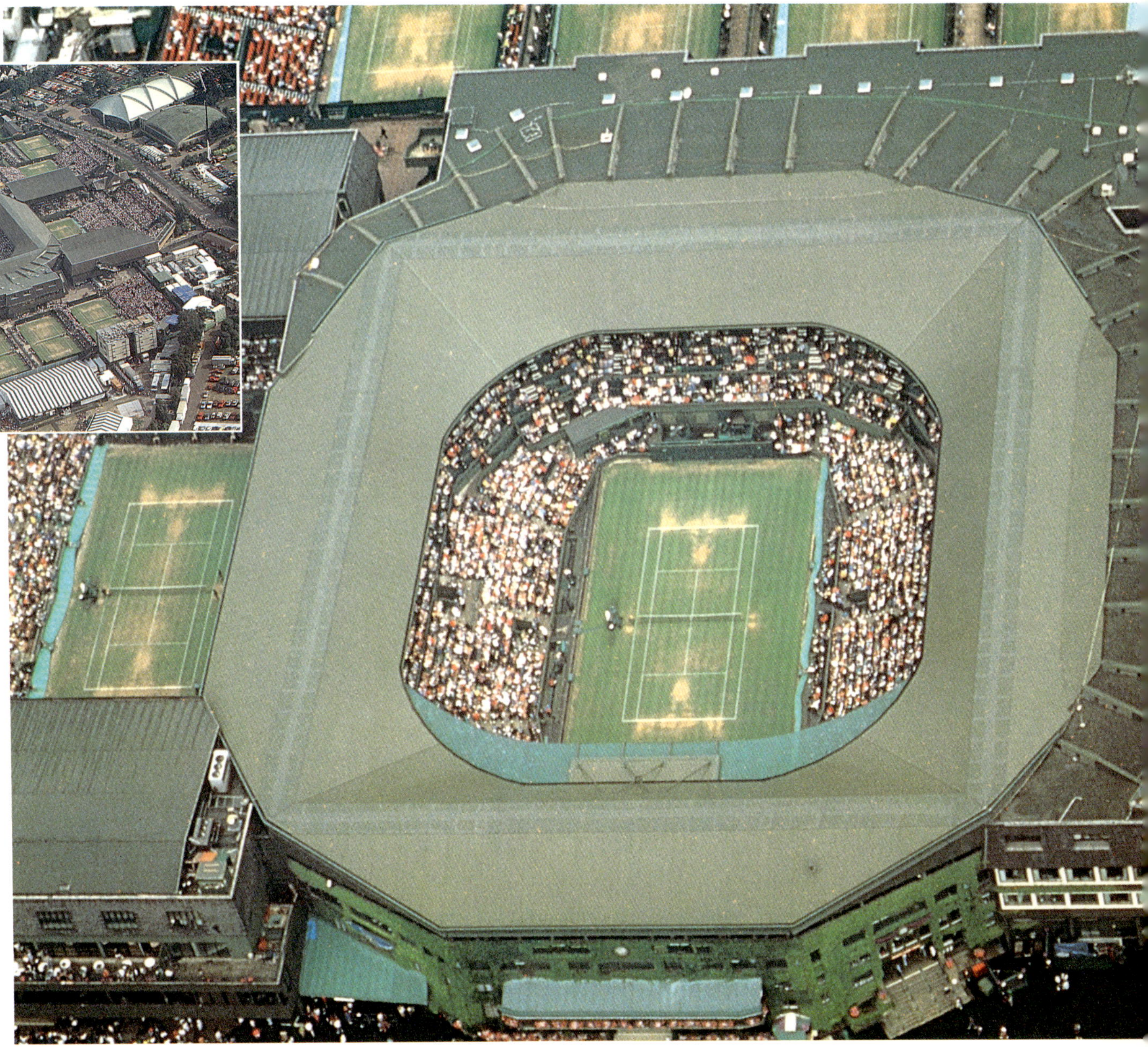

WIMBLEDON

The All England Lawn Tennis and Croquet Club in the last week of June/first week of July: 650 matches, 330 officials, 132 ball boys and girls, 2,500 balls, 370,000 spectators, tons of strawberries – and still it rains .

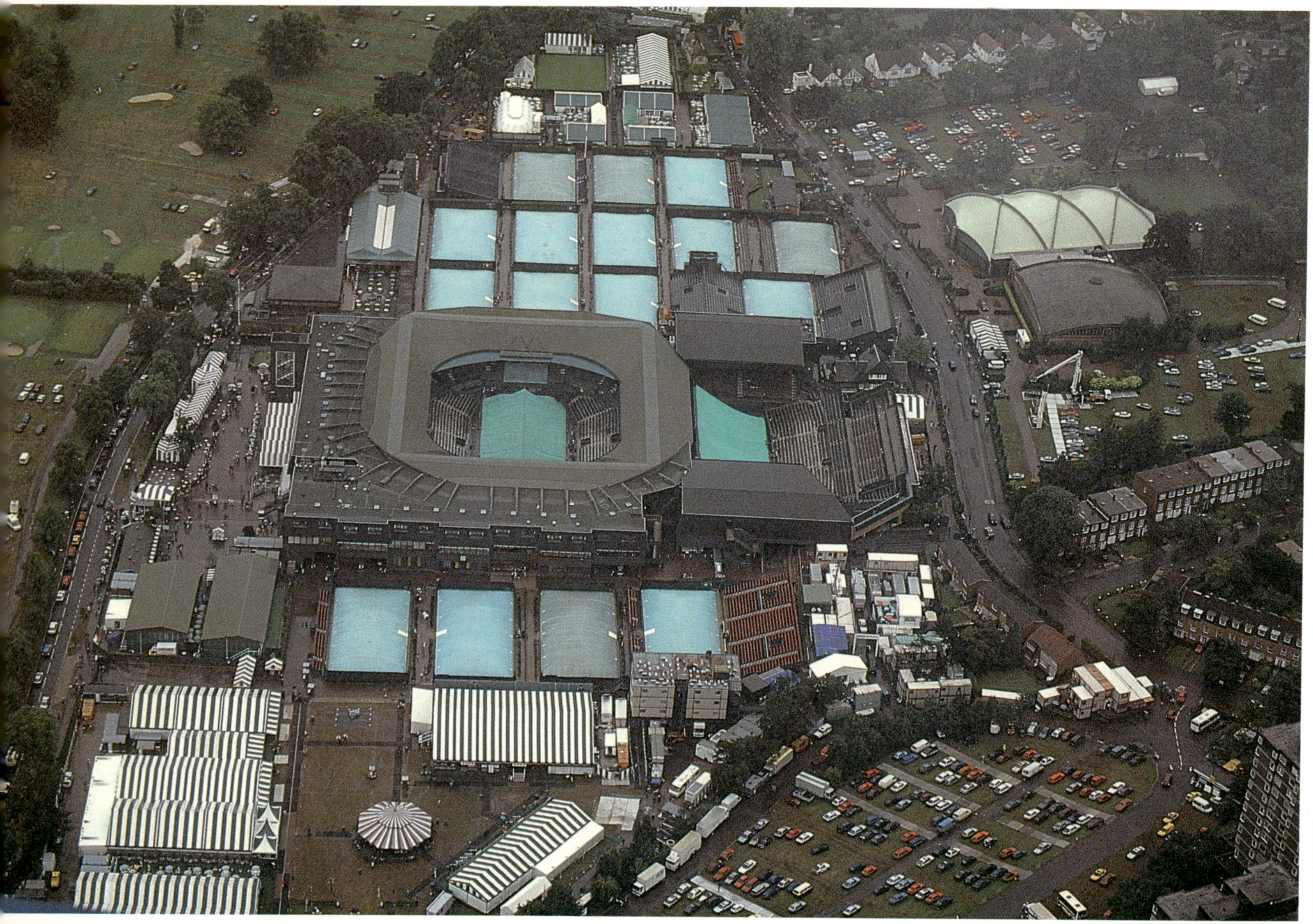

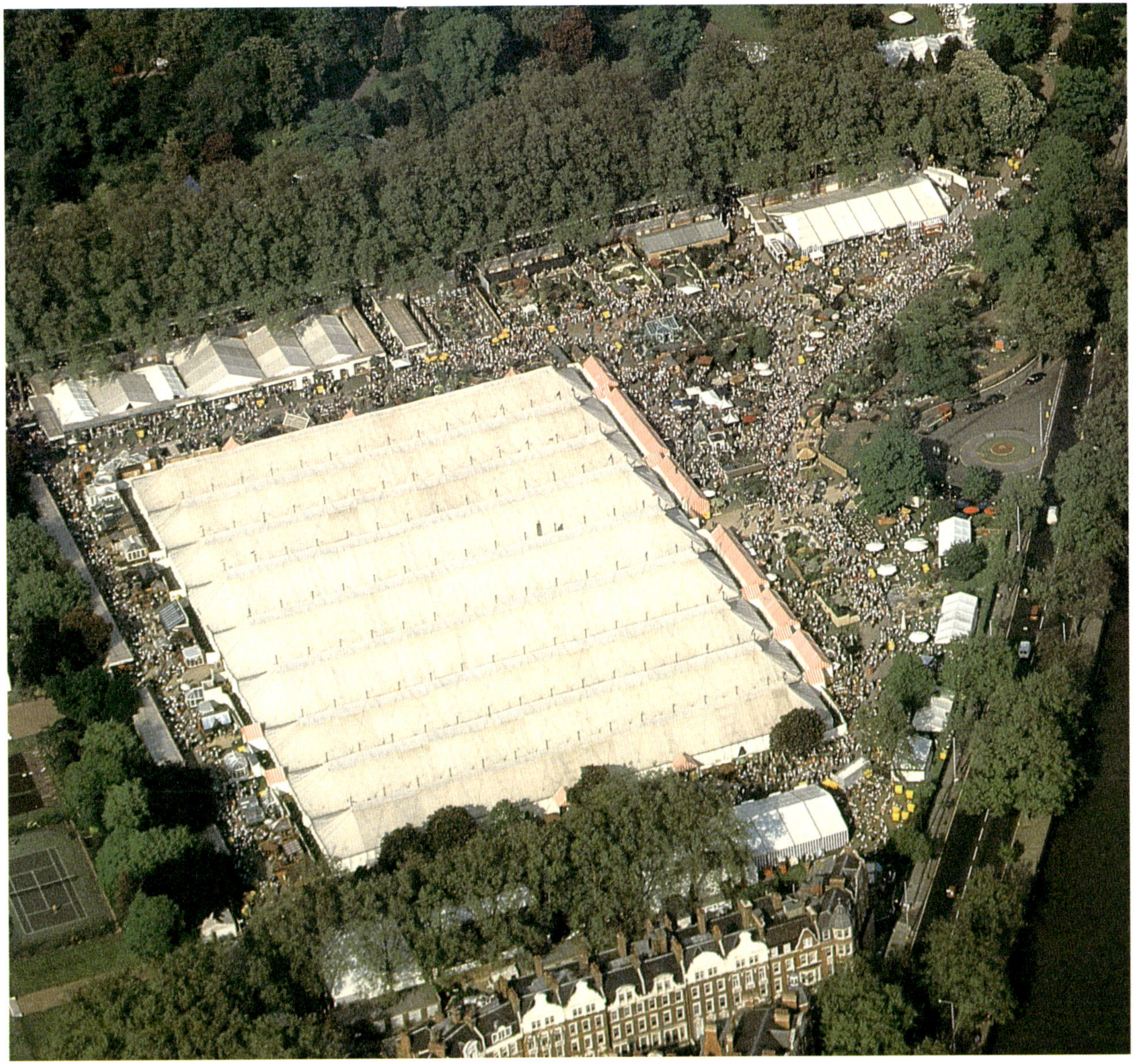

CHELSEA FLOWER SHOW

That vast three-and-a-half-acre marquee, the biggest in the world, looks even bigger from the Flying Eye.

FUN DAYS OUT
Thorpe Park and Chessington World of Adventure attract many Londoners out for an easy day's fun.

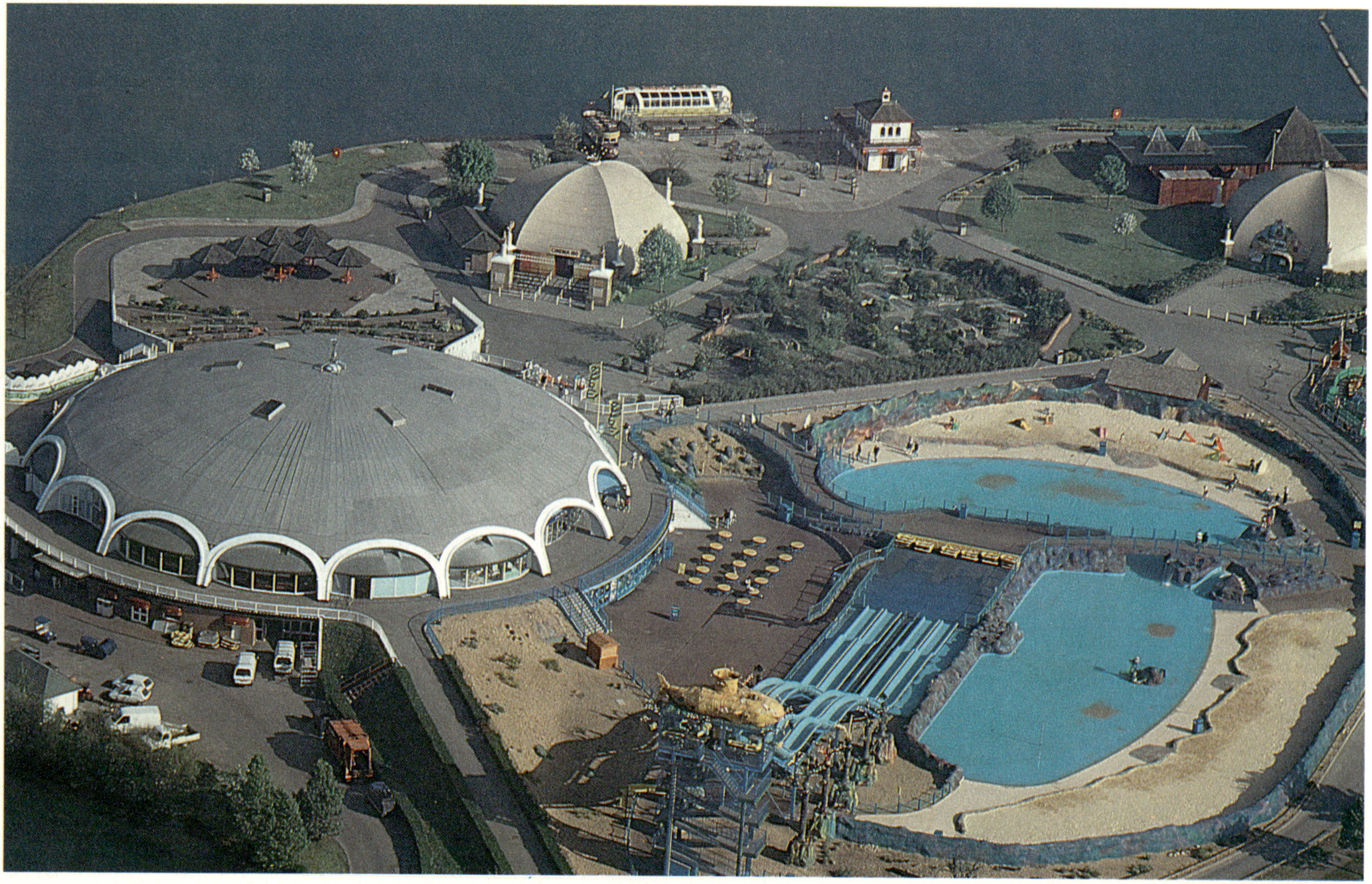

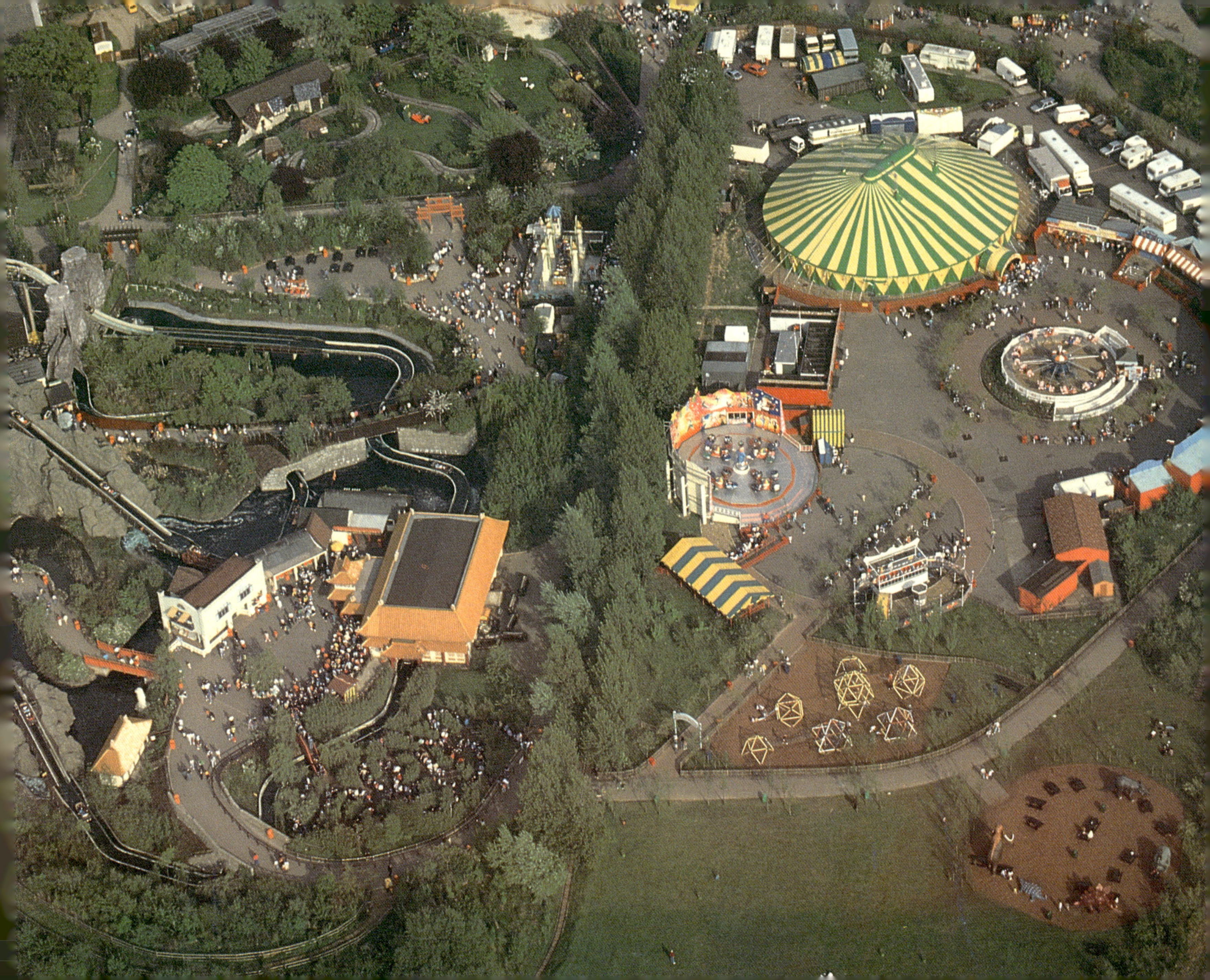

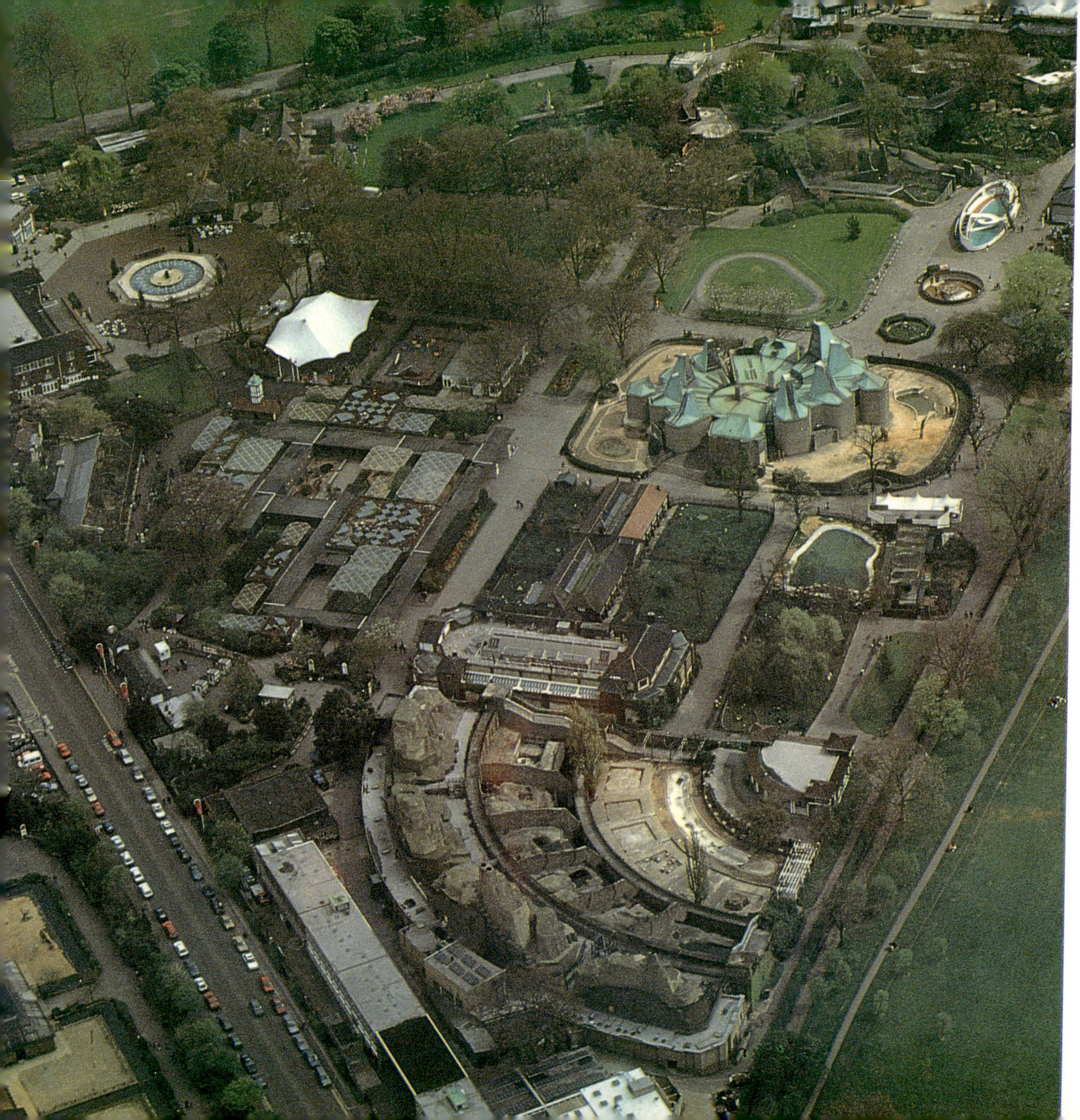

LONDON ZOO

Opened in 1877 and perilously near to closing in 1992. Some of the more streetwise inmates have a sharp eye for their visitors' possessions; in one year alone the elephants seized fourteen coats, twelve handbags, ten cameras, eight gloves and six return tickets to Leicester.

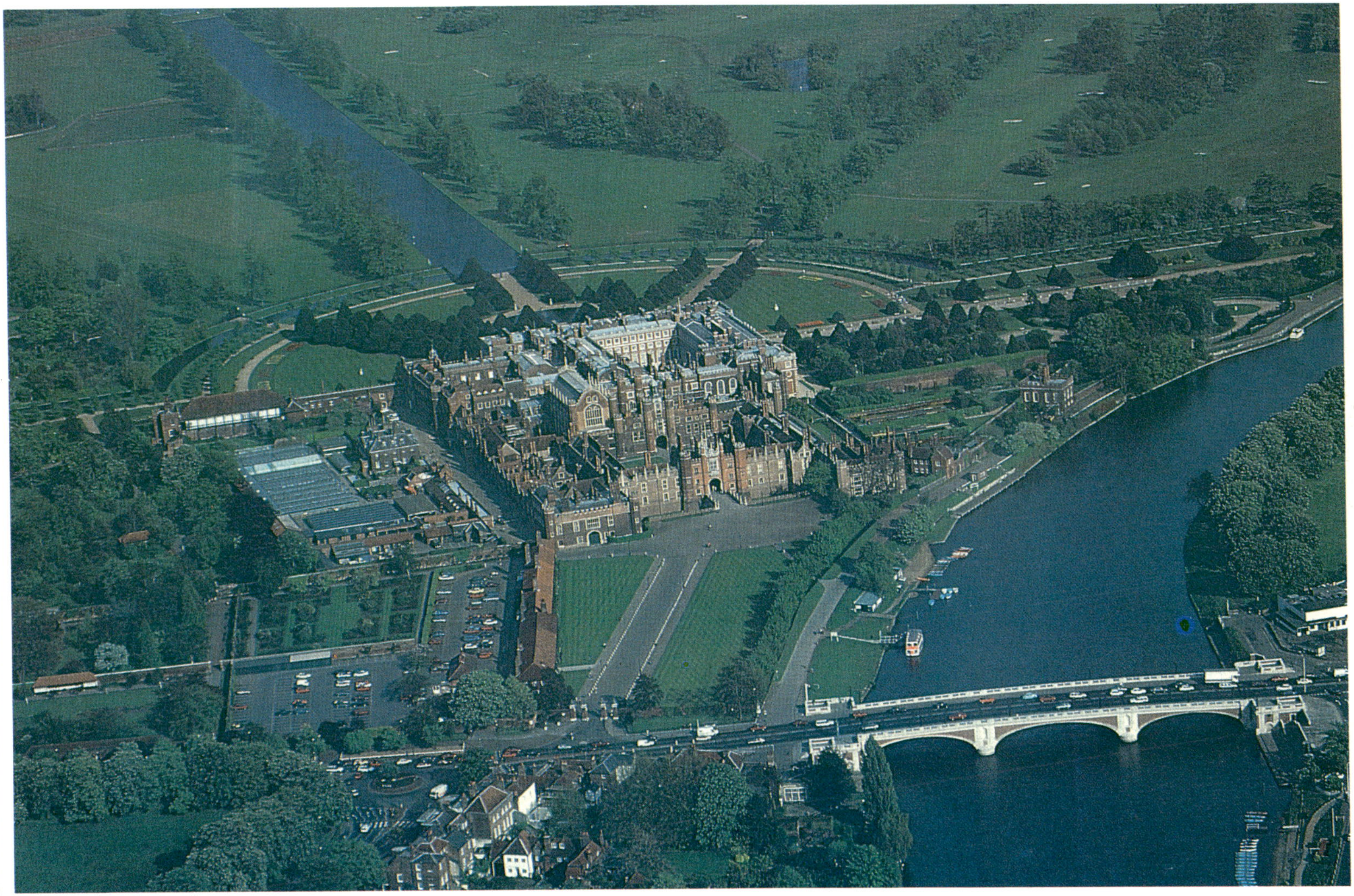

HAMPTON COURT
Cardinal Wolsey's little place by the river, a favourite tourist spot and now the setting for a big new flower show every July.

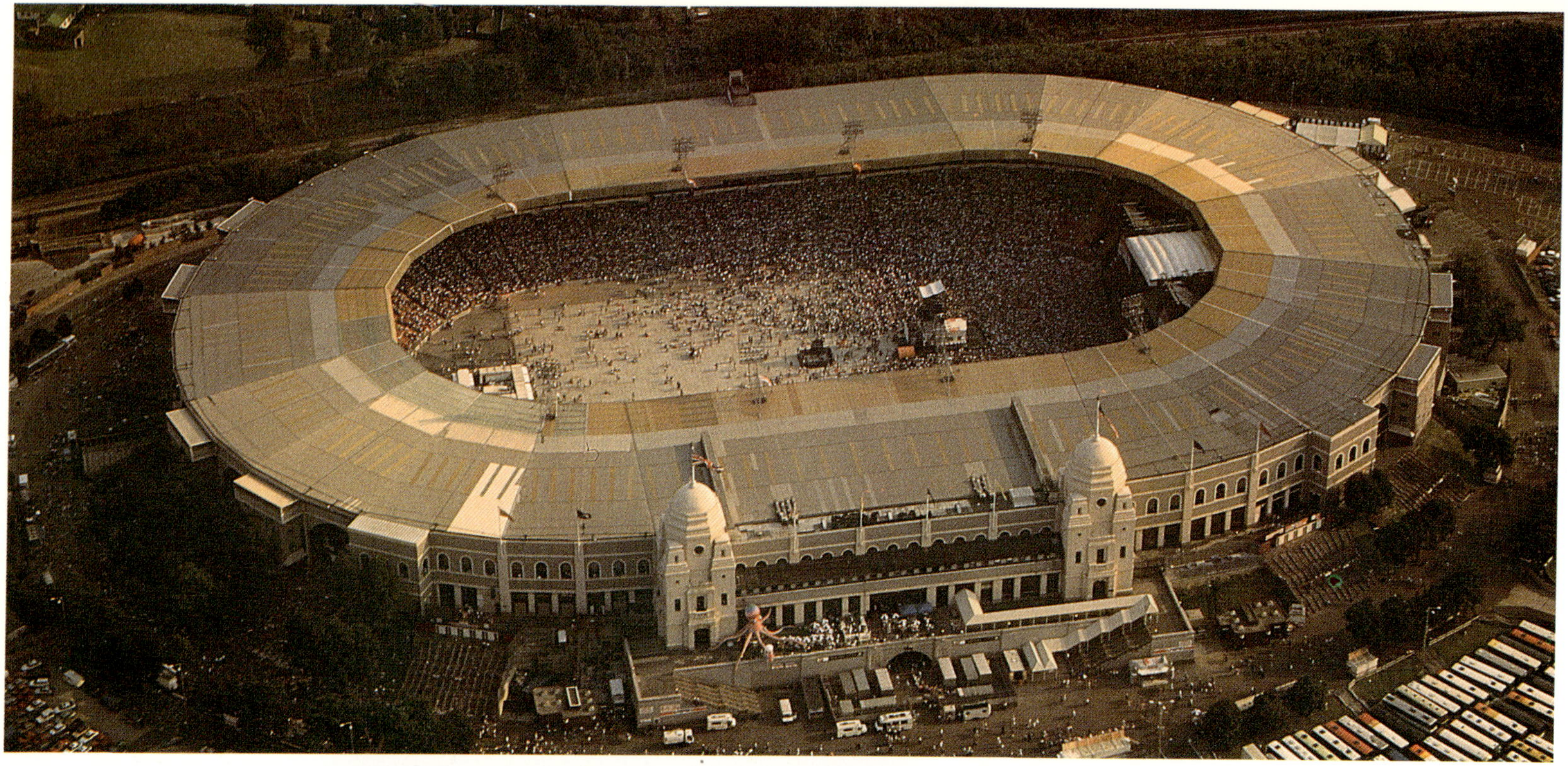

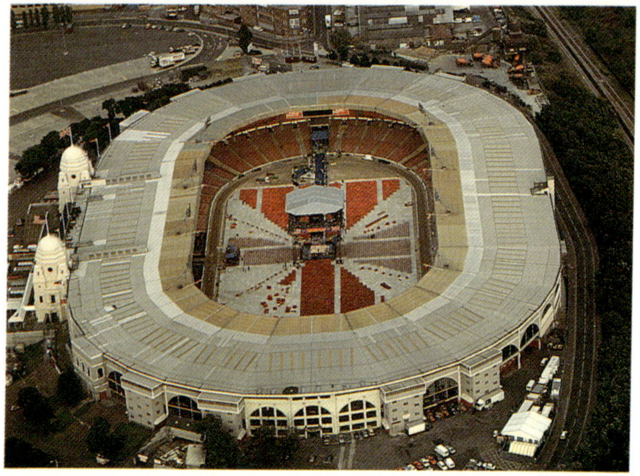

WEMBLEY STADIUM

The early build up to a Michael Jackson concert co-promoted by Capital FM. Michael's seven *BAD* shows at Wembley were seen by over 500,000 fans, an all-time record. Preparations for Summer Slam '92, the WWF wrestling extravaganza, featuring such stars as The Ultimate Warrior and The British Bulldogs, shows how well Wembley caters for all tastes!

'THE MICHAEL JACKSON concerts at Wembley were co-promoted by Capital FM, and Pat Sharp and I actually introduced them on stage. There was the most incredible atmosphere: it was the height of summer, and with 75,000 people packed in there you could actually feel the heat coming at you in waves. I swear it was about 20 degrees hotter than anywhere else in London.

It was an amazing feeling going out on to the stage and talking to the crowd – you had such power it was quite frightening. You said, 'Come on, let's do the Mexican wave,' and everyone stood up and did it. And you said, 'Let's sway,' and they all started swaying. You could have said anything and they would have done it because they were at such fever pitch before Michael Jackson came on.

It was one of the most spectacular entrances to a concert I've ever seen. I took my daughter Natalie, who was eight, and we sat there, and all of a sudden there was this enormous bang and he flew out from the stage on a kind of huge spring. The whole place gasped – you could hear this kind of indrawn breath coming from all over the stadium. That was just the start, and personally I think it was the best live show I've ever seen. It was absolute dynamite. I think it's something that anyone who was there will always remember – I'll certainly never forget it.'

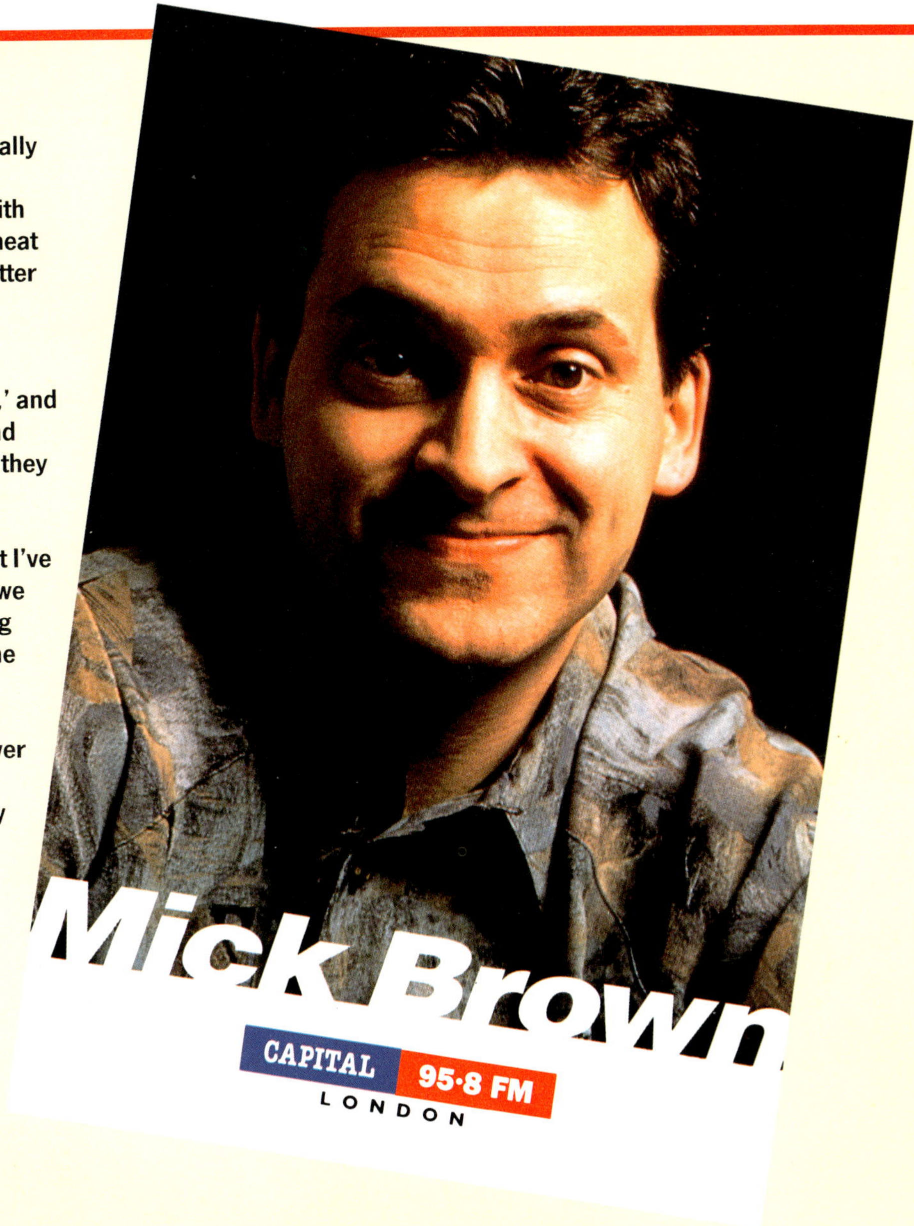

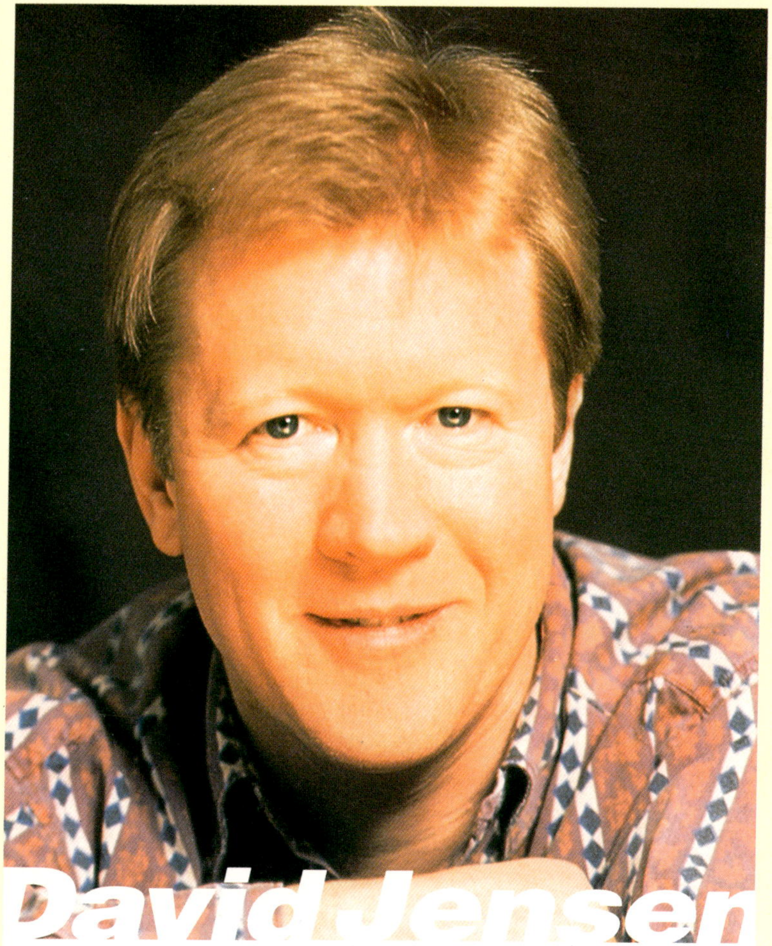

CAPITAL 95·8 FM
LONDON

'I REMEMBER THIS match vividly. It was the European Cup Final between Sampdoria of Italy and Barcelona of Spain, and there was a wonderfully colourful, carnival-like atmosphere. I was in a really enviable position: not only did I have a great seat for the game, but also I was able to do my Drivetime show from there, live between four and seven o'clock. And, of course, during the programme, Hazel took this photograph.

The crowd came into the stadium quite early, and in the first half hour of the programme (which was all played over the loudspeakers in the stadium) we played current hits from the Spanish and Italian charts – so we had the Italian fans singing along with 'Nessun dorma' and all the Spanish supporters joining in with 'La Bamba'. At one stage, Hazel did one of her traffic broadcasts while the Flying Eye was circling overhead, so I got all the fans to look up and wave at her in the plane.

Everyone was in a really good mood. There was lots of singing and banner waving, and it was an atmosphere that I have never encountered before in all my years of going to British football (I'm a Vice-President of Crystal Palace Football Club).

Once my programme was over, my son Alexander (who was twelve at the time) and I joined the Italian section and became honorary Sampdorians for a couple of hours. The weather was glorious, really hot, and it was like being on holiday. It was intoxicating because of the friendliness of the crowd – there were no hassles and no yobs. People were there, whole families of them, to have a good time, and even in defeat the Sampdoria fans were still singing. It wasn't a brilliant game, but the atmosphere was exceptional, and I found myself boring people about it for months afterwards!'

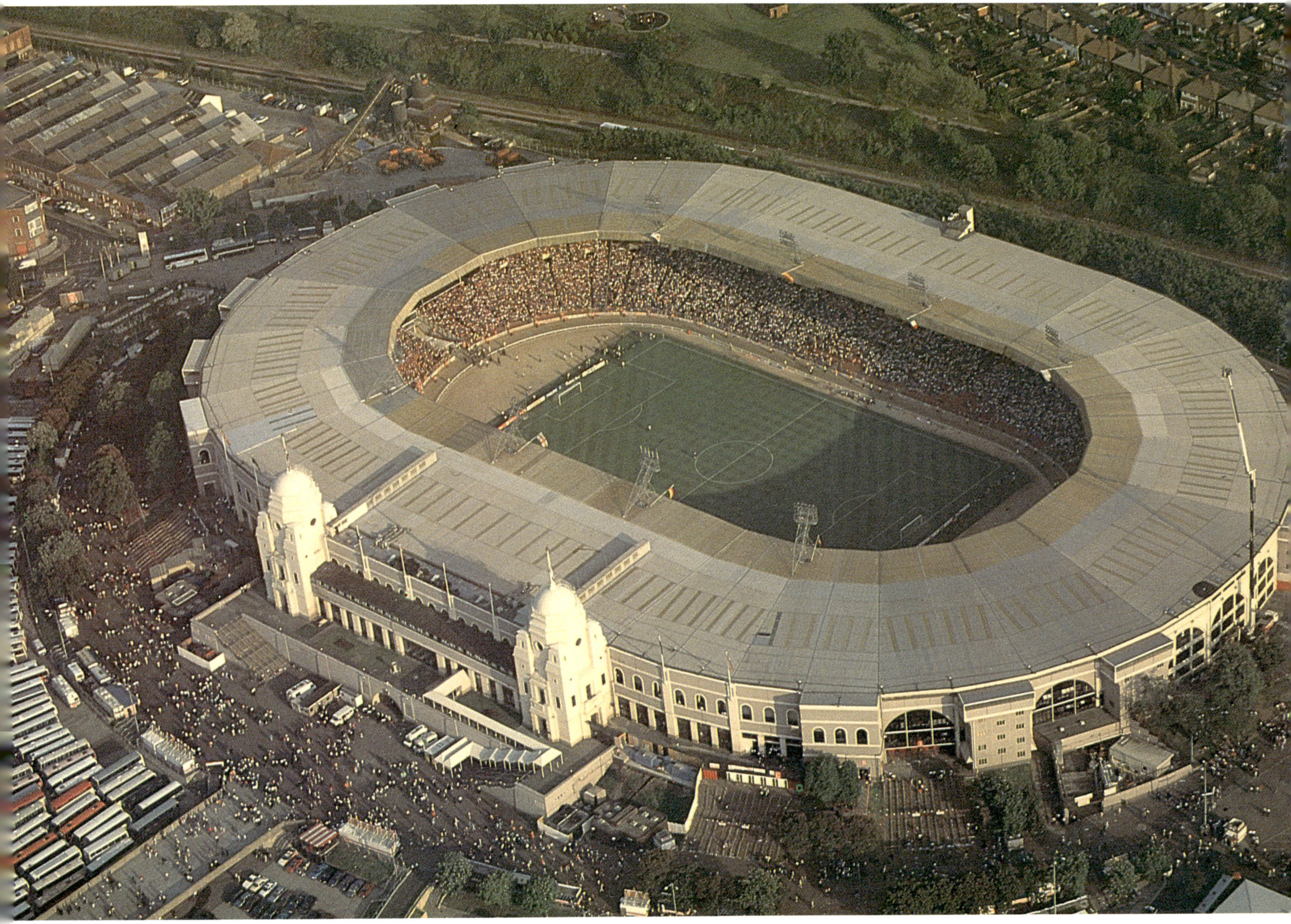

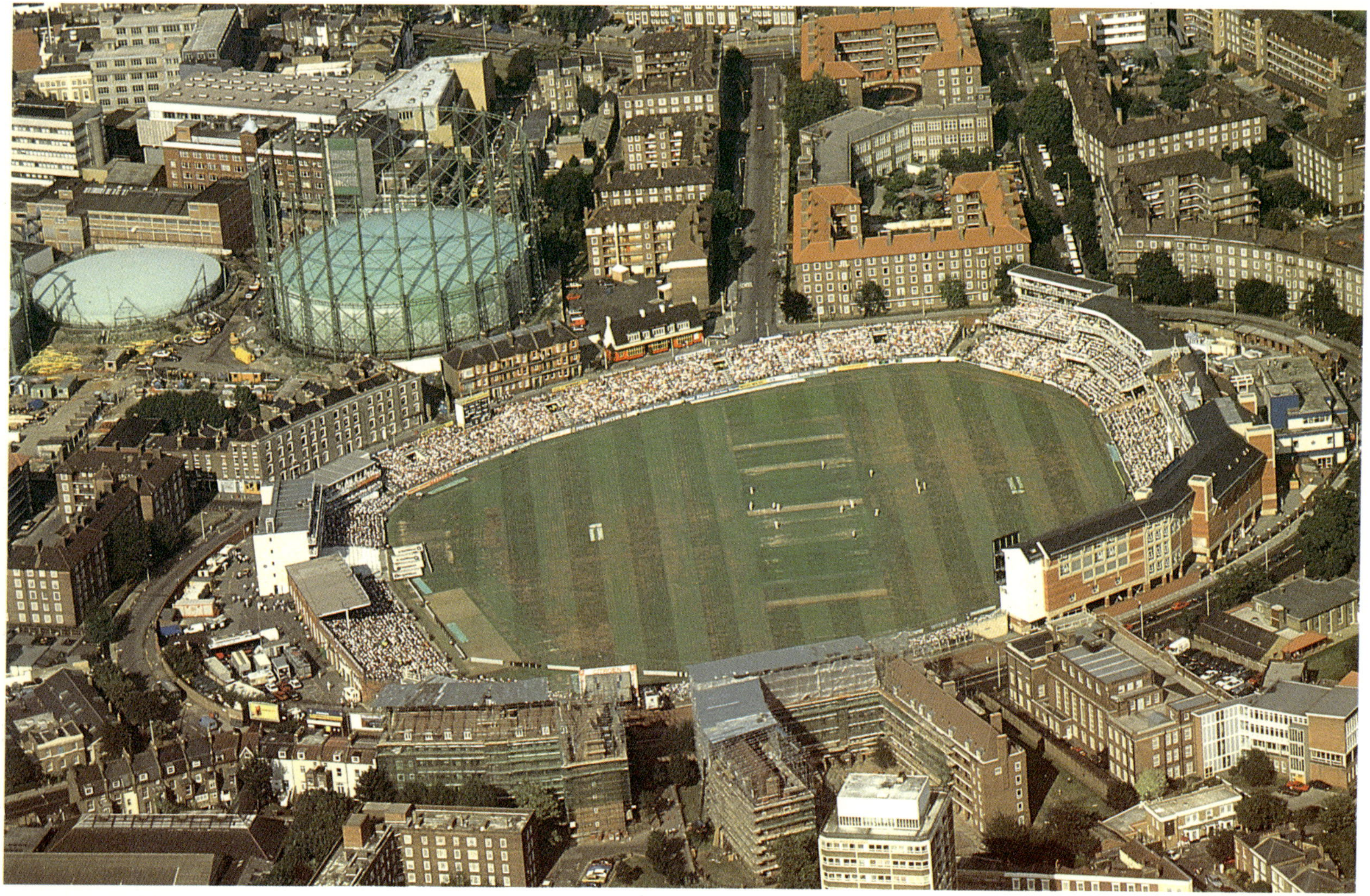

SUMMER MEANS CRICKET

Full houses at the Oval and at Lords in May 1992. Both were one-day Internationals, England v. Pakistan. England won both games!

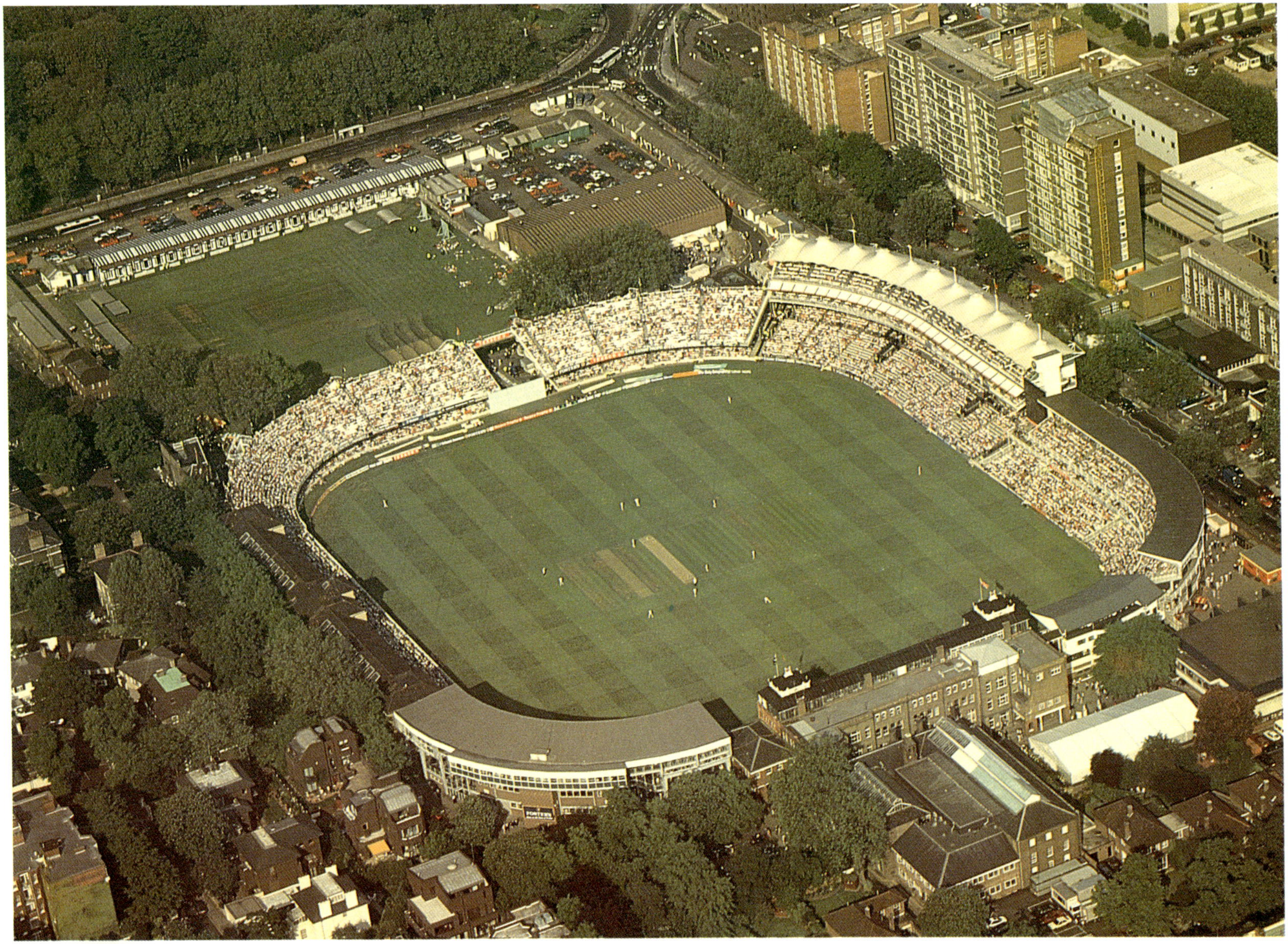

Capital Skies

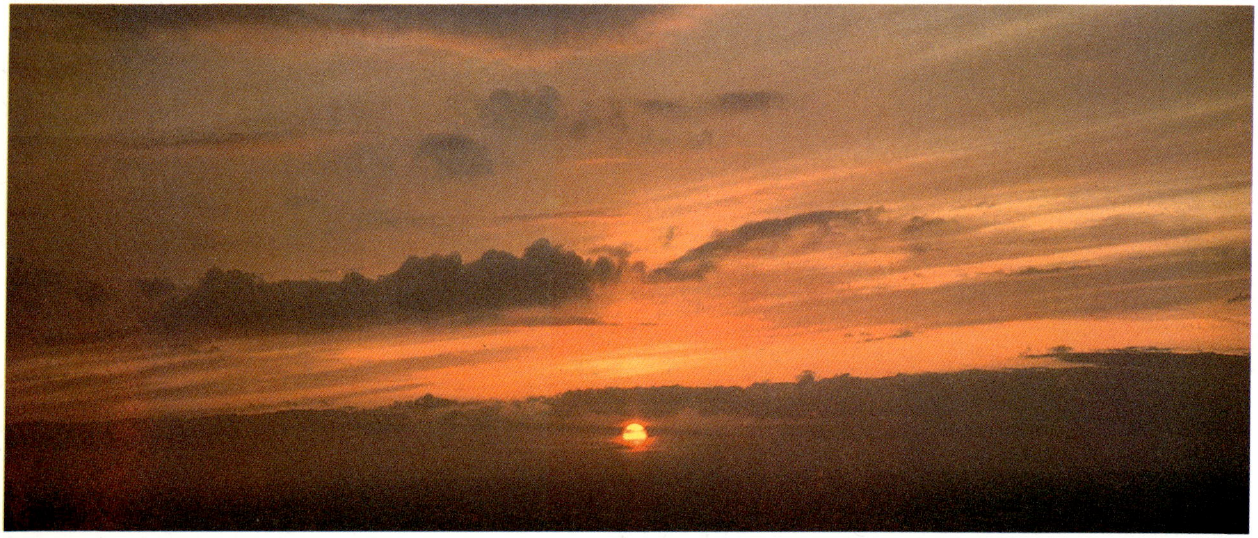

Traffic is not just confined to London's roads, there is also a fair amount of it in the air above the city, especially since City Airport got going.

At the level we fly, the airspace over London is divided into two zones, and to fly in these zones we have to have permission from the relevant air traffic control. People often ask me if we fly a fixed route. The answer is no, but we do try and follow a fairly regular pattern as it makes it easier for the controllers – after all, most air traffic just wants to go from A to B in a straight line, whereas it must sometimes seem that we buzz around like a demented fly. So we do try to cover one zone before moving on to the next, rather than constantly switching from one to the other.

Of course, there are some places we always check on – the Blackwall Tunnel, the Hanger Lane gyratory system, the A3 and all the other familiar spots where gregarious motor cars like to congregate – but our route is likely to be dictated by major roadworks, which may change from one week to the next, and by accidents; and we may have to return to one location several times during the course of a flight to make sure we have got the most up-to-the-minute details of the incident.

We can't be everywhere at once, but zapping around at over 120mph is the next best thing. However, we do sometimes have to wait our turn – for instance, if we want to check on things at the Blackwall Tunnel or around Canary Wharf we have to give way to flights in

IS IS A BIRD? IS IT A PLANE? . . .

No! It's an American Blimp Corporation A60 Lightship, advertising the *Daily Star* and vying with the moon for our attention.

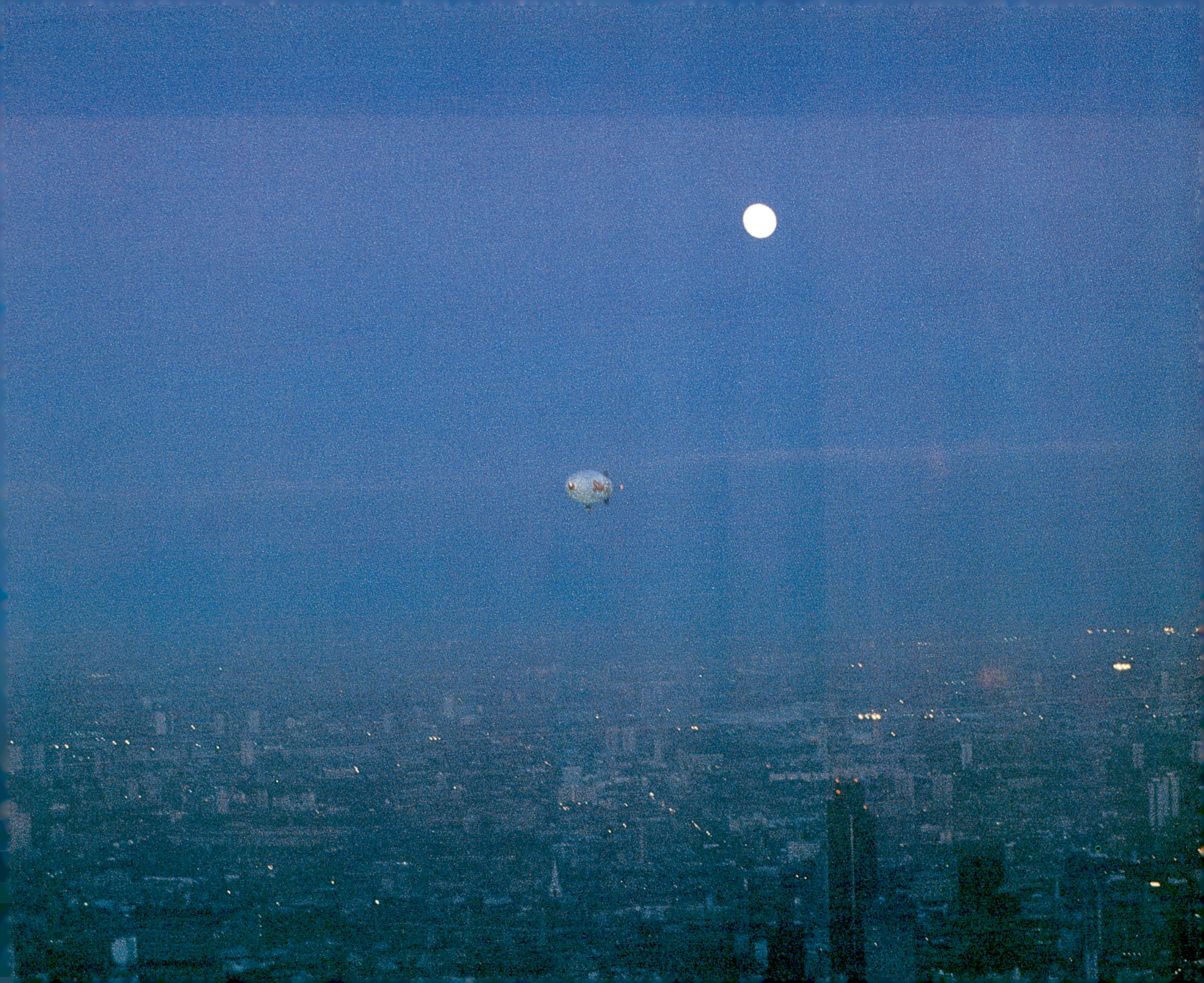

and out of City Airport. We also have to share the airspace with an assortment of helicopter traffic, including Medevac, the police helicopter and various royal flights. The controllers have to ensure that there is a safe distance between us and all the other air traffic, although most of it is, of course, flying considerably higher than we are. It's in the dark when you can really see how busy the skies are – on a clear night you can spot the lights of the planes stacking up for Heathrow – quite often it's possible to pick out nine or ten in a holding pattern around London.

Outside the zones we can go pretty well where we want, but then we need to keep an even sharper look-out for other planes. I remember once we were somewhere to the north of the Dartford Tunnel and I was in the middle of a broadcast, when we suddenly went into a steep dive. This is decidedly disconcerting when you're in full flow, but I made it to the end of the report, perhaps more quickly than usual, to discover that we had had to take avoiding action after a microlight had suddenly appeared, apparently out of nowhere.

Most of the time things are not so dramatic. We watch from a distance as Concorde makes its stately progress into Heathrow or, at the other end of the aviation scale, a gaggle of hot-air balloons drifts sedately across the sky – maybe not the most practical way of getting around but certainly the most serene.

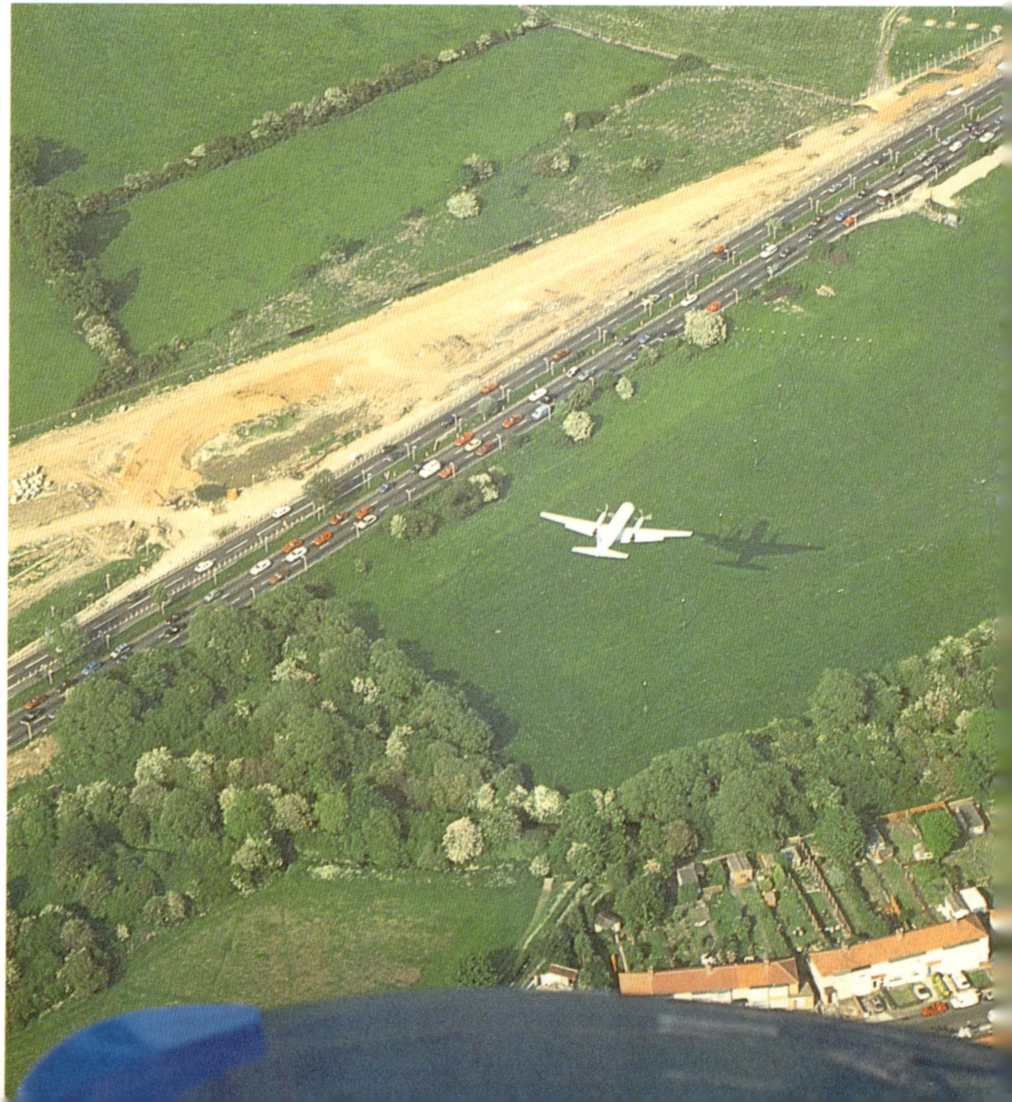

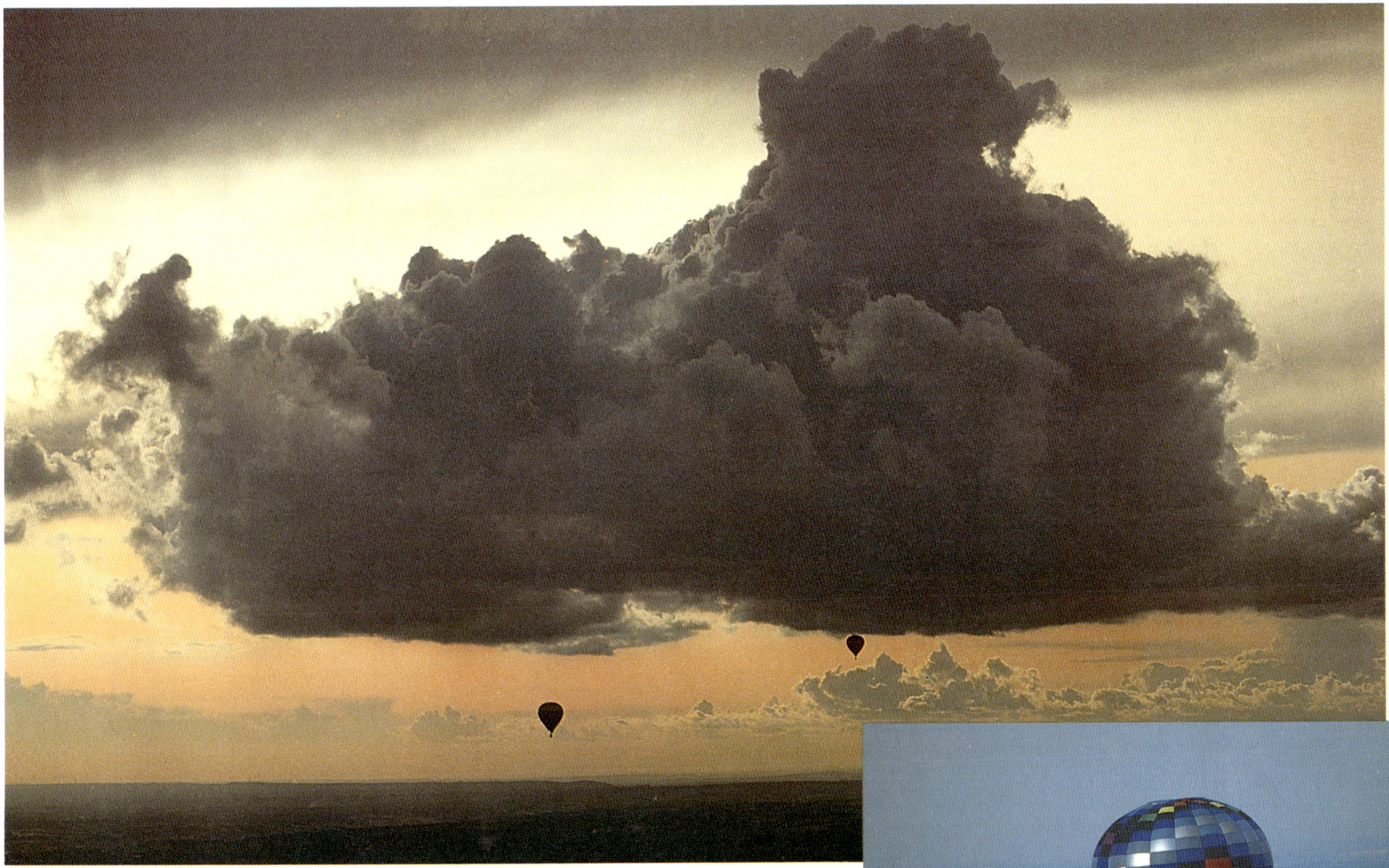

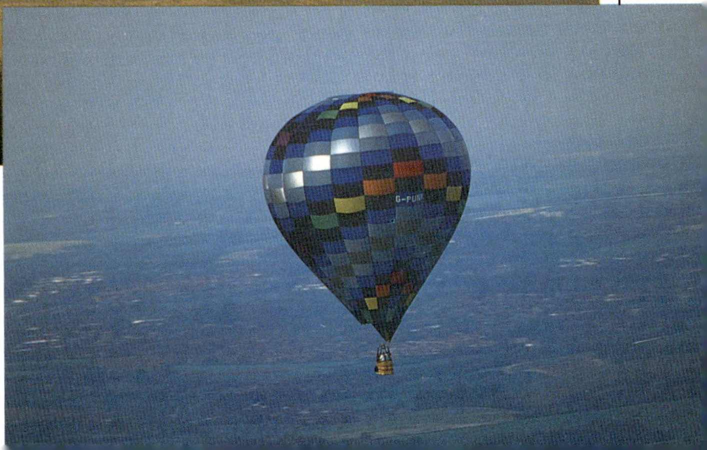

FELLOW FLIERS

We share London's skies with many other aircraft. Here we are overflying another twin-engined plane as it crosses the A40 to land at RAF Northolt, and a clutch of hot-air balloons demands a closer inspection. We needed special permission from air traffic control to fly so close.

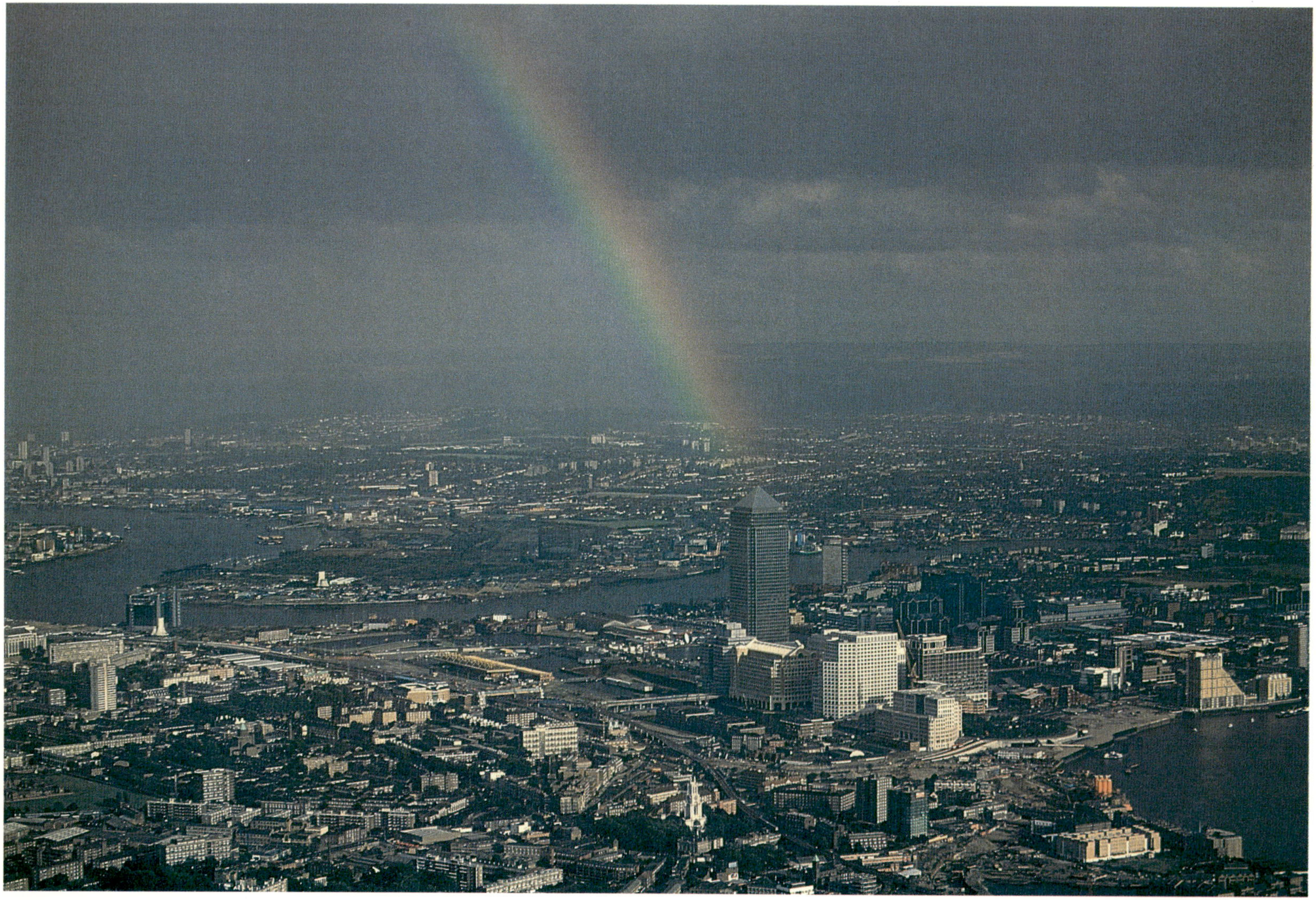

RAINBOW'S END

The pot of gold at the end of the rainbow?

AND FINALLY

It's time to come home. This is our view of Elstree just before we touch down. Another evening's reporting from the Flying Eye successfully concluded as the jams begin to clear and our listeners arrive home safe and sound, if a little traffic weary. And it all starts again tomorrow morning . . .

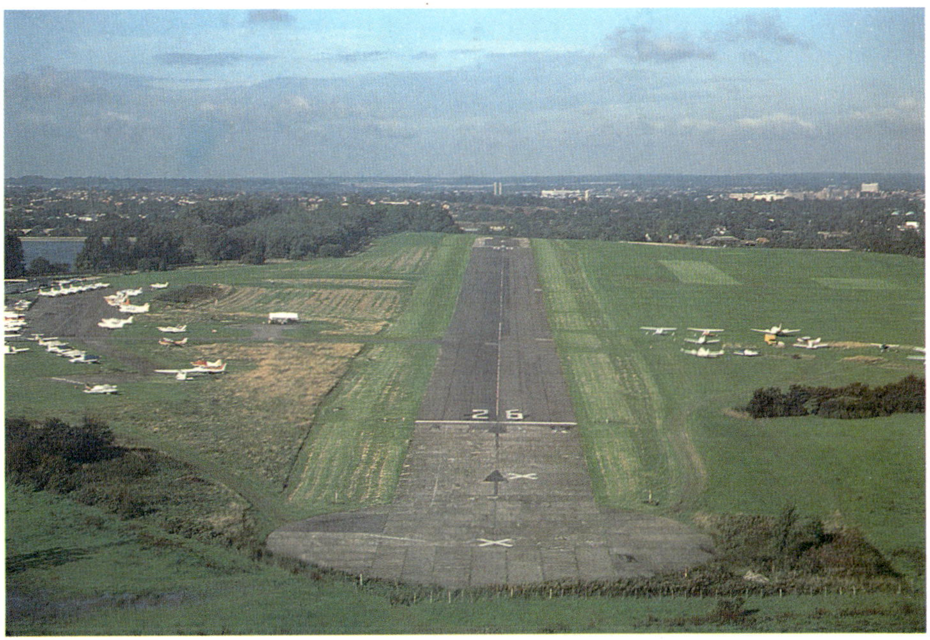

These are some of the sights and scenes that I have captured from Capital's Flying Eye over a period of about a year. Of course, most of the time our gaze is firmly fixed on London's traffic – the accidents, the hold ups, the roadworks, the queues and the congestion. Every evening brings new problems and a different set of jams. But no matter what has been going on during the flight, our last view is invariably the same – nose down for the tarmac at Elstree.

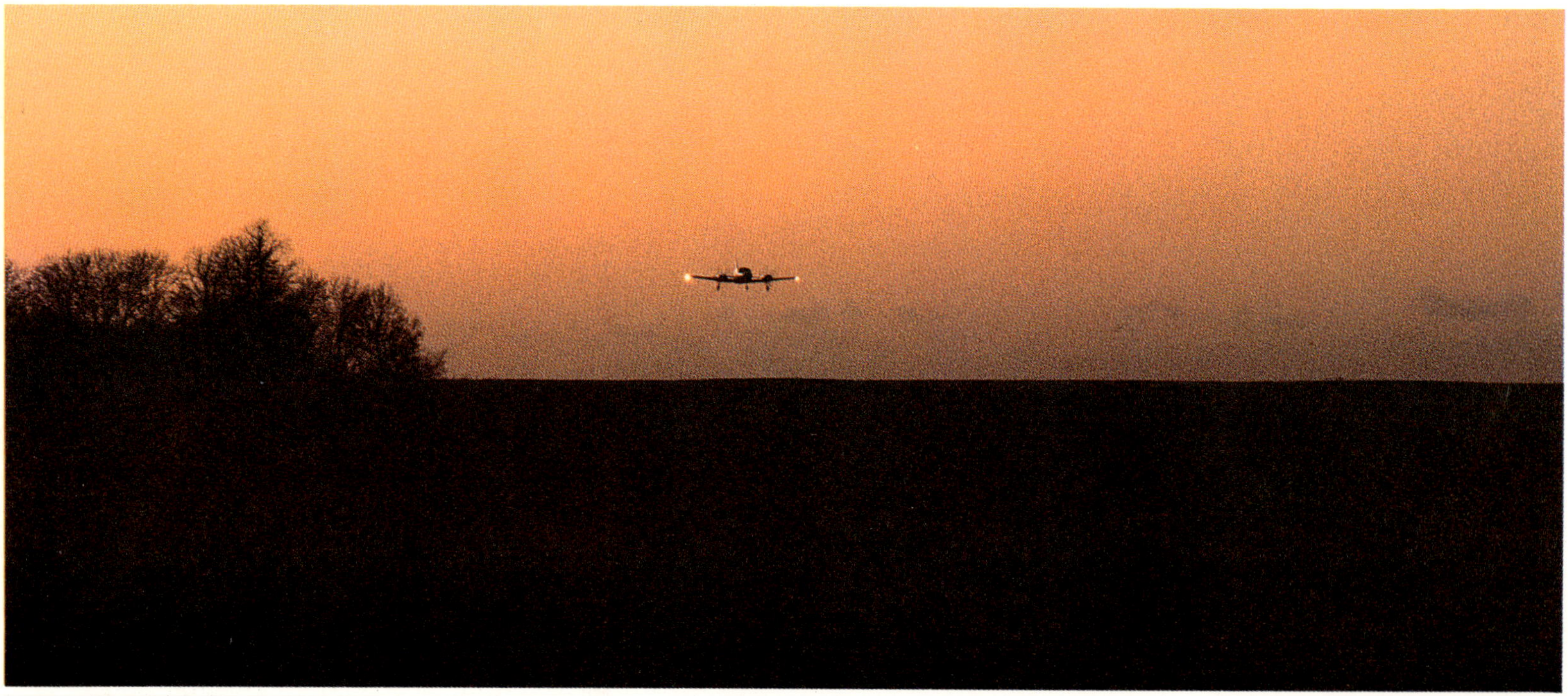